Brian Catchpole, formerly Dean of Faculty and Head of the School of Teacher Education, Hull College of Higher Education, is now a free-lance writer and lecturer in International American schools and colleges.

He has examined at O level for the Cambridge board and is the author of numerous textbooks on history including *History 1: World History since 1914*, a companion volume in this series.

Pan Study Aids for GCSE include:

Accounting

Biology

Chemistry

Commerce

Computer Studies

Economics

English Language

French

Geography 1

Geography 2

German

History 1: World History since 1914

History 2: Britain and Europe since 1700

Human Biology

Mathematics

Physics

Sociology

Study Skills

PAN STUDY AIDS

HISTORY 2:
Britain and Europe since 1700

Brian Catchpole

A Pan Original
Pan Books   London, Sydney and Auckland

First published 1987 by Pan Books Ltd,
Cavaye Place, London SW10 9PG

9 8 7 6 5 4 3 2 1

ISBN 0 330 29984 0

Text design by Peter Ward
Text illustration by M L Design
Photoset by Parker Typesetting Service, Leicester
Printed and bound in Spain by
Mateu Cromo SA, Madrid

CONTENTS

Contents

ACKNOWLEDGEMENTS

The author and publishers would like to thank the following people for kind permission to reproduce illustrations on the following pages: the BBC Hulton Picture Library for pages 21, 22, 35, 71 (London gasworks), 99, 277, 282, 310; the Mansell Collection for page 71 (Crystal Palace); British Caledonian for page 198; the Trustees of the Imperial War Museum for page 331; to Amanda Chandler for page 158; Dr Lorentz U. Pedersen for page 342; and to Col. R. Sage for page 160. The author is especially grateful to Brigadier S. N. Floyer-Acland for permission to quote from his father's First World War Diary, pages 137 and 141; and to Peter Farrar for permission to quote from the Diary of Private James Tait, page 295.

INTRODUCTION TO GCSE

From 1988, there will be a single system of examining at 16 plus in England and Wales and Northern Ireland. The General Certificate of Secondary Education (GCSE) will replace the General Certificate of Education (GCE) and the Certificate of Secondary Education (CSE) In Scotland candidates will be entering for the O grade and Standard Grade examinations leading to the award of the Scottish Certificate of Education (SCE).

The Pan Study Aids GCSE series has been specially written by practising teachers and examiners to enable you to prepare successfully for this new examination.

GCSE introduces several important changes in the way in which you are tested. First, the examinations will be structured so that you can show *what* you know rather than what you do *not* know. Of critical importance here is the work you produce during the course of the examination year, which will be given much greater emphasis than before. Second, courses are set and marked by six examining groups instead of the previous twenty GCE/CSE boards. The groups are:

Northern Examining Association (NEA)
Midland Examining Group(MEG)
London and East Anglian Group (LEAG)
Southern Examining Group (SEG)
Welsh Joint Examinations Council (WJEC)
Northern Ireland Schools Examination Council (NISEC)

One of the most useful changes introduced by GCSE is the single award system of grades A–G. This should permit you and future employers more accurately to assess your qualifications.

GCSE	GCE O Level	CSE
A	A	–
B	B	–
C	C	1
D	D	2
E	E	3
F	F	4
G		5

Remember that, whatever examinations you take, the grades you are awarded will be based on how well you have done.

Pan Study Aids are geared for use throughout the duration of your courses. The text layout has been carefully designed to provide all the information and skills you need for GCSE and SCE examinations – please feel free to use the margins for additional notes.

N.B. Where questions are drawn from former O level examination papers, the following abbreviations are used to identify the boards:

UCLES (University of Cambridge Local Examinations Syndicate)
AEB (Associated Examining Board)
ULSEB (University of London Schools Examination Board)
SUJB (Southern Universities Joint Board)
O&C (Oxford & Cambridge)
SCE (Scottish Certificate of Education Examination Board)
JMB (Joint Matriculation Board)
SEB (Scottish Examining Board)
ODLE (Oxford Delegacy of Local Examinations)
WJEC (Welsh Joint Examinations Council)

PREFACE

This *GCSE History Study Aid* deals with two popular examination periods:

1   British Economic and Social History since 1700.
2   Britain and Europe since 1789.

In both periods the examiners will be testing *you* in very specific skills. They hope that, as a result of your history studies, you have developed a very real enthusiasm for the past and that you will want to go on learning about it. They expect you to know how to use historical sources; how to spot the connections between past events and present day situations; how to detect bias, analyse data and construct a reasoned argument about a particular historical event or issue. In British history in particular the examiners will expect you to be able to look at events and issues from the point of view of people in the past so that you can understand how, over a fairly long period, our national social and cultural values have changed and what the agents of change actually were.

So you can expect a very great variety of questions. Certainly there will be some essay type questions because that is how the examiners will test your skill in recalling events and people and assembling a reasoned, critical account of, say, the Irish Famine or the effect of the Second World War on the status of women. But they will certainly provide a variety of sources of historical evidence for you to discuss and evaluate. For example, the examination paper may contain quotations from historians who lived over two hundred years ago, statistical data about climate and its effect on crops, maps and land surveys, photographs of vintage motor cars, songs and poems from the distant past, extracts from the diaries of soldiers who fought in the First World War. You will have to look at this evidence very carefully, put it into its historical context and add to it your own knowledge and comment. For example, you might be presented with a photograph of a MASH in the Korean War and be asked to locate the war on a map and to explain what a MASH was. Possibly, you will have done a lot of work on the Korean War and the effect it had upon the UN, Chinese and Korean soldiers as well as on the civilian population. The examiners will give you credit if you expand your answer with relevant comment and additional factual detail – this is how you can score a high mark by developing the answers to what may be very simple and straightforward questions.

This GCSE *History Study Aid* provides you with lots of examples of the sort of questions the examiners will set in the written examination.

All the GCSE Examining Boards offer some aspect of British Economic and Social History but over varying periods. London and East Anglia test candidates by one of three 'Schemes':

Scheme A British Economy and Society 1760–1860;
Scheme B British Economy and Society since 1870;
Scheme C Themes in Modern Economic and Social History.

These 'Themes' will include Transport, Education, Social Welfare, the Condition of the Working Classes, Women and Society, Trade, Medicine and Health.

Wales offers modules in the Textile Revolution (1730–1815), the period 1815–46 and the Edwardian Age (1901–12); while Northern Ireland emphasises Aspects of Economic History (Britain and Northern Ireland) 1919–85. The Southern Examination Group offers British Social and Economic History 1750–1975; while the Northern Examination Group's Syllabus C examines themes such as agriculture, industry, trade (from 1700 onwards), urbanisation, the response to industrialisation and social improvements. The Midland Examining Group's syllabus is the most comprehensive, covering the period 1700 to the present day in British Social and Economic History.

Three GCSE Boards test candidates on British and European History from *c*.1789:

1 Southern Examining Group: Britain and Europe since 1815.
2 London and East Anglian Group: Syllabus B – Britain and Europe from the mid-eighteenth century.
3 Midlands Examining Group: Syllabus E British and European History 1789–1914 OR Syllabus F 1867 to the Present Day. However, material in this section is of great back-up value to World History studies and to aspects of British History.

All the most important aspects of British Economic and Social History, together with British and European History since 1789, are described and tested in this *Study Aid*. For success in GCSE History examinations you will need a history textbook covering your period or option together with a good map history.

BRITISH ECONOMIC AND SOCIAL HISTORY 1700 TO THE PRESENT

BRITAIN'S PRE-INDUSTRIAL SOCIETY 1700–c.1750

CONTENTS

During the eighteenth century the British people had the unique experience of being the first ever to go through the process of an industrial revolution. What was it like on the eve of that industrial revolution?

1   Most people worked on the land, in the market towns or in the prosperous sea-ports.

2   They made a living on the good farmlands of the south where most of the biggest ports (London, Bristol, Exeter, Norwich) had developed.

3   The north was generally underpopulated and undeveloped – the only two large areas of settlement were in Lancashire and the old West Riding of Yorkshire.

4   Altogether, there were about 5.75 million people living in England and Wales in 1700 – though these numbers were destined to increase by one million over the next fifty years.

5   Moving from one village to another was difficult for a family as local parish councillors were unwilling to accept newcomers in case they became poverty-stricken and 'a charge on the parish'. In those days a family had to obtain a 'settlement certificate' stating that they would not become a financial burden in their new parish. Armed with these certificates, many families began to move to new places of work when they thought they could get better jobs.

6   Some (if they had enough capital) invested in a handloom and materials (about £120) and set up a cottage industry weaving cloth for the overseas markets. Others hired spinning wheels or stocking frames and sold their products to local merchants. In Lancashire, quite a few spinners experimented with raw cotton and tried to make up garments similar to the expensive (but beautifully made and easy to wash) cotton products imported from the Far East.

7   In other parts of England, people made nails and small iron goods at home. These were the nailers – who had a good export outlet in the American colonies but whose profits were largely absorbed by the middlemen – the nailmasters and merchants.

8   In the coal-mining areas, thousands of people – men, women and children – slaved to meet the demands of the many industries that depended on coal as the main fuel. The exploitation of coal (a fossil fuel) had begun around 1300 and the annual production by the late 1740s was around 5 million tons. It was the most dangerous industry – as the easy-to-work open-cast and shallow seam mines had been worked out by 1700.

Multiple choice questions

1 The 'soul of English manufactures' was:
- ☐ oil
- ☐ gas
- ☐ coal
- ☐ wood

2 The most productive coal mines in the country (*c.*1740) were in:
- ☐ the North-East (Northumberland & Durham)
- ☐ South Wales
- ☐ Yorks, Notts, Derby
- ☐ Midlothian

3 The increasing population was due partly to immigration from Ireland and Scotland and partly to:
- ☐ old people living longer
- ☐ better social services
- ☐ better pay
- ☐ improvements in infant mortality rates

4 The classic example of the 'domestic system of industry' was:
- ☐ glass-blowing
- ☐ soap manufacture
- ☐ charcoal burning
- ☐ woollen manufacturing

WORKING ON THE LAND

The majority of British farmers were freeholders, though substantial numbers rented their land from a landlord. There were many huge estates belonging to the aristocracy and the rich merchant class. The local squire and parson usually farmed many acres. Thousands of smallholdings existed (a few acres); while the poorest might depend on common land and waste land to feed their animals. A great deal of farming was still carried out under the 'open field' system. Nevertheless, British farmers were very successful and exported a great deal of food.

Read the following extract

Many farmers had adopted Dutch farming methods during the seventeenth century. They began to sow clover seed with their barley; once the crop was harvested, they turned cattle out to graze on the clover. The clover renewed the nitrogen in the soil, the cattle fattened on the clover and the animal manure increased the fertility of the soil. In the 1660s they began to grow turnips. Because they needed a great deal of weeding the hand-hoeing created a good tilth. The turnips provided a sound winter fodder for animals and Norfolk and Suffolk in particular became famous for their 'crop rotations'. Lord 'Turnip' Townshend (1674–1738) won his nickname by growing turnips on his Norfolk estates. He was equally well-known for his use of *marl* which he spread on fields to increase their fertility.

2 From which European country did English farmers take their farming methods?
2 Why was nitrogen so important?
3 Was turnip growing 'labour intensive'?
4 Give an example of a crop rotation (remember that wheat, barley and rye grass were widely grown).
5 Where were Townshend's estates?
6 What is marl?

WORKING IN THE PORTS

British trade was not only with the colonies and foreign countries. There was also a very profitable re-export trade – particularly in surplus sugar and tobacco. Additionally, there was the evil but highly prosperous slave trade based in particular on Bristol and Liverpool. There was a tremendous demand for merchant seamen, for dockside workers, ship's chandlers, carters and fruit and vegetable suppliers. This meant there was always a chance of a job in the port areas – though the chances of making a fortune were usually restricted to the entrepreneurs, the merchants who were willing to risk capital and 'to contrive new ways to live'.

SHIPPING MERCHANTS

These were the specialists who chartered ships, drew up deals and provided insurance. The most famous were to be found in London at Lloyd's Coffee Shop and in Liverpool at the Cotton Exchange.

BANKERS

These were the most important specialists as they 'discounted bills of exchange'. This freed the merchant from depending on large amounts of gold and silver coin and made him less vulnerable to robbery and swindling. A merchant issued a bill of exchange to a client promising to pay the cash due in three months' time. So the client became a 'creditor'. In turn, the creditor might need the money quickly. So a banker would 'discount the bill' or cash it – for a fee! Of course, he would only do this if the original merchant were 'credit worthy' and could be relied on to pay the bank (again the banker would charge a fee!)

The complexity of international trade can be seen from the diagram overleaf. It refers to the 'triangular trade' between Britain, West Africa and the West Indies – the destination of thousands of African slaves.

on the outward passage to West Africa:

brandy
rolls of cloth
muskets
gunpowder
bar-iron

— for the African kings in exchange for slaves

handcuffs, leg-irons
— to shackle the slaves

beans — food for the slaves on the middle passage

a slaver c. 1780

S
M

on the middle passage to the West Indies:
the main deck M held about 100 slaves. The ship's carpenter specially built a 'shelf' S to hold another 100 negroes, ' .... like books in a row', was how John Newton, a slaver captain, described the unhappy negroes.

on the inward passage to Liverpool:

'Load up with one hundred cask good Muscovado sugars for the ground tier, the remainder with first and second white sugars and betwixt decks with good cotton and coffee'
— and in Jamaica — 'as much broad sound mahogany as will serve for dunnage'

(Orders to a Liverpool slaver captain, 1762)

Cargoes on the 'Triangular Trade'

THE INCREASING VALUE OF A WEST AFRICAN SLAVE

1690

COWRIE SHELLS, BRASS BASINS, IRON BARS AND DYED CLOTHS TO THE VALUE OF
£3.70

1790

25 KEGS OF GUNPOWDER
2 BAGS OF SHOT, 100 GUNFLINTS
20 KNIVES, 4 CUTLASSES,
96 YARDS OF CLOTH,
4 HATS, 4 CAPS,
1 LARGE BRASS PAN,
50 HANDKERCHIEFS,
10 BUNCHES OF BEADS
2 MUSKETS

ALL MADE IN BRITAIN AND WORTH NEARLY
£100

Note the way in which slaves were crammed into the slave-ship. The beans were needed to feed the slaves – they were cooked in fresh water and that meant huge casks had to be stored on the vessel. One of the reasons for so many deaths on board the slave ships was that they had to stay for months off the West African coast awaiting the arrival of slaves (in coffles or convoys of about sixty at a time) coming in from the inland chiefdoms and kingdoms. Gradually, conditions on board ship became foul. Many thousands must have died before the ships even left for the plantations on the other side of the Atlantic.

The diagram opposite shows the remarkable increase in the value of slaves from about 1690 to 1790. Note the goods required by African leaders. There was no demand for large manufactured goods, no need in Africa for the new steam engines that were being developed – but an enormous demand for arms and ammunition.

EARLY STEAM POWER

As early as 1698 Thomas Savery had designed a steam-driven piston for pumping out water from flooded tin-mines in Cornwall. Thomas Newcomen adapted this design to allow atmospheric pressure to bear on the piston to create a working stroke. This was a giant leap in early-eighteenth-century technology. Newcomen's invention is dated 1705. It was a very crude design and it cost a lot of money – about £1000 in 1720 after it had been in production about five years. It needed capital and a great deal of fuel and was virtually restricted to being used in the coal-mines. Newcomen's invention was a great success – he was exporting his engines in kit form during the 1720s. He died in 1729.

AN EARLY FACTORY

The word 'factory' derives from French, Spanish and Portuguese expressions to denote:

1 a place of carrying on a business in a foreign country;
2 a building in which goods are made – a 'manufactory'.

The term was used as early as 1580 and was applied to the silkmills built at Derby in 1717–19. It was a sign of the future as this traditional ballad shows:

> Of come all you cotton weavers,
> Your looms you may pull down,
> You must get employed in factories,
> in country or in town.
> For our cotton masters have
> found out a wonderful scheme,
> those calico goods now wove by hand
> they're going to weave by steam.

The Domestic System
Source: BBC TV British Social History, *The Age of Steam*, Autumn 1971, p. 2

The scene, depicted in the above picture, was about to disappear.

1   The picture has been called 'idyllic'. Do you think it is an exaggeration of the domestic system as operated inside an English cottage?
2   Would you agree that the theme of the ballad quoted above is ☐ enthusiastic or ☐ sarcastic?

Generalisations about Britain's pre-industrial society

		True	False
1	The earliest factories did not depend on steam power.	☐	☐
2	The densely populated industrial towns and cities common today did not exist in those days.	☐	☐
3	The foundations of business credit as we know it today were laid in pre-industrial Britain.	☐	☐
4	The success of British farmers in the eighteenth century did not depend on the introduction of new machinery.	☐	☐
5	The gain in population (due to immigration, an increased birthrate and reduced infant mortality) was partly offset by emigration to Europe and the colonies.	☐	☐

THE PERSISTENT HANDLOOM WEAVER

This is one example of a pre-industrial technique that survived the onset of the British 'industrial revolution'.

Can you discover why this was so?

Can you find out why the handloom weavers suffered so terribly in the 1820s and 1830s – when the industrial revolution was well-established?

Source: BBC TV British Social History, *The Age of Steam*, Autumn 1971, p. 5.

AGRICULTURAL CHANGES 1750–1850

THE ENCLOSURES

The Parliamentary Enclosure movement represents the most dramatic change that took place in British agriculture during the eighteenth and early nineteenth centuries. Farming is only profitable when it is efficient and in 1700 half of England's arable land was still organised in the medieval 'open-field' system.

CHARACTERISTICS OF THE OPEN FIELD

1 Huge open fields were usually divided into strips, worked by individual owners or tenant farmers.
2 Strips were divided by 'baulks' – a waste of good land.
3 Strips owned by an individual could be widely scattered over a village's open field system, making for time-consuming travel and a drop in efficiency.
4 The persistence of strips prevented the use of modern equipment generally available in the early nineteenth century.
5 Strips were difficult to plough and fertilise efficiently.

'ANCIENT ENCLOSURES'

During medieval and Tudor times there had been a great deal of enclosure – but this must not be confused with the enclosures that went on during your period, enclosures that were most elaborate and sanctioned by Act of Parliament.

CARRYING OUT AN ENCLOSURE

A group of local landowners authorised surveyors to draw an accurate map of the village and its field-systems. They then divided up:
1 land not already enclosed;
2 common land;
3 heath/waste land.
It proved to be a costly process as the surveys and the resulting hedging and fencing ran into thousands of pounds. Of course, Parliament had to approve this major re-allocation of land, and when the appropriate Enclosure Act was passed, the lands were swiftly divided. At first, landowners didn't have to tell their tenants about the new arrangements; ordinary villagers were often ignorant of what

was happening. Some farmers, appalled by the costs, sold out in the middle of the process.

NUMBERS OF ENCLOSURES

The Parliamentary process went on from about 1720 to 1850. The Acts of 1801 and 1836 speeded up the process. Well over five million acres were enclosed mainly in:

1　the three Ridings of Yorkshire;
2　East Anglia;
3　the Midlands;
4　Wiltshire and Berkshire.

If you are studying enclosure in your district (there were over 1,200 Acts of Parliament between 1750 and 1780 alone) your County Archivist may let you have photostats of certain enclosure awards (these are not always easy to read) and enclosure maps (the most useful source of information). Remember that in the history of enclosure there were three main periods, two of them outside your period:

1　Medieval – during the thirteenth century when there was an agricultural 'boom'.
2　Tudor – when landowners enclosed large areas of land especially for sheep grazing.
3　Your period – when the main reason for enclosure was to boost food production for domestic and export purposes.

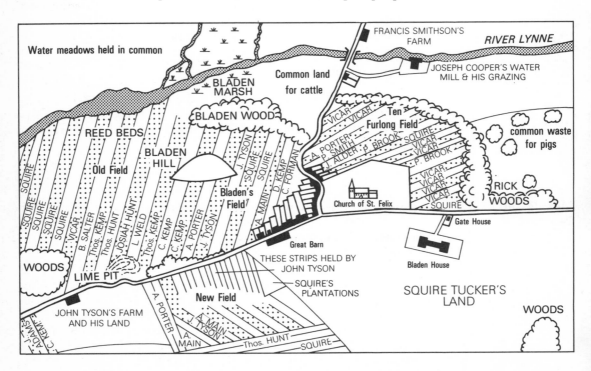

The village of Lynne in the parish of St Felix before enclosure

Using the enclosure map

You will find that the actual award is packed with details of:

1 field names;
2 the names of the new owners;
3 the location of the new farms, the plan of the village and perhaps details of grants and endowments to the local church or school house. You will not always find that the map contains a sketch of the village before enclosure – but it is usually possible to trace the boundaries of the main fields and wastelands. The diagram below shows how the appearance of a village and its surrounding farmland might change in the few years after enclosure.

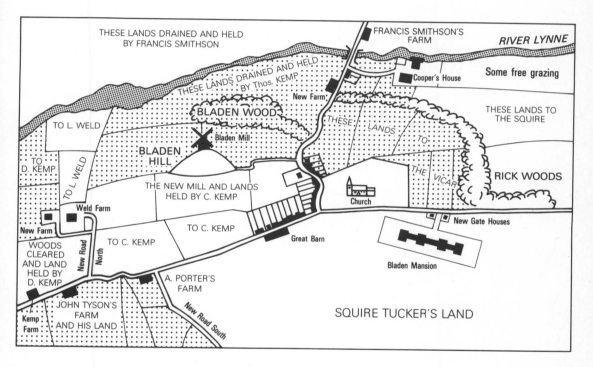

The village of Lynne after enclosure

Look at the enclosure diagram on page 26

In the village of Lynne before enclosure:

1 Who owned the water mill?
2 What was the name of the Squire's house?
3 Who owned most of the strips in New Field?
4 Who owned most of the strips in Ten Furlong Field?
5 Is it likely that the villagers were free to catch game around the water meadows and Bladen Marsh?
6 Where could the villagers graze their cattle?
7 What were the woodlands west of Rick Woods used for?

8　Most of the cottages were thatched. What material do you think the villagers used for thatch?

9　Were the villagers able to marl their strips?

10　How many strips did the Vicar own?

In the village of Lynne after enclosure:

1　Who had become the owner of Ten Furlong Field?

2　Had John Tyson sold any of his land?

3　Who had taken over the cattle common land?

4　Had his relatives done well out of the enclosure?

5　They were obviously not big landowners; so by what name might they have been known at the time. (For a clue, see below.)

6　Had there been any woodland clearance after enclosure?

7　Can you spot any improvements in communications?

8　What evidence is there that the Squire did rather well out of enclosure?

9　What seems to have happened to:

(*a*)　P. Brook

(*b*)　J. Adler

(*c*)　A. Main?

10　Name two villagers who had built new farms.

SOME EFFECTS OF ENCLOSURE

There is sometimes a tendency in textbooks to blame enclosures for much of the social hardship experienced by the British people between 1780 and 1840. Enclosures meant that wealthy merchants or traditional aristocracy were able to employ the field improvements on a large scale and, eventually, to mechanise agriculture. The overall effect was to increase the supply of food grown in Britain. One point that is sometimes made is this: that although enclosures were generally 'good', several groups of British farmers suffered. The one often singled out is the yeoman farmer – and his disappearance after 1820 is lamented. In fact, yeomen farmers did not disappear due to enclosure; there is evidence that they actually increased in parts of the country. They were, however, deeply injured by the effects of a long period of warfare – quite a different matter.

The groups who suffered

Squatters: people who did not hold land in the original open fields but who depended on heathland, wasteland and common land 'rights'. Many of these disappeared with enclosure.

Casual labourers who hired themselves out as farmworkers or shepherds. Efficient farmers preferred now to recruit a permanent workforce. Farming was still a labour intensive occupation.

The surplus labourers: it is likely that many young people (products of the rising birthrate) found it harder to find work in some rural areas and drifted away from their villages to find work and accommodation in rapidly expanding towns. This was not necessarily a bad thing but it did have an impact on contemporaries who may have exaggerated the effects of enclosure as a consequence.

Generally speaking, enclosures themselves did little harm; it was the way the enclosures operated within each village that often caused hardship though it is unlikely that Arthur Young's famous comment (1801 – when he supported enclosures) is literally true:

> By nineteen enclosure acts out of twenty the poor are injured, and in some grossly injured . . . Go to an alehouse of an old enclosed county, and there you will see the origin of poverty and the poor rates.

THE NEW FARMING METHODS

AN INCREASE IN LIVESTOCK

Turnip Townshend's famous crop rotation was copied by many other farmers and they experimented with other plants, e.g. lucerne and sanfoin instead of clover; Swedish turnips (swedes) instead of traditional turnips.

The effect was a massive increase in animal fodder and this in turn encouraged farmers to improve breeding, e.g. **Richard Bakewell (1725–95)** developed cattle, sheep and horses at Dishley in Leicestershire. His most famous breed was the New Leicestershire sheep.

Not everyone benefited:

> The country people of North Britain live chiefly on oatmeal, and milk, cheese, butter and some garden stuff, with now and then a pickled herring, by way of delicacy; but flesh-meat they seldom or never taste.*

*Smollett, writing in 1771.

NEW MACHINERY

Jethro Tull (1664–1741) invented a seed-drill and a horse-drawn hoe and in 1733 he published his *Horse-hoeing Husbandry* to publicise his ideas. Shortly after this several new types of plough were coming on the market. During the 1770–85 period farmers began using metal ploughs based on the Rotherham design. Then in 1785 Robert Ransome of Ipswich (his farm machinery business later developed into Ransomes, Sims & Jeffries) brought out a cast-iron plough. Arthur Young noticed the effect:

> ´. . . many other things from which the industrious poor derive an agreeable and wholesome variety of food have become a great deal cheaper. Potatoes . . . turnips, carrots, cabbages; things that were never formerly raised but by the spade, but which are now commonly raised by the plough.´

PUBLICISING THE NEW METHODS

Arthur Young (1741–1820) was the best known publicist – though in his youth he had failed to make a small farm profitable! He was the editor of *Annals of Agriculture*. Other important publications were:

1776   *The Farmer's Magazine;*
1787   *A Survey of the Rural Economy.*

The well-known modern agricultural show did not then exist. However, Thomas Coke (1752–1842), a wealthy Norfolk farmer, held his famous sheep-shearing competitions (Coke's Clippings) and attracted thousands of people interested in his new farming methods and the mechanical reapers, horse harrows and seed-drillers on display at Holkham.

The most distinguished supporter of modern farming methods was King George III (1760–1820). He had a show-piece farm on Windsor Great Park and deserved his nickname – 'Farmer George'.

The importance attached to farming was shown in the universities where Professorships in Agriculture were set up in Edinburgh and Oxford.

WAR AND ITS IMPACT ON FARMING

THE AMERICAN WAR OF INDEPENDENCE 1775–83

The American War (in which the inhabitants of the Thirteen American Colonies won their independence) caused the usual loss of human life and equipment. There was a great deal of sea warfare and this hampered trade just at a time when Britain's expanding population was becoming dependent on a certain amount of imported food. The war therefore caused food shortages; and, as always, shortages caused price increases.

THE REVOLUTIONARY AND NAPOLEONIC WARS 1793–1815

With one brief respite, the British fought the French throughout this period. For obvious reasons, the war caused a prolonged food shortage. This meant that harvests were crucial. Look at the following table describing the harvests during the Revolutionary War:

Year	Cost of wheat (quarter)	Comment
1792	43 shillings	'Summer and autumn were a continued series of wet weather.' Harvest was poor.
1793	49/3d	Poor haycrops; poor turnip crop. Board of Agriculture set up.

Year	Cost of wheat (quarter)	Comment
1794	52/3d	Poor harvest and a bad year for sheep-rot.
1795	75/2d	Terrible winter, poor harvests, food scarce. Food Riots – Speenhamland System introduced.

AID TO FARM WORKERS

Dreadful conditions went on until the end of the century and a modification to the Elizabethan Poor Law system took place. This is known as the Speenhamland system.

Read this extract:

> The Poor Law officials at Speenhamland in Berkshire modified their Poor Law arrangements by supplementing wages out of the Poor Rate. They thought that each family man ought to be able to buy up to three 'gallon' loaves a week. The idea was adopted or modified by other farming counties so that what had been a genuine local effort to help a few distressed families now developed into a widespread system of 'supplementary allowances' geared to current food prices and the number of children in a family.

You can see the results:

1 Some farmers began to pay low wages (especially in the south of England), confident that the Poor Law officials would make them up out of the Poor Rate.
2 As it excluded unmarried men, it encouraged even earlier marriages.
3 More and more families had to 'go on the parish' as food prices rose (wheat was 113/10d a quarter by 1800).
4 It tended to reduce the mobility of families – as parish councils were wary of letting distressed families in because this would mean an instant increase in the local Poor Rate.

PROSPEROUS FARMERS

Generally speaking, farmers did well out of long periods of warfare. Crop prices were always good and there was every encouragement to enclose more waste and common land in order to grow food. Even so, they could not provide sufficient to feed everyone in England, Wales, Scotland and Ireland – the UK population figure in 1801 (the year in which the first population census was taken) had reached nearly 16 million.

AGRICULTURAL CONDITIONS AFTER THE WAR

By 1816 agricultural labourers were earning as little as seven shillings a week. They depended on Speenhamland-style poor relief. They resorted to poaching and pilfering – but to net a rabbit or steal a bag of grain meant a minimum sentence of transportation to the Australian colonies. To make matters worse, farmers began to employ Irish immigrants who were willing to work for even lower wages; while quite a lot during the 1820s had bought the new threshing machines, thus robbing their farm-hands of some of their winter work.

THE POOR LAW AMENDMENT ACT 1834

In 1831 there were two startling statistics:

1801 Census England and Wales =   9,157,176 people
1831 Census England and Wales = 13,897,187 people

The old Poor Law, even when supported by generous charitable bequests, could not cope with the new kind of poverty emerging in towns and villages as a result of this huge upsurge in population. Poor relief was beyond the resources of many parishes and small towns – especially as the towns began to attract the unemployed and the large (but uncounted) vagrant population.

AN EXAMPLE OF POVERTY

It is unusual to find an example of a poor man's account of poverty. The following is an application for poor relief, written by Thomas Bannister who lived in Staffordshire. The spelling is as on the original document:

> 12 December 1822
>
> Jeantlemen
>   at this time I ham In grate distress my youngest son is dad and I have another vury bad and I my sealfe am hill
> Sir the coffin will be 12 shillings and the ground with the fee will be 5 shillings and sixpence and the shroud three shillings and sixpence
> Sir threugh stoping my trifle of pay I have 14 shillings in det for seame and if not paid by christmas I must be trioubled
> Jeantlemen   I hope you will not stop my trifle of pay at this time
>   your humble servant
>   Thos. Bannister

Quoted by Geoffrey Taylor, *The Problem of Poverty, 1660–1834.* Longman, 1969, p. 127.

This letter went before the Parish Council with a recommendation that Bannister receive £1. The money was paid.

THE GOVERNMENT ENQUIRY INTO POOR RELIEF 1832

As a result of a government enquiry into the extent of poverty and the way in which parishes coped, the following conclusions were drawn:

1 the existing system of poor relief was uneconomic;
2 it absorbed around 20 per cent of the national income;
3 the main problem was that able-bodied men in work did not earn enough to feed their families;
4 the best way of helping such people was to abolish the system of parish allowances;
5 in its place, they would put a system of workhouses in which the way of life was so grim that people simply wouldn't want to live in them.

THE ACT 1834

Government passed the Poor Law Amendment Act in 1834 and suggested that parishes should join together and set up 'unions' whose job was to build the workhouses. Local rate-payers would then elect guardians to run them.

The Act has often been criticised because, it has been said, that when the parish allowances (known as 'outdoor relief') were abolished the payments made inside the workhouse were lower than the lowest wages paid outside.

Certainly, the Act had many faults. But it did not abolish outdoor relief. By 1840 far more people were still 'on the parish' than were actually living inside the new 'unions' (as the workhouses were called).

The problems of poverty persisted, especially in the countryside. New problems (slums, disease) developed in the expanding towns. More and more parishes raised funds so that their poor inhabitants could emigrate to the colonies.

THE CORN LAWS

KEEPING UP THE PRICE OF CORN

In 1815 Parliament (in those days controlled by rich landowners) passed a Corn Law. It forbade the import of foreign wheat before home-grown wheat was fetching 80 shillings a quarter.

In 1828 William Huskisson changed this arrangement with his famous 'sliding scale'. Under this, the import duties on foreign wheat fell as the price of British wheat rose. This worked well when harvests were good and wheat prices were relatively low; but when harvests were poor food prices in Britain rocketed, causing all sorts of problems to the British people. Many of the new industrialists wanted to free trade from all restrictions such as the Corn Law. These 'free traders' formed an Anti-Corn Law League (1838) at a time of food shortages. Led by John Bright and Richard Cobden, both of them manufacturers, the League began its work.

THE ANTI-CORN LAW LEAGUE: AN EARLY PRESSURE GROUP

Cobden and Bright organised lectures and circularised influential people by post:

1 lecturers could travel on the newly established railway routes;
2 letters now travelled via the new postal service set up by Rowland Hill in 1839.

REPEAL OF THE CORN LAWS 1846

Prime Minister Peel was convinced that Cobden and Bright were basically right: that the Corn Laws hampered the expansion of the British economy. But many of his own land-owning supporters did not agree. It was the unexpected Irish potato famine (1845–6) that enabled Peel to force through the Repeal of the Corn Laws. He told the Tory Party that the only way to help the Irish was to end the import duties on corn. Britain had taken the first step on the road towards becoming a free trade nation.

Effects of repeal on agriculture

In the ten years after repeal (1846–56) the much-feared glut of cheap corn did not appear. No other country could compete with the efficient British farming methods and the rapidly improving system of transport that enabled food to be carried around the country cheaply and efficiently.

Look at the price of wheat 1846–56:

Year	Price of wheat per quarter	Comment
1846	54/8d	Very early spring; very hot, wet summer – enabled the potato blight fungus to flourish in Ireland.
1847	69/9d	Plentiful wheat harvest; phosphates (for fertilisers) found in East Anglia.
1848	50/6d	Wet harvest – poor yields.
1849	44/3d	Excellent harvest.
1850	40/3d	Harvest damaged by high winds and mildew. Horses used to operate the big buttermaking churns needed to supply the expanding towns and cities.
1851	38/6d	A late but very good harvest.
1852	40/9d	Another good harvest – some damage due to rain.

Year	Price of wheat per quarter	Comment
1853	53/3d	Poor harvest due to 'very disastrous summer floods'. Corn crops flattened – much grain lost.
1854	72/5d	A good harvest – corn prices high because cheap Russian corn ordered that year not available because of Crimean War.
1855	74/8d	Rains damaged a good wheat harvest.
1856	69/2d	Good harvest.

Questions

1 Compare the tables on page 30 and page 34.
  (a)   In what year did the price of wheat reach its peak?
  (b)   What was the main reason for poor harvests?
  (c)   What appeared to be the main threat to sheep rearing during these years?
2 Why did Thomas Bannister (p. 32) make his application for relief?
3 Did the 1834 Poor Law Amendment Act end all 'outside relief'?
4 Document 1

Barrett and Co.'s Four-horse power Thrashing Machine.

Source: L. F. Hobley, *Living and Working*. OUP, 1964, p. 83.

This is one of the early horse-powered threshing machines available in the 1820s.

(a)   How many horses could be used to operate this particular machine?

(b)   When was the threshing usually done?

(c)   Why did farm labourers in the south particularly oppose the installation of these machines on the farms?

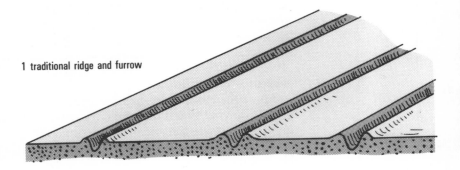

1 traditional ridge and furrow

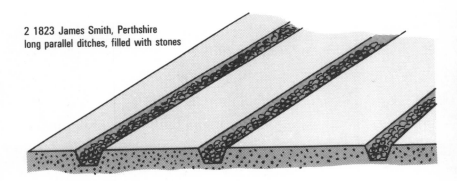

2 1823 James Smith, Perthshire
long parallel ditches, filled with stones

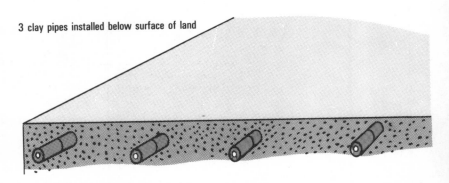

3 clay pipes installed below surface of land

Soil drainage techniques

5 Document 2

(a)   What were the disadvantages of the traditional method of draining fields?

(b)   Why was James Smith's technique better?

(c)   Does it have any particular disadvantages?

(d)   Why was the use of clay pipes superior to other drainage systems?

(e)   On what kind of soils would farmers now be able to improve their productivity?

6 Document 3

This is a map to show the division of Britain into

(a)   the high wage area;

(b)   the low wage area

for agricultural labourers.

(a)   Describe how this division came about.

(b)   Mark the village of Speenhamland on the map.

(c)   Describe the Speenhamland system.

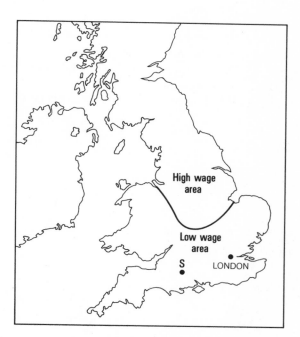

(d)   Was it ever intended to apply to the whole country?

(e)   Why did other parishes make use of the idea?

(f)   For what reason was the system abolished?

(g)   Name the Act of Parliament that changed the system in 1834.

(h)   Explain the significance of these two old English sayings:
          (i) 'I'll have to go on the parish.'
          (ii) 'It'll drive me to the workhouse.'

7 Document 4

The beginning of the artificial fertiliser industry

During the period 1835–50 British farmers were able to make
use of some of the latest chemical research into the use of
artificial fertilisers. Peruvian guano, rich in phosphates, was
imported in 1835 and by 1840 its use was common on British
farms, supplementing the phosphate deposits that had been
tapped in East Anglia. The most famous agricultural chemist
was Sir John Bennet Laws (1814–1900). He began his
experiments at Rothamsted Manor in Hertfordshire (1837).
He first treated bones (often used as a fertiliser) with
sulphuric acid and calcium phosphate and realised that this
would make a much better fertiliser. However, his problem
was how to mass produce stocks for sale. He found that if he
used sulphuric acid to treat mineral rock phosphate he had a
completely new form of fertiliser. Manufacturers now began
to offer 'superphosphate of lime' to farmers and this marks
the beginning of Britain's important artificial fertiliser
industry.

(a)   Where did the guano come from?
(b)   Was this an artificial fertiliser?
(c)   Where did Sir John Bennet Laws begin his experiments?
(d)   Why was the treatment of bones not a commercial prospect?
(c)   What name did Laws give to his new artificial fertiliser?

INDUSTRIAL CHANGES 1750–1850

CONTENTS

THE STEAM AGE

Once the miners had exhausted the shallow coal pits it was necessary to work the deep seams – and as the miners went deeper so the hazards increased:

(a)   the 'sulphurous vapour' of firedamp (methane gas);

(b)   constant flooding of shafts and seams.

Savery's engine and Newcomen's engine paved the way for the expansion of the coal industry. Without the ability to pump water from flooded mines, that expansion would have been impossible.

THE NEWCOMEN ENGINE

It was very simple to operate and maintain and was generally called the 'common engine'. Its effectiveness can be gauged from the performance of the engine installed by the Earl Fitzwilliam at Elsecar (outside Barnsley) in 1795:

(a)   13 strokes a minute;

(b)   could pump 748,800 gallons out of flooded seams every 24 hours;

(c)   this gave access to approximately 4 million tons of coal.

WATT'S STEAM ENGINE

James Watt (1736–1819) was a Scottish instrument maker who worked on modifications to the Newcomen engine. He discovered ways of making it far more efficient. The great saving, he discovered, came in the use of a separate condenser. However, his great contribution came in 1781 when he added 'rotary motion' to the engine through a 'sun and planet' gear system to drive a variety of mechanical devices. His engine, a major technological breakthrough, was of enormous benefit to coal mining and many other industries. But because it was a low pressure steam engine it was still relatively inefficient.

The challenge was: how to design an efficient high pressure steam engine?

TREVETHICK'S STEAM ENGINE

Richard Trevethick (1771–1833) was a Cornish engineer who patented a high pressure steam engine in 1802. In 1804 he used this engine to power a railway locomotive – the world's first successful example. His engine was used in rail and road transport; it carried out the dredging operations in a tunnel under the Thames (1806). He is best remembered for building the world's first passenger locomotive – the Catch-me-who-can. It ran on a small circular track close to the modern Euston Square station and people paid a shilling a time to ride on this extraordinary vehicle. Later Cornish engines were immensely powerful – producing about 150 bhp.

Example (from coal-mining)

Year	Time	Pit output
1835	12 hours	300 tons using rotary engines
1850	12 hours	800 tons using Cornish engines

SIGNIFICANCE OF THE STEAM ENGINE

The steam engine was probably the most important single invention in the period often termed the Industrial Revolution. Why? Because it supplied power – power to drive spinning machines in cotton factories, power to drive the corn mills, power to drive rolling mills and bellows in the expanding iron industry. Power enabled the British people to 'take off' into a period of sustained economic growth ahead of any other nation in the world. It began around 1780; by 1851 Britain was able to hold its 'Great Exhibition' at the Crystal Palace to demonstrate that it was 'the workshop of the world'.

THEORIES OF TRADE AND INDUSTRY

The long period of warfare (American Revolutionary War 1775–83 and the Revolutionary and Napoleonic Wars against France 1793–1815) had dislocated the British economy at the precise moment
(a)   it was 'taking off' into a period of rapid trade and manufacturing expansion;
(b)   when the population was expanding so that feeding the extra millions proved an almost impossible job for the ill-equipped and insensitive governments of the day.
Government governed the country according to the established rules of 'mercantilism' – the trade theory of the seventeenth and eighteenth centuries. By this, goverment regulated trade and controlled food prices to preserve the financial well-being of the State. It had no concern for the well-being of the masses of poor people and regarded their protests as a sign of potential revolution and crushed them without mercy.
    Mercantilism therefore came under a great deal of attack from

economists at the end of the eighteenth and the beginning of the nineteenth centuries. Three are especially important:

Adam Smith (1723–90) was a widely travelled and highly respected political economist. He challenged mercantilism and wrote a very famous book called *Inquiry into the Nature and Cause of Wealth of Nations*.

(a)   Navigation Acts and monopoly organisations controlling trade should be removed.

(b)   The reverse of this – *laissez-faire* (leave things alone to take their own course) – was not advisable.

(c)   The producer should assess the wants and interests of the consumer – consumption of goods is the keynote of prosperity.

(d)   Hoarding money/gold is of no value – it should be invested in expansion and this expansion would need specialisation i.e. there should be a division of labour in a modern industrial society.

(e)   This new society needs a reliable currency.

These were some of Adam Smith's ideas and they had a great impact upon his contemporaries. Many of these ideas are no longer relevant – nevertheless, Adam Smith may be regarded as the founder of 'political economy'.

Thomas Malthus (1766–1834) did not agree. In his *First Essay on Population* he said that the key to the problems facing society was the rapidly expanding population. Government had agreed with the policy of handing out more food subsidy and poor relief. This was actually causing people to marry earlier and have bigger families. Having smaller families would increase the standard of living; for the standard of living was always low in countries with large populations. Otherwise, population would increase faster than the means of feeding the people. Of course, he was not to know that the flowering of British manufacturers, and the agricultural improvements (especially the use of artificial fertilisers) would eventually cope with the increased population.

David Ricardo (1771–1823) produced his *Principles of Political Economy* in 1817. He believed in *laissez-faire* and claimed that, left alone, wages, profits and taxation would take 'a natural course'. He at first suggested that the value of goods must be determined by the amount of labour put into making them. He had an influence on the later Free Traders and, as a matter of interest, was often read by the German philosopher, Karl Marx.

Despite the economists, the interests of the producers remained paramount in British society. Not until the middle of the century was there any deep concern for the welfare of the masses – the consumers. Your studies of the coal, cotton and iron industries will give you plenty evidence of that.

THE COAL INDUSTRY

THE DEMAND FOR COAL

1700 annual tonnage of coal produced = about 2.5 million
1800 annual tonnage of coal produced = over 10.0 million

Why?

1 Demand from the ironmasters – mineral fuel had virtually replaced timber in the iron industry by 1800.

2 Expanding population and movement into towns needed coal to keep warm; while the industries in which the workers were employed needed a constant supply of coal.
e.g. London's import of coal via the coastal trade:

1834	2,078,000 tons
1846	3,392,000 tons

THE LIFE OF THE MINERS

It is very important to understand that no single invention transformed the mining industry during the nineteenth century. The massive demand for coal was met through the muscles of men, women and children – often under very harsh conditions, especially when rapid expansion in a new mine took place. In most mining communities men had taken their wives and children along to carry the baskets and look after horses and pit ponies. Though working conditions were always unpleasant, there had been plenty of rests between shifts and lots of holidays. Moreover, pay was often good. As late as 1832 William Cobbett had noted that in the Sunderland area 'everything seems to be abundant'.

Violent death and injury

Exact figures of miners' deaths in the period 1750–1850 are not known. It is thought that before 1812 disasters were on a relatively small scale. Pit accidents did not often cause more than ten deaths. Then in 1812 came the Felling Colliery disaster in County Durham. Ninety-one men died – most of the labour force. In 1813 the Sunderland Society for Preventing Accidents was formed and in 1815 it contacted Humphry Davy (1778–1829) an eminent chemist. He promptly designed the Davy's safety lamp (1815) – adopted by many coal-miners. This helped to solve the problem of firedamp.

Ventilators were well-established in many deep mines. Compound ventilation was common – ventilating shafts (often operated by child 'trappers') created air currents underground.

The use of mechanical ventilators

A variety of mechanical ventilators came on the market between 1800 and 1850:

1807   John Buddle's air pump
1837   William Fourness built his Rotary Air Drum
1849   William Brunton's new ventilator

These ventilators helped control the dreaded firedamp explosions but did not help the two other main hazards:

1 coal dust explosions;
2 roof falls.

PUBLIC CONCERN

This was not truly awakened until the publication of the *First Report of the Children's Employment Commission (1842)*. It had pictures, drawn on the spot, by the artist Binney; these, together with the descriptions of work that women and children had to do, shocked MPs.
This is part of the report:

> We find:
> 1 That instances occur in which Children are taken into these mines to work as early as four years of age, sometimes five, and between five and six, not unfrequently between six and seven, and often from seven to eight, while from eight to nine is the ordinary age at which employment in these mines commences.
> 2 That the great body of the Children and Young Persons employed in these mines are of the families of the adult workpeoples engaged in the pits, or belong to the poorest population in the neighbourhood, and are hired and paid in some districts by the workpeople, but in others by the proprietors or contractors.
> 3 That the nature of the employment which is assigned to the youngest Children, generally that of 'trapping', requires that they should be in the pit as soon as the work of the day commences, and, according to the present system, that they should not leave the pit before the work of the day is at an end.
> 4 That in many cases the Children and Young Persons have little cause of complaint in regard to the treatment they receive from the persons in authority in the mine, or from the colliers; but that in general the younger Children are roughly used by their older companions.
> 5 That in general the Children and Young Persons who work in these mines have sufficient food, and, when above ground, decent and comfortable clothing, their usually high rate of wages securing to them these advantages; but in many cases, more especially in some parts of Yorkshire, in Derbyshire, in South Gloucestershire, and very generally in the East of Scotland, the food is poor in quality, and insufficient in quantity . . . notwithstanding the intense labour performed by these Children, they do not procure even sufficient food and raiment; in general, however, the Children who are in this unhappy case are the Children of idle and dissolute parents, who spend the hard-earned wages of their offspring at the public house.

Do you consider this to be a balanced report? Does your textbook point out that miners, their wives and children often secured good wages?

The Report also spoke of girls who carried the coals on their backs up steep ladders. Look at the illustration below. The Report described this girl as wearing a wide leather strap 'to which is attached a ring and about four feet of chain terminating in a hook'.

Girl shackled to coal barrow

Questions

1   Name the first steam engine that was able to pump floodwaters from mines at a very high rate?
2   Why did the towns need so much coal?
3   Why were mine disasters before 1812 'on a relatively small scale'?
4   What name was given to the children who operated the ventilating doors?
5   Give two examples of major hazards besides firedamp in the mines.
6   To whom did most of the children working in the pits belong?
7   Is there evidence that the majority of the pit owners behaved harshly towards the children?
8   Who in particular behaved badly towards children in the pits?
9   Why were some children so ill-fed and badly dressed?
10 List the dangers facing the girl in the illustration.

THE 1842 MINES ACT

Lord Ashley (Anthony Ashley Cooper, 7th Earl of Shaftesbury) was an MP 1826–51 and involved in many aspects of reform. He introduced the bill that became the 1842 Mines Act:

1   Women and girls not to work underground;
2   Boys under ten not to work underground;
3   Mines Inspectorate appointed – but with very limited powers. In 1850 another Mines Act ensured that inspectors were practical engineers. So by 1850 Parliament, under the pressure of public opinion, had investigated social conditions within one major area of work and ordered improvements.

It is important to remember that the early inventors in the textile industry brought out improvements to speed up production in the home – not in a factory. One of the main problems was how to speed up spinning processes. It is interesting to note that the first invention actually speeded up the weaving process.

John Kay of Bolton – the 'flying shuttle' (1733)

Kay was born in 1704; his date of death is in dispute (now thought to be 1781). His 'flying shuttle' (a spring-loaded shuttle) speeded up weaving in the home and created a demand for more weavers.

James Hargreaves – the 'spinning-jenny' (1764–70)

Born about 1720, died 1778. He invented the 'spinning jenny' (the word jenny is possibly a corruption of 'engine'). It could spin eight threads at once. Other spinners attacked his house as they were afraid that the invention would put them out of work. However, most spinners could see its advantages and bought their own spinning jennies – widely used in the domestic system until the 1790s.

Richard Arkwright – the water frame (1768–70)

Richard Arkwright (1732–92) constructed a water frame that could produce yarn ideally suited to the Nottingham stocking knitters. He went into partnership with Jedediah Strutt and built a spinning mill (powered by water) at Cromford. This was a great success. Shortly afterwards, Arkwright opened another mill at Belper.

Samuel Crompton – the 'mule' (1779)

Samuel Crompton (1753–1827) combined the spinning techniques developed by Hargreaves and Arkwright. The mule could produce large quantities of very fine yarn.

You will note that Hargreaves, Arkwright and Crompton had all produced machinery that increased the quality and quantity of spun cotton. What was desperately needed was some mechanical device to carry out the weaving process. For many years this eluded the inventors and during that time thousands of extra handloom weavers were hired.

Edmund Cartwright – the power loom (1787)

His power loom operated by steam was a great success – except that it constantly broke down because its main moving parts were made of wood. After 1800 iron equipment was being introduced into the new spinning and weaving factories being built in the towns. The men who get the credit for improving Cartwright's original designs were:

1 **William Horrocks** of Stockport – devised a crankshaft drive mechanism for the loom in 1803.

2 **Richard Roberts** made cast iron parts for the textile industry in 1822.

THE SOCIAL SIGNIFICANCE OF THE TEXTILE REVOLUTION

1   At first, the new factory owners found it hard to get people to work for them. The domestic worker gave up his freedom to work his own hours with great reluctance. Many domestic workers regarded the first factories as the same as going in the army – there were so many petty regulations to observe.

2   However, there was a huge floating population in Britain. Many people came from Ireland and Scotland to work in Lancashire and Yorkshire. Many farm labourers, unable to earn a living wage in the countryside, settled in the textile communities.

3   The textile industry offered a lot of jobs to women and children – children found ready employment as 'pieceners' because their nimble fingers could join broken threads on the new equipment.

4   As well as attracting a huge labour force, the textile industry encouraged the expansion of other trades – mining, engineering, industrial chemistry and, of course, building.

5   This helped to create the new communities in which people had to live close together and experience a new way of life sometimes highly unpleasant because of the lack of hygiene.

6   The mass production of cotton goods created new markets at home and abroad and put Britain on the road to industrial prosperity as far as the factory owners and merchants were concerned.

7   By 1810 cotton had outstripped the traditional woollen industry. The East Anglian wool trade declined; so did the south-west producers around Exeter.

8   The handloom weavers began to lose their jobs. They could not compete with the power looms – though they tried. To some extent, their feelings show in this weaver's folk song:

> Poverty, poverty knock
> Me loom is a-saying all day.
> Poverty, poverty knock.
> The Gaffer's too skinny to pay.
> Poverty, poverty knock,
> Keeping one eye on the clock.
> Ah know ah can guttle
> When ah hear me shuttle
> Go: Poverty, poverty knock.
> Up every morning at five.
> Ah wonder that we keep alive.
> Tired and yawning' on the cold mornin'
> Its back to the dreary old drive.*

*Quoted by John Addy, *The Textile Revolution* (Oxford 1976) p. 90.

9   Relationships between master and worker – never very good in the domestic system – began to worsen. This polarisation between employer and employee was apparent in the Luddite riots (see pp. 56–8).

CONDITIONS IN THE FACTORIES

In some, conditions were appalling. In others – where the factory owners could see the benefit of providing workers with good conditions and pay – life was tolerable. There was widespread demand for a ten hour day (John Fielden, one of the world's most prosperous cotton spinners, granted a ten hour day before it was legally required) and a Parliamentary Select Committee interviewed people who worked in the textile industry to discover their conditions. One of the most famous interviews concerned 23-year-old Elizabeth Bentley:

What time did you begin work at a factory?
When I was six.

What was your business in that mill?
I was a little doffer.*

What were your hours of labour in that mill?
From five in the morning till nine at night, when they were thronged.†

You are considerably deformed in your person in consequence of this labour?
Yes, I am.

At what time did it come on?
I was about thirteen when it began coming and it has got worse ever since.

Were you perfectly straight and healthy before you worked at a mill?
Yes, I was as straight a little girl as ever went up and down town.

Interviews such as this made a great impact; and in 1833 the famous Factory Act was passed (see p. 61).

*A doffer took the full bobbins off the spindles and replaced them with empty ones.
†This means there were lots of people about, working hard, i.e. the factory was busy until late at night.

Questions

1 Why were the early spinning factories not situated in the towns?
2 What encouraged factory owners to move to the towns?
3 Read the weaver's song on page 48. Why does he constantly repeat the words: 'Poverty, poverty knock'?
4 What is his main complaint?
5 Look at the evidence given by Elizabeth Bentley (above). How long had she worked in a factory before she noticed she was deformed?
6 Why do you think factory work caused deformity among young workers?

IRON

Read the following extract:

The best English iron had once come from the Weald, where the charcoal-fired furnaces were just ending their long history. The main reason for this was the steep rise in charcoal prices; as farmers cleared the woodlands and other industries clamoured for timber fuel, the iron workers' costs soared until, by 1746, charcoal accounted for 80 per cent of their overheads. However, in the Midlands iron production was increasing. Quality bar-iron came in from Sweden – costs actually fell after the improved Hull–Bawtry river route was completed in the seventeenth century. There was plenty of water power and the small blast furnaces poured forth a steady stream of pig-iron which, after forging and slitting, became the material for thousands of nailers. But the major expansion in the Midlands – and later on in the North and in South also – awaited the developments that would enable the iron industry to use not only local ore but local coal as well.

1　Where is the Weald?
2　Why were the charcoal furnaces in decline?
3　Where was iron production increasing?
4　Which country supplied a great deal of bar-iron?
5　Explain the term 'pig-iron'.
6　What development was needed to expand iron production?

Abraham Darby (1677–1717)

Though everyone agrees that Darby's discovery in 1709:
(a)　　'changed the course of history';
(b)　　'brought about Britain's supremacy as an iron-producing country';
the exact circumstances of how he did it remain uncertain. He discovered how to smelt iron by using coke made from local coal. It is possible that he had learned about coking methods when he was apprenticed to a maltings construction firm. He was certainly good at keeping secrets though he passed his knowledge on to his son, Abraham Darby II.

Abraham Darby II (1711–63)

He expanded the family firm at Coalbrookdale and discovered how to make good quality bar-iron. The firm also made parts for Newcomen engines. The firm's techniques became more and more sophisticated and Abraham III built up Coalbrookdale into the biggest iron-works in the country.

Abraham Darby III (1750–91)

He is famous for building (with the help of John Wilkinson) the first iron bridge in the world (across the Severn at Coalbrookdale).

MASS-PRODUCING BAR-IRON

The Darby family had a secret way of producing quality bar-iron using coke but they made it in very small quantities. Many other ironmasters experimented along their lines but met with no success.

Henry Cort (1740–1800) discovered a method called 'puddling and rolling' (1783–4) to produce thin plates of iron.

1. Pig-iron was heated in a furnace but kept quite separate from the coke.
2. A skilled puddler stirred the molten iron, cooling it and, at the same time, removing carbon impurities.
3. The puddler then removed the iron (in chunks called 'blooms') and it was then hammered prior to being passed through a series of rollers.

Cort's techniques enabled ironmasters to locate themselves on the coalfields. One of the most famous ironmasters was John Wilkinson.

John Wilkinson (1728–1805)

He was one of the most successful of the eighteenth-century entrepreneurs. His special skill was boring cylinders:

(a) iron pipes for the Paris water supply;
(b) special cylinders for the new Watt's rotary engine;
(c) cannon for the Royal Navy (his rival here was John Roebuck whose cannon (as supplied to the Royal Navy) were known as 'carronades', after the Scottish ironworks at Carron).

STEEL

Techniques for making cast steel developed during the period 1750–1850.

Benjamin Huntsman (1704–76) invented the crucible method of producing steel – a lengthy and expensive process. He had many rivals, and by 1850 cast steel was widely used for precision instruments (watches, machine tools) and high quality cutlery. But it could not be produced cheaply and in large quantities. Brass continued to be used – a common feature of early Victorian products.

THE GROWTH OF TOWNS

The population explosion continued into the nineteenth century, and between 1801 and 1851 the population of England and Wales actually doubled.

Thousands of people became town-dwellers and raised their families in the towns:

Town	1801 figure	1851 figure
Leeds	53,000	172,000
Manchester	75,000	400,000
Bradford	13,000	104,000
London	1,117,000	2,000,000+

In the manufacturing towns the location of the factory was critical. It needed to be near a canal or river; it needed to have good road access – and later it needed to have good rail links. It also had to have a labour supply located close to it. Factories didn't have canteens. So if the work-force came on to the first shift at six in the morning it would be forced to walk home for breakfast!

Blocks of terraced houses with no proper sanitation and no running water were built close to the factories. Above the houses the air hung heavy with pollution. Between the houses ran open cesspools. Sometimes the people who lived in houses such as this – or in cellars or in one room – were thrown out of work due to depressions in their particular industry. They were as helpless as the farm labourers, with no way of redressing their complaints. So, in Britain during the period 1810–50 there developed:

1   Terrible diseases, often due to the squalor of the new towns:

(*a*)   *cholera* – the worst. The first onslaught began in Sunderland (1831), spreading to Tyneside, Hull, York and Liverpool. The second attack came in 1849 – over 53,000 cases. 5000 people died in overcrowded Liverpool.

(*b*)   *typhus* – epidemics raged in 1837, 1839 and 1849 (the worst year when thousands died all over the country);

(*c*)   *smallpox* – a terrible period 1837–40. Over 10,000 died in 1840;

(*d*)   *respiratory diseases, scarlatina, whooping cough and measles* – these were the diseases that struck down infants whose chance of survival in the unhygienic conditions of the new towns was limited.

2   Urban violence – mob action (for all sorts of reasons) and petty crime were the main problems. Law and order problems were met by Robert Peel, Home Secretary, when he began the Metropolitan Police Force (1829), an idea that rapidly spread to other cities. In 1839 a Rural Constabulary Act extended the idea to the counties.

Why was there so much disorder?

Apart from the misery of life in the town and countryside during periods of severe economic crisis, there was a constant sense of frustration that the ruling classes either didn't care about or couldn't understand the problems of an industrialised society. The condition of the consumer was not actively improved. Fundamentally, the consumers could not express their point of view – they wanted to form trade unions and they wanted to put their representatives into Parliament. There was a clamour for reform and improvement that was only partially met during this period.

PROTEST AND REFORM TO 1851

CONTENTS

Most protest during the eighteenth century – and much of this was spontaneous – took the form of food riots. However, there were exceptions such as the Gordon Riots of June 1780.

THE GORDON RIOTS 1780

Lord George Gordon (1751–93) was a professional agitator. He was violently anti-Catholic and headed the Protestant Association. He led a campaign of systematic protest against Catholics in London and claimed to have evidence that there was a plot to massacre Protestants in the City. Heading a huge crowd of hooligans, he marched to Parliament and tried to present a petition deploring the Catholic 'plans'. Riots began that night, but it was on the following Sunday that matters got out of hand. Mobs set fire to many Irish houses in East London and eventually burnt down Fleet Prison. John Wilkes – himself a skilful agitator and a constant thorn in the side of King George III – won fame by defending the Bank of England against Gordon's mob. Gordon was acquitted – despite the fact that the authorities hanged twenty-five of his supporters. Imprisoned for a later offence, Gordon died in jail from typhus.

EFFECTS OF THE FRENCH REVOLUTION

In 1789 the revolutionary crowd in Paris stormed the Bastille and sparked off the revolution that led to the formation of the French Republic in 1792.

During the 1790s some British extremists (they were called 'radicals' because their political beliefs were quite different from those held by most educated people) openly admired the Revolution. John Thelwall was a radical:

> That which I glory in, in the French Revolution, is this: . . .
> that man has rights which no statutes or usages can take
> away . . . that thought ought to be free . . . that intellectual
> beings are entitle to the use of their intellects . . . that one
> order of society has no right, how many years soever they
> have been guilty of the pillage, to plunder and oppress the
> other parts of the community . . .

Tom Paine (1737–1809) was a British political writer who went to America where he published *Common Sense* (1776) in which he advocated complete independence for the thirteen American colonies. He came back to Britain. There he wrote *The Rights of Man* – and was forced by the authorities to flee to France.

People who read the works of people such as Thelwall and Paine wondered about their own lack of political rights.

1   Some formed 'corresponding societies' (these began in 1792 in many of the expanding British towns) so that ideas could be exchanged. Very well known in the capital was Thomas Hardy's London Corresponding Society.

2   Others formed 'Combinations' (early trade unions) in an effort to protect their own trades and skills. One Leeds combination was fearful of the way 'aristocrats' could control their affairs and punish any tradesman who 'stepped out of line'. One member wrote this (original spelling):

> We are chiefly Working Mecanicks as those tradesmen hear who are friends to our cause have few of them Virtue enough to come Publickley forward as the Aristocratic influence is so great that they have got all the trade under their own hand so that they have got Power to distress any tradesmen who exposes the Villany of a Corrupt System.

GOVERNMENT REACTION

Fearful that there were signs in Britain of support for France (Britain was at war with France in 1793), Prime Minister Pitt passed a series of repressive laws:

1   **Habeas Corpus** suspended 1794–1802.
2   **Treason Act 1795** – forbade criticism of government.
3   **Seditious Meetings Act 1795** – no meeting of over fifty people without permission.
4   **Combination Acts 1799–1800** abolished all trade unions and corresponding societies (many continued to flourish in secret).

The Luddites 1811–12

Luddites were originally stockingers who smashed up sixty stocking frames in Arnold, Nottinghamshire, in 1811. They were organised and led by well-trained machine-breakers who timed their attacks on Nottingham's outlying villages in such a way as to mislead the local magistrates and soldiers who were trying to capture the Luddites in action. The name Ludd is supposed to have been taken from Ned Ludd, a Leicestershire textile worker who smashed a piece of machinery in a fit of rage.

Document 1

> *General Ludd's Triumph*
> The guilty may fear but no vengeance he aims

*Quoted by E. P.
Thompson, *The Making of
the English Working Class*
(Pelican, 1968). Read
pp. 605–59 for a first class
account of the Luddite
Revolt.

At the honest man's life or Estate,
His wrath is entirely confined to wide frames
And to those that old prices abate.
These engines of mischief were sentenced to die
By unanimous vote of the Trade
And Ludd who can all opposition defy
Was the Grand executioner made.*

Document 2

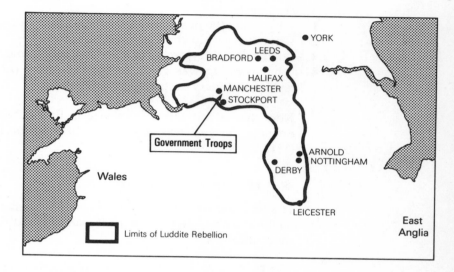

The Luddite Rebellion

Document 3
Extract from the *Leeds Mercury*, 1812

> As soon as the work of destruction was over, the Leader drew
> up his men, called over the roll, each man answering to a
> particular number instead of his name; they then fired off
> their pistols . . . gave a shout and marched off in regular
> military order . . . One of the party having asked the Leader
> what they should do with one of the Proprietors, he replied –
> not hurt a hair of his head; but that should they be under the
> necessity of visiting him again they could not show him any
> mercy.

Questions
Document 1
1 Were the ordinary working men at risk from General Ludd?
2 What was the main object of attack?
3 Explain the term 'these engines of mischief'.

4   Is there evidence that Luddism was popular?
5   Explain the term 'Grand executioner'.

Document 2
1   On the map, shade in the area of Luddite activity.
2   How many counties were involved?
3   Seventeen Luddites were hanged. Where were the sentences carried out?
4   How did the government try to restore law and order?

Document 3
1   Why didn't the men use their names during the roll call?
2   What did they do immediately after roll call?
3   What evidence is there that they were well trained?
4   What warning was given to the Proprietor (i.e. the owner of the textile machinery destroyed by this band)?

Note that at this time of violence in British history Prime Minister Spencer Perceval was shot by a lunatic in the House of Commons (1812).

RIOTS AFTER THE NAPOLEONIC WARS

1816 Farm workers in East Anglia demanded a minimum wage of two shillings a day. These were the 'Bread or Blood' riots – suppressed by the authorities.

1816 Spa Fields Riot – Parliament reacted by passing the 'Gagging Act' to prevent mobs forming and suspended Habeas Corpus. The government also became quite skilful in sending in 'undercover' agents to work among the tradesmen and textile employees. Because of this, the demonstrations known as the 'March of the Blanketeers' and the Pentridge March (1817) made little impact. Government agents were able to tip off the military where and when these demonstrations were to be held.

1819 The Peterloo Massacre This resulted from the first post-war attempt to secure a reform of Parliament, to allow a democratic system of government to exist in Britain. Radicals had wanted annual elections and universal suffrage in the eighteenth century; so had the corresponding societies. Now, after the Napoleonic Wars, radicals such as William Cobbett and Henry 'Orator' Hunt were demanding parliamentary reform.

About 50,000 people went to St Peter's Field on 16 August 1819. They went to hear Orator Hunt. The local magistrate ordered his arrest and ordered the mounted Yeomanry to do the job. Many of the Yeomanry were local employers – manufacturers, publicans, butchers – and they were infuriated by the presence of so many of their employees at St Peter's Field. They eventually arrested Hunt after being jostled by the crowd and then a fight broke out leading to massive confusion as regular cavalry (the 15th Hussars) and the Yeomanry began to use their sabres against the people. Ten were killed; hundreds were wounded.

Parliament's reaction to the Massacre

Parliament rushed through the Six Acts (1819):

1 no military training allowed;
2 no seditious meetings allowed;
3 fines and transportation to be the punishment of those found guilty of seditious libel;
4 newspapers to carry stamp duties;
5 houses could be searched for weapons;
6 speedy justice – the law courts to deal instantly with agitators.

The Cato Street Conspiracy 1820

This was a plot to blow up the Cabinet. The main conspirator, Arthur Thistlewood, was betrayed by an undercover agent. Thistlewood was executed.

Repeal of the Combination Laws

Francis Place, a London tailor, was deeply interested in the way in which the 1799–1800 Combination Laws had been used against workers. He liaised with a sympathetic MP named Joseph Hume to coach witnesses for a Parliamentary inquiry into the misuse of the laws. This was so skilfully done that the Committee recommended the repeal of the Combination Laws, carried out in 1824. This enabled workers to form unions and to go on strike.

However, a second law (1825) seriously restricted these rights when it defined 'intimidation to strike' as an offence. Nevertheless, several trade unions did operate 1829–33, for example:

– the National Association for the Protection of Labour (textile workers – failed in 1832);
– the Builders' Union brought together over 30,000 workers but that too failed (1833).

The Swing Riots 1830

This was a farm labourers' revolt against mechanisation – similar to the Luddite revolts of 1811–12. The rioters wrote 'Swing Letters' to their intended victims and then moved in to burn threshing machines. It was a serious revolt and spread across the 'low wage' counties and parts of Yorkshire. Cornstacks and hayricks were destroyed as well as farm machinery. Nineteen Swing rioters were hanged; over 500 were transported to Australia. There is strong evidence that farmers were wary about mechanising their farms for several years after the Swing Riots.

REFORM

THE FIRST REFORM ACT 1832

THE VOTERS BEFORE 1832

Although there were over 24 million people in Britain by 1832 only 440,000 had the right to vote in parliamentary elections. Some of these voters had very curious qualifications:

The Forty Shilling Freeholders: all who owned land worth forty shillings a year had the vote.

Freeman of boroughs , together with councillors, usually had the vote.

Potwallopers – in some constituencies those who had a fireside big enough to take a cooking pot had the vote.

Burgage-holders – a person whose house carried certain voting rights.

Scot and Lot – in some boroughs a householder who still paid these ancient taxes had the vote.

Some of the constituencies or boroughs as they were then known were curiously organised:

1   A 'pocket' borough was controlled by one man – usually through bribery i.e. it was in the man's pocket.
2   A 'rotten' borough perhaps didn't have any people living in it – yet it might send two MPs to Parliament!

THE REFORM CRISIS

By 1830 the clamour for reform, for the improvement of the British people through constitutional means, was unending. Lord Grey, the British Prime Minister, brought in a reform bill in 1831 and it secured a majority of one vote. Grey thought he should hold a general election to discover how the 440,000 voted really felt. Re-elected, Grey brought in a second reform bill which passed the House of Commons. However, the Lords rejected it.

This led to riots all over the country – especially serious in Bristol. Grey's reaction was to ask King William IV to create enough peers to outvote the opposition in the House of Lords; or, alternatively, accept his resignation.

King William IV accepted Grey's resignation.

The fear of revolt

For the next nine days there was no effective government in Britain. It was expected that Birmingham militants would march on London and soldiers were ready to stop them. The threat reached its peak on 13 May 1832. Next day the King agreed to co-operate with Grey – and this forced the surrender of the House of Lords.

THE REFORM ACT 1832

1   In the boroughs all men owning property worth £10 a year won the vote.
2   In the counties the forty-shilling freeholders kept the vote; as did all leaseholders and those who paid £10 annually as 'copyholders'.
3   Most 'rotten boroughs' abolished.
4   Forty-two new MPs for the industrial towns.
5   Each county to have two MPs.

Significance

Less than a quarter of a million new voters had been added. There was no universal suffrage (that would have to wait nearly a hundred years) and no secret ballot. But at least it did enable caring MPs to exercise some influence on Parliament – as the work of the new Parliament (called the Reform Parliament) shows.

The work of the Reform Parliament

Many of the MPs were followers of 'Benthamism' – the ideas put forward by the British philosopher Jeremy Bentham (1748–1832). Widely travelled, he believed that all laws passed by Parliament should be aimed at doing the greatest good for the biggest number of people possible – this should be the criterion of all legislators. Benthamism, called 'utilitarianism' by many of his followers, encouraged careful investigation of conditions on scientific and humanitarian lines. Certainly, his influence is apparent in both:

(*a*)   the methods;
(*b*)   the legislation of the Reform Parliament.

FACTORY AND SCHOOL LEGISLATION

THE 1833 FACTORY ACT

Many humanitarian factory owners had already pointed the way reform should take.

Robert Owen (1771–1858) was by 1800 manager and part-owner of some huge factories in Scotland – the New Lanark Mills. He was active in improving housing and working conditions for his employees and brought in some teachers to educate the younger children. He was determined to improve the environment of the people and urged government to take radical steps to bring about change. In many ways, Owen was the first practical socialist in British industrial society. Government had taken two tiny steps already:

1802 Factory Act (Health and Morals of Apprentices Act) said that young people shouldn't work more than twelve hours a day – usually ignored by industrialists.

1819 Factory Act abolished nightwork for children and no child to work more than twelve hours a day – again, usually ignored.

1833 Factory Act tried to put matters right by appointing inspectors to ensure:

1   No children under nine to be employed in textile mills (there were some exceptions in the silk trade).
2   Children not to work longer than a forty-eight-hour week.
3   Between ages of thirteen and eighteen children could work a sixty-nine-hour week with a maximum of twelve hours a day.
4   No night work for anyone under eighteen.
5   No cleaning of machinery when it was working permitted.
6   Two hours a day schooling for children aged nine to thirteen.

Significance

1   Government had shown it was taking responsibility for the welfare of children in industry.
2   It provided the bedrock for further acts – gave reformers a chance to campaign for more improvements in working conditions, notably the Ten Hour Day

PROVISION OF EDUCATION

Again, the government took a tiny step forward. It had before it the example of philanthropists and the Church of England.

Robert Raikes had introduced some formal education into Sunday School teaching.

Joseph Lancaster had begun teaching children using the 'monitor' system (teacher teaches the monitors, the monitors then teach the children). Lancaster was a Quaker and his work interested the nonconformists in Britain.

Andrew Bell had also operated this system in India and he recommended it to the Church of England.

Results

1   Nonconformists founded the British and Foreign Schools Society – often called the 'Brits'.
2   The Church of England founded the National Society – often called the 'Nats'.

Government action 1833

It awarded £20,000 annually to these two societies, boosted to £30,000 in 1839. The main shortage was teachers and Dr Kay-Shuttleworth led the way by opening the Battersea Training College (1840).

THE POOR LAW AMENDMENT ACT 1834

This Act attempted to deal with the problem of paying the Poor Rates – a problem that was quite out of hand in some villages where the Poor Rate had increased by up to 800 per cent since the beginning of the century. The Act made no attempt to deal with the causes of poverty and was content to set up workhouses where poor men had to seek relief – or none at all. There was a great deal of resistance to the idea in the North and it was almost impossible to abolish the old 'outdoor relief' north of the Trent.

For details concerning the Act and its application see page 32–3.

THE MUNICIPAL REFORM ACT 1835

The Whig government set up a Commission to inquire into the state of municipal (i.e. town) government. On the basis of its findings it abolished nearly all the old corporations that had run British town life since the middle ages. In their place the Act set up 179 municipal boroughs.

How they worked

Ratepayers received the franchise, i.e. the right to vote in municipal elections. The rates they paid had to be used for the benefit of the people living within the borough – they were not to use any of this cash for their own purposes, as had happened before reform. Each year the borough's accounts had to be professionally audited to ensure that everthing was above board.

Significance

The new municipal arrangements were very popular and the first elections were held within three months of the Act becoming law. However, the new councils had very few powers in 1835 and the importance of the Act is that it extended the idea of 'parliamentary representation' to the municipal boroughs.

THE ABOLITION OF SLAVERY 1833

Britain had abolished the slave trade in 1807. This was as a result of pressure from men of the calibre of the Rev. Thomas Clarkson and William Wilberforce (1759–1833) MP for the great trading port of Hull.

THE 1807 ACT

Wilberforce had helped to found the Society for the Abolition of the Slave Trade (1787) and persuaded Parliament to abolish the slave trade in 1807. From 1 January 1808 dealing in slaves or shipping them from Africa was 'utterly abolished, prohibited and declared to be unlawful'.

THE 1811 ACT

This made slave trading an offence punishable by transportation to the convict island of Van Diemen's Land (Tasmania).

THE ACT OF 1833

The Act for the Abolition of Slavery throughout the territories of the British Empire became law on 29 August 1833. Wilberforce had died the previous month but not before he heard that the government intended to pass the law and compensate the slave owners. 'Thank God,' he said, 'that I should have lived to witness a day in which England is willing to give twenty millions sterling for the abolition of slavery.'

LAW AND ORDER TO 1851

CRIME

Though the death penalty still existed, in 1822 it had been abolished for over a hundred offences. This had not proved much of a deterrent before 1822; after 1822 crime rose to unprecedented levels, notwithstanding the creation of the Metropolitan Police Force and a number of borough and county police forces. The 1839 Constabulary Report described the situation and calculated that there were 40,000 full-time criminals in Britain and hosts of petty criminals.

Some statistics:

1827–31	17,000 commitments to prison (1 per 700 of the population)
1837–41	25,000 commitments to prison (1 per 640 of the population)

About 90 per cent of all crime was crime for gain – essentially petty thieving. Typical punishments were:

stealing some silver spoons	14 years
passing counterfeit notes	20 years
stealing £15 and two pistols	15 years

About 20 per cent of all convicted people were transported and these unfortunates usually spent some time in one of the prison hulks at, for example, Woolwich or Chatham. During this period, most convicts went to New South Wales or Tasmania (altogether about 188,000 men and women).

THE POLICE

The Metropolitan Police had set the trend: British police forces were not to carry guns, only truncheons. There were plenty of jobs for policemen now that the new municipal boroughs were required to set up a police force with its own stations. However, setting up police forces was a slow job and not all the counties had proper police forces by 1851.

Who joined the police?
Most of the early policemen were the former night watchmen and day watchmen. Quite often a former chief watchman became the chief constable overnight! Society did not value the police highly. Chief constables and superintendents were usually well paid by early Victorian standards; but sergeants and constables were not. The Criminal Investigation Department began with eight men in 1842.

Average weekly wages

Typical Victorian worker with family:	28 to 30 shillings
Labourer on a building site:	20 to 22 shillings
Police constable on joining:	16 shillings
Experienced police constable:	19 to 20 shillings

Turnover
Many policemen did not stay in a job for long. There were many charges of grave indiscipline – showing that a lot of police misused their special position. The position of the police did not improve until 1856 – and by then Britain had become a much less tumultuous society.

THE TRADE UNIONS

The 1825 Act forbade strike action – and though union leaders tried to organise strikes their actions were usually broken up by the employers and the new police forces.

Robert Owen and the GNCTU
Robert Owen had the idea of forming the Grand National Consolidated Trade Union in 1833 and soon had a large number of members – possibly as high as half a million. But GCNTU strikes were forbidden and their union 'lodges' were declared illegal if their members administered 'oaths' to bind one another together.

The Tolpuddle Martyrs 1834
Several farmworkers formed a branch of the GCNTU in their village of Tolpuddle, Dorset. They hoped to be able to prevent their masters from cutting their wages even further – a tendency since the failure of the Swing Riots. Wages were a mere 7 shillings a week in Tolpuddle and the Tolpuddle branch asked for a rise of 3 shillings. The government responded, the labourers were arrested and tried in Dorchester. Found guilty of administering illegal oaths they were sentenced to

seven years transportation. Today they are known as the 'martyrs' and their Tolpuddle village is a shrine for the Labour Party. There were six martyrs: George Loveless, James Loveless, Thomas Standfield, John Standfield, James Brine and James Hammett. All six were pardoned (1836) and eventually returned to Britain.

THE NEW MODEL UNIONS

The Rochdale Society of Equitable Pioneers

Some Rochdale weavers banded together in 1844 in an effort to become independent of manufacturers and retail shops. Members paid 2d a week, rented a warehouse in Toad Lane, bought stock and sold it at cut-prices. At the end of the year, the members shared out the profits among themselves. The Society renamed itself the Equitable Co-operative Society and set the fashion for scores of other societies up and down Britain. This was the beginning of the co-operative movement in Britain.

The status of Friendly Societies

From 1846 onwards the 'co-ops' could register as Friendly Societies. Many featured savings funds, created bookshops and libraries, and gave instruction to their members.

Significance

Such developments gave participants an air of respectability in the eyes of other Victorians. After all, they seemed to uphold the virtues of Victorian society: thrift, education, self-help, law-abiding, gainfully employed. They seemed to indicate that times were changing for the better, with less violence and mob-rule. On the whole, this assessment was correct – apart from the story of the Chartists (see pages 67–9).

The Amalgamated Society of Engineers

Several trade unions began in the 1840s. All were dedicated to maintaining the status quo, i.e. they were not revolutionary bodies trying to overthrow the establishment of the day. They stressed education and self-help; paid officials to organise their affairs; published their own newsletters and trade journals; and were not noted for their calls to strike action. The most famous of these was the ASE – the Amalgamated Society of Engineers – formed in 1851. Over 10,000 people joined in the first few months. The subscription was high – a shilling a week. Most members were skilled workers and they were the first to build up large reserves of cash – invaluable when the union went on strike or when the union wanted to pay compensation to injured or sick members. These were the characteristics of the new model unions – though they would have to overcome many legal hurdles before they became a recognised aspect of Britain's rapidly industrialising society.

THE CHARTISTS

If you think of the long period of protest
-      riots in 1800
-      the Luddites 1811–12
-      the 1816 riots
-      the Swing Riots

it is clear that they were all 'anti' something – they were not constructive. In fact, the climax was during the 1830 Swing Riots when the rick-burning and threshing machine destruction were designed to stop mechanisation. In some ways the famous Chartist movement was in the same vein. The Chartist leaders wanted to change the shape of things to the advantage of the ordinary people. The methods they adopted were both peaceful and violent. As a movement, the Chartists failed, though some of their ideas saw fruit in the years to come.

The Charter and its Six Points

The Charter was a means to an end: how the working man could improve his standard of living within British society.

The Six Points represented the way he could achieve this through universal suffrage:

1   all men (over 21) to have the vote;
2   secret ballots;
3   no property qualifications to enter Parliament;
4   MPs to be paid;
5   constituencies to be of equal size;
6   Parliaments to be re-elected annually.

The Chartist leaders

William Lovett 1800–76: he published the *People's Charter* in 1838.

Feargus O'Connor 1796–1855: published the radical Leeds newspaper *Northern Star*. Considered various means of bringing pressure on Parliament – but did not agree with the idea of a General Strike. Eventually developed the idea of petitions to Parliament (1839, 1842, 1848).

John Frost 1794–1877: led the miners in the 'Battle of Newport'.

Chartist actions

Chartism flourished in the period 1837–42 and in locations where industrial change had brought misery and unemployment, e.g. among handloom weavers, nailmakers and frame-knitters.

There was a serious trade depression during 1837–42 but there was not widespread hunger. Yet a great deal of propaganda about hunger (the 'Hungry Forties') was put out by the Anti-Corn Law League (a much more sophisticated form of pressure group, see pp.34–5) – and has been mentioned in later history books. Some parts of the country were undoubtedly suffering – but by no means all. The evidence is interesting:

Productivity	1832	1850
Coal	26 million tons	60 million tons
Iron	0.7 million tons	2.35 million tons

Tobacco and tea consumption

Year	Tobacco consumption in millions of tons	Tea consumption in millions of tons
1842	22.2	37.4
1843	23.0	40.3
1844	24.6	41.4
1845	26.2	44.2
1846	26.9	46.7
1847	26.7	46.3
1848	27.3	48.7

Consequently, there was not widespread support for Chartist actions.

1839 Charter – petition rejected by Parliament.

1839 Newport Uprising – about twenty-four miners died when Frost led them in an unsuccessful attack on Newport Jail where a local Chartist leader was languishing.

1842 Petition – again Parliament rejected it.

'Plug Riots' in Lancashire (Lancashire workers knocked out boiler plugs in the factories) during 1842.

Rebecca Riots 1842 – led by a man dressed in woman's clothing. Targets were local toll-gates.

The 1848 Petition 1848 was the year of revolution in Europe and government feared that Chartism might well take a revolutionary turn when the Chartists assembled on Kennington Common (South London) in April 1848. The Duke of Wellington was in control and the Chartists behaved peacefully, bringing their petition to the Parliament at Westminster. On examination, the petition was found to contain many false names and that the six million claimed signatures were closer to two million.

Results

Chartism rapidly declined as a social and political movement in Britain partly because of its lack of credibility in 1848 and partly because the trade recession ended and prosperity returned 1849–50.

**PUBLIC HEALTH
LEGISLATION**

Edwin Chadwick (1801–1890)

Edwin Chadwick was one of the most important social reformers of the Victorian period. He distinguished himself in his work for the Poor Law Commission (1832–46). He helped to draft both the 1833 Factory Act and the 1834 Poor Law Amendment Act. His great contribution was to public health and in 1842 he produced his Report into the Sanitary Condition of the Labouring Populations. Cholera was the greatest menace of the day and Chadwick believed that the disease originated in the heaps of uncollected rubbish and sewer filth that polluted so many towns and cities. He was accurate in his assessment of the problem, made worse by inadequate cemetery facilities and the lack of pure drinking water. It was customary for people to queue for hours to collect their water supplies – often in pails and other containers that were dirty and contaminated.

The British government was impressed by his 1842 report and asked Chadwick to carry out a further investigation into the burial of the dead. Chadwick published his results in 1843.

Public opinion

A Health of Towns Association, on which famous personalities such as Disraeli and Lord Shaftesbury served, made sure that Chadwick's discoveries and recommendations were not overlooked. However, although public opinion was in favour of massive change its attention was diverted by the Irish potato famine and the political crisis over the Repeal of the Corn Laws (see p. 34).

THE HEALTH OF TOWNS ACT 1848

This was the first Public Health Act passed by Parliament and created a Board of Health (to last five years). Its members were:

Lord Morpeth (government representative);
Chadwick (a paid commissioner);
Shaftesbury (an unpaid commissioner).

Powers of the Board of Health

These were very limited. It was allowed to set up local Boards of Health provided that at least 10 per cent of the ratepayers requested this. Otherwise, it could only intervene in public health matters where the death rate exceeded twenty-three per thousand. At first it had the power to take over all the burials in London – but it had to give this up in 1852 when a new act:

(a)   enabled the Home Secretary to close unsuitable cemeteries;
(b)   gave individual parishes the right to buy lands for use as cemeteries away from the main centres of population.

THE GREAT EXHIBITION 1851

Read the following extract:

> While some men such as Chadwick were determined to solve the problems of Britain's industrial society, others were equally concerned with promoting the quality of Britain's industrial products. Such a man was Henry Cole, civil servant and member of the Royal Society of Arts – the President of which was Prince Albert, consort of Queen Victoria. Cole wanted the Prince to back a national industrial exhibition, along the lines of one he had seen in Paris during 1849. Albert agreed, so long as it would be an international exhibition 'The Great Exhibition of the Works and Industries of all Nations'.

1   Who was Prince Albert?
2   Why was Cole keen to have an exhibition in Britain?
3   Albert agreed with Cole, on one condition. What was that?

Location and style

Prince Albert headed a Royal Commission to plan the exhibition. This gave the job of designing the exhibition hall (to be built in Hyde Park) to Joseph Paxton (1806–65). He was Superintendent of the Duke of Devonshire's great gardens at Chatsworth House and a specialist in the building of giant conservatories. His design for the 'Crystal Palace' (as the building was generally known) marked another technological breakthrough in the design of steel structures.

Impact

Paxton's creation was unique and a sight surpassing anything that the ordinary people of Victorian times had ever seen. They came to London literally in their millions – using cheap excursion tickets on the new railway system – and were fascinated by new inventions such as the sewing machine (imported from the USA). Undoubtedly, the industrial and technological achievement by Britain (the Workshop of the World) was in advance of most other nations of the world and the Exhibition seemed to herald a new era of peace and plenty.

Aftermath

After the Exhibition was over workmen dismantled the Crystal Palace and rebuilt it at Sydenham where it could be seen until 1936 – when it was destroyed by fire.

Look at the two photos below

Write an account by a London child living in the street shown in Photo 1 of his/her impressions of the building shown in Photo 2.

PLAGUE SPOT NEAR THE LONDON GAS-WORKS, SOUTH LAMBETH

Source: BBC TV British Social History, *The Age of Steam*, Autumn 1971, p. 15

Source: BBC Radio for Schools, *Stories from British History*, Autumn 1964

The following extract is taken from a guide to the Exhibition:

> Appoint someone to act as a leader, one who has visited the exhibition, if possible, and if a little higher in station or influence than the rest, the better.

1   Why did the guidebook want a leader to a party of visitors? After all, people don't need them to visit a museum or festival nowadays.

2   Why did the guidebook suggest a person 'higher in station or influence than the rest'?

Multiple choice questions

1   The 1819 Peterloo Massacre was followed almost immediately by:
- ☐   The Six Points
- ☐   The Six Acts
- ☐   The Spa Fields Riot
- ☐   The First Reform Act

2   The main conspirator behind the 1820 Cato Street Conspiracy was:
- ☐   Feargus O'Connor
- ☐   Ned Ludd
- ☐   Arthur Thistlewood
- ☐   Orator Hunt

3   One of the following groups did *not* have the right to vote in parliamentary elections before 1832:
- ☐   The Forty Shilling Freeholder
- ☐   The Copyholder
- ☐   The freemen of boroughs
- ☐   Burgage-holders

4   The Prime Minister at the time of the Reform Bill crisis was:
- ☐   The Duke of Wellington
- ☐   Sir Robert Peel
- ☐   Benjamin Disraeli
- ☐   Lord Grey

5   The 1832 Reform Act enfranchised new voters to the total of:
- ☐   approximately 0.25 million
- ☐   approximately 2.5 million
- ☐   approximately 5 million
- ☐   approximately 10 million

6   The utilitarians followed the teachings of:
- ☐   Thomas Malthus
- ☐   David Ricardo
- ☐   Lord Ashley
- ☐   Jeremy Bentham

7   In 1833 the Government awarded the two Church societies the sum of:
- ☐   £10,000
- ☐   £20,000
- ☐   £30,000
- ☐   £40,000

towards their provision of education.

8   William Wilberforce was MP for:
- ☐   Liverpool
- ☐   Bristol
- ☐   Hull
- ☐   Plymouth

9   Dealing in slaves was illegal with effect from:
- ☐   1 January 1806

□   1 January 1807
□   1 January 1808
□   1 January 1809

10 Convicts were transported mainly to:
□   Canada
□   USA
□   New South Wales and Tasmania
□   New Zealand

11 The 1825 Trade Union Act forbade:
□   the formation of trade unions
□   the payment of trade union officials
□   strike action
□   lock-outs

12 The three Chartist petitions were presented in
□   1838, 1839, 1848
□   1840, 1841, 1848
□   1842, 1846, 1848
□   1839, 1842, 1848

INDUSTRIAL CHANGES 1850–1914

CONTENTS

THE SMOKESTACK INDUSTRIES

Apart from the Crimean War (1854–6) Victorian Britain was not involved in any major European conflict that drained her resources. In fact, right up to 1914 most of Britain's military efforts concerned the preservation and expansion of her overseas empire. Consequently, Britain truly became the workshop of the world. By 1914 her 'smokestack industries' – coal, textiles, iron and steel – were at their peak.

Remember:

1 The British were free traders.
2 Before 1870 they had very little foreign competition.
3 Britain had been the first industrial nation, therefore she had the expertise, the technology and the best developed areas of raw materials, e.g. the coal-mines and iron ore deposits.
4 These advantages enabled her to produce textiles, coal, pig iron and steel far more cheaply than other nations.
5 In turn, these enabled her to undercut her competitors and to sell her products cheaply.
6 1851–75 were the boom years in industrial production.
7 During those years Britain developed a financial base. Her industrialists could secure credit, raise cash and sign cheques with relative ease. As you will see, it hadn't been like that for long.

THE DEMAND FOR CAPITAL

Ever since the foundation of the Bank of England in 1694, the government had always intervened to protect its position. From the beginning, it had been a joint-stock bank. This means that a number of investors had pooled their money to create the bank. These had then persuaded others to deposit their money in the bank. Large sums of cash could then be lent at high rates of interest – and one of the best borrowers was the British government!

THE RISE OF OTHER JOINT-STOCK BANKS

Up to the 1830s the Bank of England enjoyed a monopoly in London (this was taken to be within a radius of sixty-five miles of the City). Then other joint-stock banks were allowed to operate in the London area, provided they adopted the London practice of using cheques and a clearing house.

What was the main problem?

The expansion of trade and industry meant that merchants and factory owners were constantly doing deals; and often these deals needed large sums of cash. Many banks traditionally issued banknotes – and these, of course, could legally be exchanged for gold bullion. Sometimes – especially when there was a sense of political crisis in the country – people would rush to the bank to change their notes into gold. This was 'a run on gold' – and it might cause a bank to fail.

THE 1844 BANK CHARTER ACT

The government determined that only one bank should issue notes and that the bank should have adequate reserves of gold to meet demand. This was easier said than done, but the 1844 Bank Charter Act began the process:

1   No new bank may issue notes.
2   The Bank of England would have the monopoly of issuing notes (this did not happen until 1921).
3   It could issue notes (its smallest note was £5 until 1914) up to the value of its current gold reserves.
4   The government would support an additional issue of up to £14 million. This is the famous 'fiduciary issue', i.e. these notes were issued in good faith.
5   When another bank lapsed (i.e. folded up) the Bank of England could issue up to two-thirds of the value of the lapsed issue.

Now read the following account:

Of course, the 1844 Act did not give the Bank an immediate monopoly of note-issuing. Nor was the Act an answer to the kind of problem that beset bankers during the nineteenth century. Peel was confident that it would stop 'reckless speculation' and ensure that businessmen could depend on cheques and the banknotes in circulation. Fraudulent deals and the misuse of customers' deposits could not always be prevented and government had twice (in 1857 and 1866) to suspend the 1844 Act. But there was no doubt that Peel's Act had ensured 'a safe system of currency' that lasted up to 1914 – when the ten shilling and one pound notes were issued by the Treasury and not by the Bank of England.

1   Who was Peel?
2   What did Peel think was the most worrying aspect of finance in the period before 1844?
3   When did the government have to suspend the 1844 Act?
4   Give one reason for the cause of such a crisis.
5   When did the Treasury begin to issue notes?

Multiple choice questions

1   The standard gold coin or sovereign was worth:
- ☐   twenty shillings
- ☐   ten shillings
- ☐   five shillings
- ☐   twenty-one shillings

2   The 1816 Gold Standard Act fixed the rate at which gold bullion could be made into gold coins at £3. 17s. 10½d an:
- ☐   ounce
- ☐   grain
- ☐   gram
- ☐   quarter

3   The fiduciary issue allowed the Bank of England to issue additional notes up to the value of:
- ☐   £11 million
- ☐   £12 million
- ☐   £13 million
- ☐   £14 million

4   A 'run on gold' was when people rushed to:
- ☐   increase their gold deposits
- ☐   offer higher prices for gold bullion
- ☐   do their deals in gold not notes
- ☐   change their notes into gold

5   When a bank lapsed it meant that:
- ☐   it fell behind with payments to the Bank of England
- ☐   it would not cash cheques instantly
- ☐   it could not lend any more money
- ☐   it failed totally

THE COAL INDUSTRY

Despite the fact that industrialists, bankers, merchants and mine-owners recognised that coal was the basis of Britain's extraordinary industrial vitality, very little money was spent on research and development, so necessary to speed up the mechanisation of the mines. It is a sad fact that Britain allowed the USA to overtake her coal production between 1900 and 1914.

SAFETY: THE 1855 ACT

The 1855 Mines Act introduced seven basic safety rules that applied to every coal-mine in the country. Additionally, individual collieries were permitted to write extra safety rules for the proper conduct of their pits. All of these had to be approved by the Home Office and penalties were imposed on those who broke the law. Interestingly, miners who disobeyed the safety regulations could be sent to jail; but mine owners were only fined.

THE 1860 MINES REGULATION AND INSPECTION ACT

No boy could work underground below the age of twelve unless he could produce evidence that he could read and write. The 'winding engine boys' now had to be eighteen.

THE 1872 COAL MINES REGULATION ACT

Just after the 1860 Act had been passed, accidents in pits received a great deal of public attention. People were constantly calling for further reform. Their voices were heard in 1862 when there was a particularly shocking accident at the Hartley Colliery (Northumberland). The huge beam on the pumping engine broke and it fell into the shaft, taking with it all sorts of mining equipment. This blocked the shaft and none of the men could get out. Two-hundred and four miners died because there was no second shaft to escape through. It became illegal to work a single shaft mine in 1862 and ten years later the 1872 Act increased the number of basic safety rules to thirty. Explosions were the cause of many disasters 1862–72 – a decade in which over 1600 miners had died.

THE 1877 MINES ACT

This dealt with the detail of safety and the methods of coping with disasters – concerning ambulance provision, methods of shot-blasting and the ways of dealing with coal-dust explosions.

Document 1

Here are two examples of special rules used in a colliery during the post 1855 period:

1   The miners are to build packwalls, and set sufficient quantities of props for safely supporting the roof, and to renew them as often as necessary, or when ordered by the under-viewer or his deputy. Anybody disobeying this Rule must be reported to the agent.

2   No person shall try the workings or the goaves [i.e. the space left after the coal pillars holding up the roof of the seam have been cut away] for firedamp with a candle, and any person smoking tobacco, or having a naked light or lucifer matches, where safety lamps are ordered to be used, must be reported to the agent or under-viewer.

Document 2

This is an extract from a remarkable book by Richard Fynes and reports the words of a protest meeting held after the Hartley Colliery accident in 1862. The miner is talking to a pit inspector:

MINER: Were you satisfied with one shaft at this colliery? If so there is an end to the matter. If not, what steps did you take to remedy the defect? Did you apply to the Secretary of State, showing him that it was defective?

INSPECTOR: At this moment there are three of the largest collieries in Northumberland – Seaton Delavel, North Seaton and Newsham – managed by the most talented men in Northumberland. Now what would you have me do? Do you think it is my duty to call in question the management of these pits?

MINER: Am I to understand this is an answer to my question?

INSPECTOR: Well, I am not so well satisfied as if they had two, but I have not the power to alter it.

1 In Document 1 what does Rule 1 require the miners to do?
2 What does Rule 2 forbid?
3 Name two types of safety lamp in use by the 1850s (a clue: in the north-east, one was called a 'Geordy').
4 In Document 2, why was the miner so concerned about the fact that there was one shaft at the colliery?
5 What point was the inspector trying to make in his answer?
6 Why do you think the miner was dissatisfied with that answer?
7 What did the inspector really think about pits with single shafts?

THE TEXTILE INDUSTRY

Though not the biggest employer during the 1850s and 1860s (most people still worked in agriculture) the textile industry nevertheless employed over 0.5 million workers in rather more than 2000 factories. Its exports were primarily to the under-developed world – about 75 per cent went to India, Africa, Asia, Latin America and the West Indies every year. The industry seemed to be highly efficient. In 1830–90 the labour force grew by 50 per cent but productivity per mill worker grew by over 400 per cent.

Undoubtedly, cotton was 'king' and cotton manufacturers did not hesitate to pour their money into further investments in (a) new factory sites and (b) new machinery. Then came a devastating blow – the cotton famine of the 1860s.

THE LANCASHIRE COTTON CRISIS 1861–5

Many new mills had come into production during 1860–61 – the year in which the crisis in the United States came to a peak. Most Lancashire factories depended on cotton imports from the slave-owning plantations in the southern United States. These states formed a breakaway Confederacy in 1861 and their ports were soon blockaded by the Union warships. It seems that no manufacturer had ever considered the possibility of losing access to the cotton-producing states. They had no contingency plans (i.e. ideas for dealing with such a situation).

Effects

Prices rocketed when cotton merchants holding large stocks of imported cotton began selling them off at high prices. To try to keep down costs, manufacturers put their workers on short time. Some resorted to a three-day week – not unknown in Britain just over a hundred years later. Others had to close down their mills altogether. Many mill-workers had to turn to poor relief; private charities (e.g. the Garnets of Clitheroe and the American International Relief Committee of New York) sent donations and food-supplies to Manchester, one of the worst hit areas.

*From the Historic Society of Lancashire and Cheshire, Vol 105 and quoted in John Addy, *The Textile Revolution*, Longman 1976, p.111.

Read this extract from the diary of a textile worker, John Ward, 1864* (original spelling and punctuation):

> 10 April 1864
> It has been a poor time for me all the time owing to the American war, which seems as far of being settled as ever. The mill I work in was stopped all last winter during which time I had 3 shillings per week allowed by the relief committee which barely kept me alive. When we started work again it was with Surat cotton, and a great number of weavers can only mind two looms. We can earn very little. I have not earned a shilling a day this last month and there are many like me . . . I can't go much further with what I am at.

1   When did the mill in which John Ward worked shut down?
2   How much relief did he get each week?
3   Explain the term 'Surat cotton'.
4   Why were the weavers hard hit?
5   What do you think John Ward's dearest wish was?

The American Civil War ended in 1865 and the cotton crisis was soon over. But a new crisis was looming up. Can you detect what it was from these figures?

Britain's percentage of the world's spinning factories

1884	54%
1900	43%
1913	40%

The woollen industry

This ancient textile industry was very slow to mechanise, largely because of the complexity of the operations involved in woollen manufacture. The traditional processes were:

scouring – removing impurities from the wool;

carding – combing the wool to straighten the fibres.

slubbing – drawing and twisting the fibres prior to spinning;

spinning – twisting the fibres to form warp (thread running the length of the cloth) and weft (thread running the width of the cloth);

dyeing – colouring the threads, often before weaving;

weaving – interlacing the weft and warp.

fulling – beating the cloth in water or fuller's earth to thicken the weave and improve the texture;

shearing – after stretching a piece of a tenter frame the shearer brushed it to raise the nap and then cropped it to make a smooth surface.

There was now far more wool available, mainly from the huge sheep stations being opened up in Australia. Imports of raw wool roughly balanced wool exports – just before the outbreak of the First World War Britain was buying raw wool worth £37.75 million; and exporting woollen goods worth £37.5 million.

By the 1860s mechanisation of woollen manufactures was largely complete except for the most difficult of the hand operations – carding and slubbing.

New textiles

Flax Grown in Yorkshire, Scotland and Ulster; mechanised by about 1860.

Jute Indian jute was imported to undercut the expensive hemp – used in ropes and sacking.

Rayon The first man-made fibre or artificial silk. Developed by Courtaulds, it did not make much impact on the textile industy before 1914.

IRON AND STEEL

THE BLAST FURNACES

The production of cheap, easy to forge iron, plus the advantage of steam-operated hammers, meant that the industry was able to meet the huge demand for railway building and construction materials generally. But the demand was really for steel and the blast furnaces currently used were inadequate for this. Certainly, the new blast furnaces were efficient in that they increased iron production and reduced costs. But until Henry Bessemer's discovery that you could decarbonise iron by blowing air across molten iron, the blast furnaces made little contribution to steel manufacture.

The Bessemer converter 1856

Henry Bessemer (1813–98) built a 'converter' to make steel from non-phosphoric ore imported from Sweden. He decarbonised the iron (thus removing the impurities) and then added a small amount of carbon to produce steel. Tests in 1859 showed that this process was commercially profitable – but as most British iron is phosphoric Bessemer couldn't use domestic supplies.

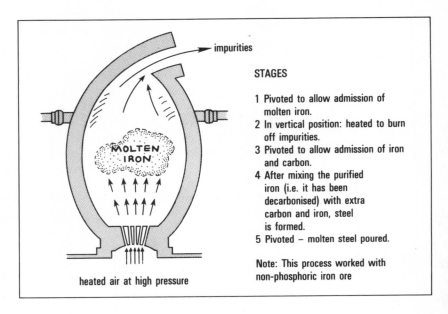

impurities

STAGES

1 Pivoted to allow admission of molten iron.
2 In vertical position: heated to burn off impurities.
3 Pivoted to allow admission of iron and carbon.
4 After mixing the purified iron (i.e. it has been decarbonised) with extra carbon and iron, steel is formed.
5 Pivoted – molten steel poured.

Note: This process worked with non-phosphoric iron ore

MOLTEN IRON

heated air at high pressure

The Bessemer Converter

The Siemens-Martin 'open hearth' process

William Siemens (1823–83) was a German scientist who settled in Britain because he could patent his inventions there more easily than he could in Germany. He had invented a gas-fired 'regenerative furnace' in 1848 and developed it into the 'open hearth' where very high temperatures could be obtained. Pig-iron – even scrap iron – could be transformed into steel – as the French scientist Pierre Martin later demonstrated. Siemens opened a steelworks in Swansea (1869) and began the mass-production of steel.

The Gilchrist-Thomas process

Scientists still searched for a way of using British iron ore in steel manufacture. Sidney Gilchrist Thomas (1850–85) and his cousin Gilchrist hit on the idea of lining the Bessemer converter with limestone to absorb the phosphorus element in British iron ore. The process was tried successfully in 1879 and this meant that the British ironfields could look forward to a period of prosperity.

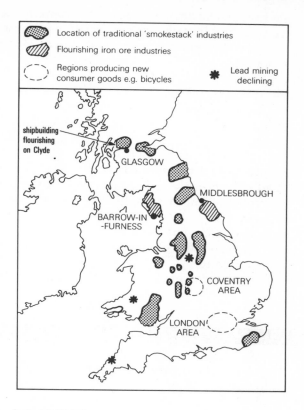

Industrial Britain

The engineers

Technical and engineering education has always lagged behind in Britain. There were no formal opportunities for aspiring engineers to learn their skills in nineteenth-century Britain. Therefore, engineers had to learn through practical experience.

Joseph Bramah (1748–1814) was a remarkable inventor who worked in many factories and engineering shops. He invented such diverse machines as a hydraulic press and a printing machine for putting serial numbers on banknotes.

Joseph Whitworth (1803–87) was one of the nineteenth century's most brilliant toolmakers. His famous screw thread – the Whitworth thread – became standardised; and he could manufacture machine tools capable of measuring accurately to one millionth of an inch.

William Armstrong (1810–1900) was a lawyer who turned inventor. His main interests were military and he concentrated on rifled barrels for weapons and developed new forms of artillery. His firm amalgamated with Whitworth's in 1897 to become Armstrong-Whitworth – a name commemorated in the Armstrong-Whitworth Whitley, one of the mainstays of Bomber Command in the early years of the Second World War.

Michael Faraday (1791–1867) was a self-taught scientist who became a laboratory assistant to Sir Humphry Davy. Faraday's experiments led to the generation of electricity and to the building of the first electric motors.

The significance of the new inventions

Gradually industry saw the advantage of research. New ideas could be applied to improve production or actually create new products, for instance:

> artificial fertilisers, artificial silk;
>
> by-products from coal such as gas for domestic and street lighting;
>
> electrical engineering – electric light bulbs and telephones.

THE NEW INDUSTRIES

THE ELECTRICAL INDUSTRY

The electrical industry provided power and revolutionised communications.

POWER

Faraday had produced the simple dynamo in 1831. In 1873 at the Vienna Exhibition it was demonstrated that it was possible to link two dynamos to create the electric motor. Electric motors were economical and easy to instal. Electrical manufacturing firms sprang up and some of the best known were Crompton's (Chelmsford 1878), the Thomson Houston Company (1896) and Ferranti's (1896).

THE MANUFACTURE OF ALUMINIUM

The first electrical resistance furnace was built by the Cowles brothers in the USA (1885). They patented the idea in 1887: introduce into the path of an electric current some form of resistance and the temperature will go up. Resistance furnaces were invaluable for the metallurgical industry, especially for aluminium. The map opposite shows the early processes and locations for the manufacture of aluminium in Britain.

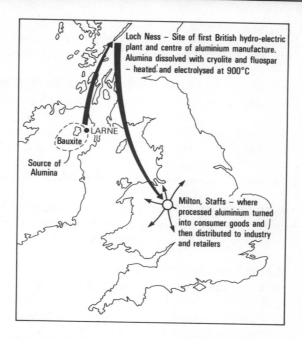

The new British aluminium industry, based on Ireland, Scotland and England

LIGHTING

About 1878, Joseph Swan (working in Britain) and Thomas Edison (working in the USA) invented the electric incandescent lamp – quite independently of one another. Dazzling arc lighting had been used earlier – the Trinity lighthouse used it in 1857 and London Bridge was floodlit in 1863 to celebrate the wedding of Edward Prince of Wales (later Edward VII). However, this was unsuitable for indoor illumination. The first public supply of electricity was in 1881 – at Godalming, using the power of the River Wey. The electricity company had to lay the cables in the gutters as the council would not grant permission to put them underground.

THE 1882 ELECTRIC LIGHTING ACT

This was Parliament's first attempt to deal with the implications of electricity. It gave local councils the power to set up electrical companies and for many years these small companies were the only source of supply. Their range was small – so gas lighting persisted well into the twentieth century in many houses, shops and factories.

COMMUNICATIONS

Samuel Morse (1791–1872) studied art in England and became a highly successful inventor. From 1832 onwards he began the transmission of messages using electricity. He invented the Morse Code and patented the electric telegraph in 1837. In 1844 he demonstrated its use by sending a message from Washington to Baltimore. His ideas were rapidly adopted by the new railway companies all over the world.

Sir Charles Wheatstone (1802–75) – working quite independently, Wheatstone patented an electric telegraph in Britain.

Submarine cables – In 1851 a submarine cable connected Britain and France; and in 1866 the *Great Eastern* laid the Atlantic cable. The ability to pass messages around the world was gradually developing – awaiting only the telephone and wireless telegraphy.

Alexander Graham Bell (1847–1922) – a Scotsman by birth, he became a US citizen. He demonstrated the telephone in 1876 and the following year set up the Bell Telephone Company.

G. M. Marconi (1874–1937) – an Italian inventor, he managed to transmit radio signals between two points in 1895 and interested the Post Office in his ideas. In 1898 he could send radio signals to France, and in 1901 sent signals from Cornwall to Newfoundland. He set up the Marconi Telegraph Company in 1897 – a company that was destined to manufacture some of the first radios.

THE SLOWING DOWN OF ECONOMIC GROWTH – THE DEPRESSION 1873–96

BRITAIN – A FREE TRADE COUNTRY

After the Repeal of the Corn Laws in 1846 Britain committed herself to dependence on exports. When W. E. Gladstone was Chancellor of the Exchequer (1852–5, 1859–66) he virtually ended the idea of 'protection' of British trade:

1 1853 Budget removed duties on over one hundred articles;
2 his 1860 Treaty with France (negotiated by Cobden and often called the Cobden Treaty in the history books) enabled the two countries to reduce or end duties on one another's goods;
3 1860–64 Budgets abolished customs duties on most other imports.

THE EMERGENCE OF TRADE RIVALS

Up to 1873–4 Britain assumed she was the world's industrial leader – and with a great deal of justification. She had led the way in the construction of steam locomotives and railways and had exported them all over the world. But now the countries who had bought them were using them to open up new farmlands in, for instance, the American prairies and the Ukrainian steppes. Similarly, German, American, Belgian, French and Japanese industrialists were applying all the research and development (much of it carried out in Britain) to their own factories. They were able to challenge British manufactured goods and undercut them in price.

EFFECTS

More and more goods appeared on the world markets; more and more food became available. This did not mean that there was immediate suffering in Britain as the word 'depression' tends to convey. In fact, the reverse was true. There was an abundance of cheaper food; the prices of manufactured goods came down even though the volume of production was going up. In other words, at a time of falling prices and decreasing dividends, the standard of living tended to rise in Britain. Overall, the rate of *growth* in the British economy was slowing down.

*By Sidney Pollard and David W. Crossley (Batsford, 1968) p. 227.

Read the following extract from The Wealth of Britain*:

> It was inevitable that the rate of growth of old-established industries should at some stage slow down, as otherwise they would grow to infinite size, but in a progressive economy this is more than balanced by new industries in their earliest and fastest growth stages. Unfortunately, it was precisely in the new developments, in machine tools and motor cars, in electrical engineering and chemicals, that Britain was farthest behind her leading competitors.

1 Which of the old-established industries would you expect to be slowing down during this period? Try to give five examples.
2 What do the writers mean when they talk of 'infinite size'? Is this a sensible statement?
3 Why do you think new industries are quick to grow?
4 In what new industries was Britain lagging behind?
Now you have read this, consider the actions that Britain took.
1 In the main, her industrialists turned their backs on modernisation, on investment in the new industries, on research and development.
2 Instead, they invested a great deal of capital overseas in foreign industry.
3 They tried to sell their products in the markets of the under-developed countries – especially the Far East, Latin America, India and Australia.
4 They tried and failed to sell their goods in the new industrial nations, Germany and America. These countries were not only overtaking Britain. They were equally ready to erect barriers against British imports.

Conclusions

So, as a result of the 'depression' 1873–96, the pattern of British trade radically changed; and because British industrial 'plant' was in many cases obsolete her chances of competing successfully with the new industrial giants diminished every year.

THE FACTORY ACTS

Very gradually opinion in Parliament was moving towards the idea that women and young persons should work in factories for no longer than ten hours per day. It was slow to develop and you might think that the 1844 Factory Act was almost a backward step.

THE 1844 ACT

1 Children between eight and thirteen could only work 6½ hours per day.
2 Young persons (between thirteen and eighteen) and women could work only twelve hours per day.
3 Factory owners had to take steps to see that their machines were safe – until now there had been harrowing tales of accidents in factories when people had been caught up by the machinery.
Have you noticed one unusual feature about section 1? The age when a child may enter a factory has been reduced from nine to eight. The reason for this is probably due to the fact that in 1836 an Act had compelled parents to register the date of birth of all babies. So a factory owner could now check the precise age of a potential child worker.

THE 1847 FACTORY ACT (THE FIELDEN ACT)

Up to now Shaftesbury had been the driving force behind factory reform. The leadership now passed to John Fielden, a cotton manufacturer, and he pushed through the 1847 Act:
1 No person under eighteen shall work in any mill or factory for more than eleven hours a day – and not more than sixty-three hours a week.
2 From 1848 no one under eighteen would have to work more than ten hours in one day or more than forty-eight hours a week.
3 These rules would apply to all women workers.
You will note that nothing is said as to how factory owners should reduce the hours of men. By working the women and children in shifts the employers could force the men to work long hours. This led to the 1850 Act.

THE 1850 ACT

This limited the time a factory could be open; in return employers demanded that women and young persons should work 10½ hours per day. But it did establish the idea of a 'Saturday afternoon off'.

Later legislation
Now that the principle of the Ten Hour Day had been established and that the hours of work a man could do were limited by factory opening times, it was possible for later governments (spurred on by

the indefatigable Ashley, Lord Shaftesbury) to improve working conditions in many – but not all – of Britain's industries:

> Lace Workers Act 1861
> Workshops Regulation Act 1867
> 'Climbing Boys' Act 1875 (prohibiting the employment of children to climb and clean chimneys)
> Employers Liability Act 1881

THE TRADE UNIONS 1851–1914

The formation of the Amalgamated Society of Engineers (1851) had heralded the beginning of a new and important stage in the history of the trade union movement. However, several events during the 1860s seemed to block that development, despite the fact that the leaders of the New Model Unions after 1851 had formed their famous 'Junta' (committee) to ensure that they had a good public image.

The Sheffield outrages 1866

Several violent incidents in Sheffield (the bombing of a factory and the murder of a workman) were undoubtedly linked with members of local trade unions. A Royal Commission sat to investigate these outrages and to establish the precise position of trade unions under the law.

THE HORNBY v. CLOSE LAW CASE 1867

In 1855 a Parliamentary Act had given protection to the funds of friendly societies in the event of one of their officials committing an act of theft or fraud against the society. The trade unions hoped they were covered by that Act and when the treasurer of the Bradford branch of the Boilermakers' Society took some money the trade union embarked on legal proceedings against him. The local magistrates said there was no case to answer – a trade union wasn't a friendly society! So the Boilermakers appealed and the judge ruled that the magistrate was right on the grounds that friendly societies had no political objectives but that a trade union might act 'in restraint of trade' – an illegal act!

Significance

The 1867 ruling meant that trade unions were now unlawful unions. The Junta therefore had to persuade Parliament that they were not. They were successful in 1871.

THE TRADE UNION ACT 1871

Gladstone legalised the position of trade unions.
1 The fact that unions might act 'in restraint of trade' no longer made them illegal.

2   Trade union money and property came under the protection of the law.

THE CRIMINAL LAW AMENDMENT ACT 1871

On the same day, this act was passed. It was largely concerned with picketing (the Royal Commission on Trade Unions 1869 had been very concerned with this development):

> 'workmen desirous to accept work are often subjected, through the agency of the pickets, to molestation, intimidation, and other modes of undue influence, and in effect are prevented from obtaining employment'.

Consequently, the Criminal Law Amendment Act made picketing illegal. Here are some of the definitions of picketing – for which the offender received three months in jail:

1   If he persistently follow a person from place to place.
2   If he hide any tools, clothes or other property owned or used by such person, or deprive or hinder him in the use thereof.
3   If with two or more persons he follow such person in a disorderly manner in or through any street or road.

THE CONSPIRACY AND PROTECTION OF PROPERTY ACT 1875

This Act legalised 'peaceful picketing' when, during a trade union dispute with employers, the trade unionists carry out acts that were legal if committed by one person. This Act encouraged the rise of unskilled unions and, eventually, the formation of a political party designed to represent their interests. The London Dock Strike (1889) hastened the process.

The London Dock Strike 1889
The London Dockers formed their union in 1887 and watched with interest the success enjoyed by other groups of workers in improving their pay and working conditions, for example:

Bryant & May's Match Girls Strike 1888 – they paraded through London to show a horrified public their 'phossie jaw' condition (the result of working with phosphorus for prolonged periods).

The London Gas Workers threatened a strike in 1888 – and won a pay increase.

The dockers' leaders were Ben Tillett, Tom Mann and John Burns. They went on strike in 1889 for an extra penny per hour – the 'dockers' tanner'. They won great support – including a £30,000 donation from Australian dockers. The strike ended in a complete victory. By 1884 1.5 million people had joined trade unions affiliated to the Trades Union Congress (TUC) formed back in 1868.

THE INDEPENDENT LABOUR PARTY

This was formed in 1893 by Keir Hardie, one of the first working-class men to win a seat in Parliament. He wanted the support of the TUC – and won this at the 1899 TUC assembly (carried by 546,000 votes to 434,000). Almost immediately, this new political union suffered a severe setback in the law courts.

The Taff Vale Judgement 1901

Members of the Taff Vale Railway Company came out on strike in 1900 and were supported by the Amalgamated Society of Railway Servants. The Railway Company then sued the union and eventually the union had to pay £23,000 compensation (the Taff Vale Judgement brought by the House of Lords). This meant that every time a union went on strike the employer could claim compensation from union funds – a situation that would rapidly ruin the unions.

Reversal of the judgment – the 1906 Trades Disputes Act

One of the first acts of the newly elected Liberal Government was to reverse the Taff Vale Judgement. But within two years the Amalgamated Society of Railway Servants was in trouble again – this time over the famous Osborne case.

The Osborne case 1908

Osborne was a branch secretary of the Amalgamated Society of Railway Servants and argued that it was not right that the union should use its funds to support the Labour Party. He took the matter to law. The judge ruled that trade unions must not fund political parties. This was a serious blow to the Labour Party but was put right by:
(*a*) the decision to pay MPs (1911);
(*b*) the 1913 Trade Union Act that allowed unions to contribute to political parties, provided they allowed their members to contract out should they so wish.

Trade union militancy 1910–12

A rash of strikes in 1910 worsened during the long, hot summer of 1911 when over one million men were unemployed. There was considerable violence in many parts of the country – especially in the ports. Both the TUC and the Labour Party dissociated themselves from this and encouraged the formation of the big unions, more capable of exerting political pressure. In 1913 militancy declined and the famous 'Triple Alliance' emerged:
1 Transport Workers' Federation;
2 Miners' Federation;
3 National Union of Railwaymen.

Multiple choice questions

1 William Siemens opened his steelworks in:
☐ Glasgow
☐ Cardiff

☐   Scunthorpe
☐   Swansea

2   The process by which steel could be made using British phosphoric iron ore was developed by:
☐   Gilchrist Thomas
☐   Henry Bessemer
☐   Pierre Martin
☐   Henry Cort

3   The scientist whose experiments led to the building of an electric motor was:
☐   Sir Humphry Davy
☐   Joseph Swan
☐   Thomas Edison
☐   Michael Faraday

4   The Cowles brothers developed a resistance furnace in:
☐   Britain
☐   France
☐   Germany
☐   USA

5   The inventor of the telephone was:
☐   Marconi
☐   Alexander Graham Bell
☐   Samuel Morse
☐   Ferranti

6   The depression of 1873–96 led to:
☐   an increase in prices for food and manufactures
☐   a decrease in industrial production
☐   a decrease in the standard of living
☐   a decrease in the cost of food and manufactured goods

7   The 1850 Factory Act established:
☐   the Ten Hour Day
☐   the idea of shifts for women and child workers
☐   limited times for the opening of factories
☐   restrictions on the use of climbing boys

8   The Criminal Law Amendment Act (1871) prohibited:
☐   strikes
☐   lock-outs
☐   picketing
☐   boycotting

9   The terrible disease known as 'phossie jaw' was characteristic of:
☐   the gas industry
☐   the coal industry
☐   the hat makers
☐   the match girls

10   The 1906 Trades Disputes Act reversed:
☐   the Osborne Judgement 1908
☐   the Conspiracy and Protection of Property Act 1875
☐   The Taff Vale Judgement 1901
☐   The Hornby v. Close Judgement 1867

AGRICULTURAL CHANGES 1850–1914

CONTENTS

In many parts of rural Britain, conditions remained almost unchanged for much of the twentieth century. The winding lanes, leafy walks, meadows, cornfields and grazing cattle presented a picture that seemed idyllic compared with conditions inside many British factories before the Factory Acts brought improvements both in pay and safety. In fact, there was greater poverty in the countryside than there was in many of Britain's rapidly growing towns.

THE DEPRESSED STATE OF BRITISH FARM LABOURERS

Women and children continued to work on British farms during the nineteenth and into the twentieth century – frequently as members of gangs, most prevalent in the East Anglian counties. Their employers – the farmers – had little concern for the well-being of their workers, most of whom migrated from village to village in search of work. They deliberately kept down the pay of the men, simply because they could hire women and children so cheaply. Young farm labourers always found it hard to keep a stable job so they tended to marry early and then supplemented their own miserable pay with the pay of their wives and children. As long as this system operated, there was little chance of radical improvement in the countryside. As one farm labourer put it, 'Ain't life at all, and I often wish I was out of it.'

THE CONDITION OF THE FARMERS

After the fierce treatment meted out to the Tolpuddle Martyrs, the farmers had few problems with their employees. Mechanisation came very slowly – it was some years before the farmers had generally adopted threshing machines (the target of the Swing rioters in 1830), and well into the 1860s and 1870s before they used steam tractors and steam engines to speed productivity. Those were the peak years for corn growing – when the price of corn was consistently high and when the demand for meat from the cities made rearing livestock worthwhile. Of course, farmers had to tie up a lot of their money in this 'intensive farming'. Nevertheless, most appeared prosperous and the 'rich agriculturist' was envied by ordinary farm workers. But before 1872, farm labourers were relatively passive – they desperately wanted to keep their jobs and many lived in 'tied cottages'. To offend their farmer-landlord might mean the loss of both job and home.

GRADUAL CHANGE

PUBLICITY FOR FARM WORKERS

The interest in the exploitation of women and children continued after the Factory Acts and public pressure prompted the government to set up a Royal Commission to investigate working conditions. The result was the 1868 Gangs Act which ruled that:

(*a*)   children under eight should not work in rural gangs;

(*b*)   women and children should always work under the super-vision of a woman overseer.

THE NATIONAL AGRICULTURAL LABOURERS UNION 1872

This was the achievement of the remarkable Joseph Arch (1826–1919). Arch was a farm labourer in Warwickshire and a Primitive Methodist preacher. He formed an agricultural union in his own county (1872) and then went on to form the national union the same year. The main objective was to boost the pay farmers paid their workers.

Average wages 1870	8–9 shillings per week (with little or no chance of overtime)
Hourly rate for women	8 pence
Hourly rate for children	5 pence
Average diet 1870	*Breakfast* (usually taken in the field): cold tea, bread, sometimes cheese *Dinner:* cold tea, ale, meat pie, potato *Supper:* Tea, cheese or bacon, butter (rarely in the poverty-stricken south).

THE STRIKE 1872

Newspapers gave wide coverage to the Warwickshire strike of 1872 when the men demanded the chance of overtime by working an eleven hour day; and a minimum wage of sixteen shillings and sixpence. The movement spread all over the country and some farmers offered to give an extra shilling or two per week. Generally, most labourers were rewarded with lock-outs and this proved highly effective. The technique was to tell strikers they had lost their jobs and to give these jobs to migrants – especially Irish labourers. The worst-hit areas were East Anglian counties where very few workers received a pay rise.

The situation in the 1870s
Read the following extract:

Estate owners were beginning to offer better accommodation.

Some provided allotments at nominal rents. A few cottage hospitals and village schools began to appear. Many families, attracted by relatively high wages in industrial towns, had left the land and thus reduced the hazard of unemployment for those who remained behind.

Moreover, as the farm labourer had also shared in the general rise in real wages there was less need for his wife and children to slave in the work-gangs, planting, thinning and pulling crops. Of course, plenty of misery and poverty existed; the standard of life in the countryside, especially in the south, was a national disgrace.

1 How did estate owners try to improve conditions for their workers?
2 What social amenities appeared in some villages?
3 Why did the hazard of unemployment diminish slightly during this period?
4 What sort of work did the agricultural gangs do?

Look at this picture
1 What work are the children doing?
2 What do you think has happened to the boy?
3 What sort of help can he expect?
4 What does the attitude of the overseer appear to be?

" GANG SYSTEM " OF FARMING. (See p. 452.)

Source: L. F. Hobley. *Living and Working.* OUP, 1964, p. 181.

THE EFFECT OF THE DEPRESSION 1873–96

Just as the depression helped to lower the prices of manufactured goods during this period, so it brought down food prices. This was due almost entirely to foreign competition as the following graphs show:

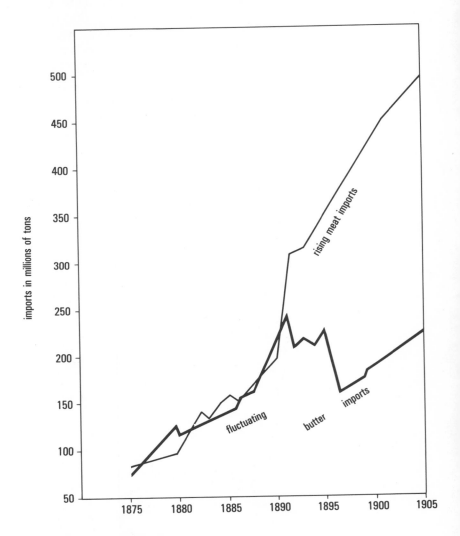

Food imports rise: 1875–1900

1   What do you notice about the imports of meat?
2   What do you notice about butter imports after 1891/2?
3   These graphs are a rough indicator of the nation's diet. Would you say, by modern standards, that the diet was healthy?

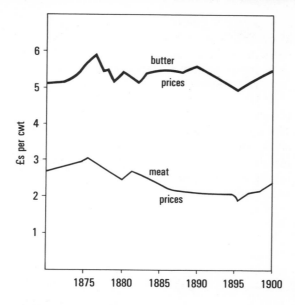

Food prices drop: 1875–1895

4 Which commodity seemed to maintain an even price during this period?
5 What do you notice about prices in 1896?

THE FUTURE

Around 1893 farm labourers were spending just over half of their income on food (very little of this being meat or fish). By 1896 diets in the countryside had marginally improved – with more families buying milk. At this stage in British agricultural history the farmers

A M'Laren engine made in Leeds during the 1890s. Winding drums underneath boiler barrel worked by bevel gearing from crankshaft; each drum held up to 500 yards of steel-wire rope.

had to accept that theirs was no longer the most important industry. More and more young people were leaving the countryside to find work in the towns and one sign that farmers were beginning to experience a labour shortage was the revival of the use of steam power. A few wealthy farmers introduced efficient wind-pumps and electricity. The two main targets for British farming were now:

1　Greater efficiency to compete with the foreign challenge.
2　The important and ever-growing consumer market in the towns and cities. Here farmers struggled to change their old emphasis on arable farming to stock-rearing (especially pigs for bacon and cows for the booming dairy industry) and vegetable/salad crops that so appealed to the urban housewife.

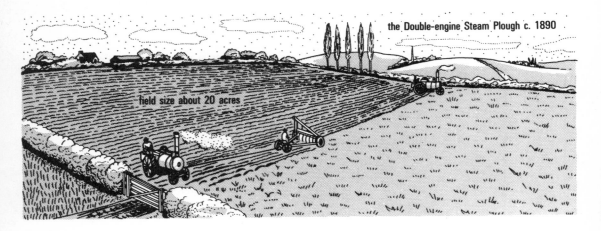

The double-engined steam plough, c.1890. A pair of ploughing engines could haul either a five-furrow balance plough or a nine-tine cultivator and a five-frame flat harrow. The equipment shown here would take a day to plough fifteen acres and, in 1890, would cost a total of £1,750

Document 3

> 7th February
> My wife came in to me and said, Joe, here's three men come to see you . . . They wanted to get the men together and start a Union directly. I told them if they did form a Union they would have to fight hard for it, and they would have to suffer a great deal; both they and their families. They said things couldn't be worse; wages were so low, they must join together and strike.

1　Document 1 depicts a typical well-built Victorian steam engine. What do you think its main weakness on a farm was?
2　What job is this particular engine designed to do?
3　What sort of fuel would a farmer need to purchase?

4 Document 2 shows two steam engines at work. Explain briefly precisely what is going on.

5 Look at the cost of the equipment. How could a farmer share his costs? Do some farmers share their costs today, e.g. at harvest time?

6 In Document 3, who is Joe?

7 Why did the men want to form a Union?

8 Did Joe warn them about what they were doing?

TRANSPORT: CHANGES TO 1914

CONTENTS

ROAD BUILDING

TRAVELLING CONDITIONS IN THE 1700s

Among the Christmas cards you had last year there was probably at least one that showed a scene of road travel in the eighteenth century – probably a loaded stage-coach making its way along snow-covered roads. Road travel wasn't often as romantic as the Christmas cards show. Arthur Young (1741–1820) once travelled on the road between Wigan and Preston:

> I know not in the whole range of the language, terms sufficiently expressive to describe this infernal road. To look over a map and perceive that it is a principal one, not only to some towns but even to whole counties, one would naturally conclude it to be at least decent . . . People will break their limbs by overthrows or breaking downs. They will meet with ruts, which I have actually measured 4 feet deep, and floating with mud only from a wet summer; what, therefore, must it be after winter?

1   Why did Arthur Young expect the road to 'be at least decent'?
2   What did he mean by an 'overthrow'?
3   How deep were some of the ruts?
4   Did he think the road conditions could get worse?
5   When would this happen?

Looking after the roads

In 1555 Parliament had ordered all parishes to appoint a local overseer of roads. He had to serve one year without pay. His job was to make sure that the parishioners looked after the roads in their parish. Everyone was supposed to give up a few days to do this work every year. It was highly unpopular – no one ever received any pay! Some parishes used the local paupers for the job; others levied a rate to employ professional labourers. This was how most roads were maintained right up until 1835 when householders had to pay highway rates.

The need for better roads

As industries developed and towns grew, manufacturers desperately needed better long-distance transport facilities to move raw materials and finished goods. There was also the problem of getting food to the towns – especially those with rapidly expanding population figures.

The turnpike roads

People with money to invest formed trusts to build new roads to attract the growing traffic they anticipated. The traffic would have to pay toll charges and from these tolls the investors would:

(*a*)   maintain the roads in good condition;
(*b*)   secure a profit on their investment.

The name 'turnpike' referred to the gate or bar across a road. This gate was often topped with spikes (pikes) and was turned or opened when you paid your toll. This picture shows one of the stage-wagons approaching a toll-gate along one of the new turnpike roads built by the famous engineer, Thomas Telford.

Section through a typical Telford road. An eighteenth-century waggoner approaches the toll gate at the beginning of a newly constructed turnpike

The turnpike builders

Parliament created the first turnpike trust in 1706 and in 1753 ruled that the minimum width of a carriage wheel was nine inches (23 cm). The turnpike trusts employed professional roadbuilders to design roads capable of taking the expected volume of traffic.

John Metcalfe (1717–1810) known to his contemporaries as 'Blind Jack of Knaresborough'; he built turnpikes in Yorkshire, Lancashire and the Peak District. He used a high camber on his road surfaces so the rain would run off easily. He often used heather to build the road foundations.

Thomas Telford (1757–1834) a Scotsman who imitated Roman road-building techniques. He concentrated on very strong foundations. He built the Holyhead–London Road (the modern A5). Telford was also famous for the suspension bridge over the Menai Straits, linking North Wales with Anglesey.

John Macadam (1756–1834) a Scottish engineer. He devised the all-important rainproof surface made of tiny stones compacted by the weight of passing wagon wheels.

Military roads

This period saw the final rebellions in West Scotland against British rule (the Act of Union between England and Scotland dated from 1707). After 1754 General Wade had the job of building new military roads to permit the easy transportation of troops and military stores.

The stage-coach age

Although horseback was still the quickest form of travel, more and more businessmen and commercial travellers used the stage-coach routes that sprang up in the 1700s. The stage-coach (named because it picked up and put down passengers at regular stops) was usually pulled by four horses and carried six people inside the coach and up to twelve on top in the cold (where you travelled at half-fare). With stage-coaches, long-distance travel was now a reality, e.g. as early as 1706 you could catch the London to York coach and then pick up the Newcastle coach. By 1772 there was a daily coach service between Newcastle and London. There were some dangers from breakdowns and hold-up men (footpads). But the system grew safer every year and in 1784 the Royal Mail coaches replaced the daredevil post-boys who had ridden on horseback to deliver mail all over the country.

THE EDINBURGH Mail *Snowbound in 1831*

Commemorative postage stamp issued 1984

    This postage stamp (issued in 1984) commemorates the first Royal Mail coaches and depicts a typical hazard on the Edinburgh run in 1831.

Now read the following account:

Road-building did not attract so much investment as did the canals, mainly because the advantages of bulk carriage and quick profits were absent. However, the roads enabled Matt Pickford to move freight from Manchester to London in 'flying wagons' in a record-breaking 4½ days. In 1706 a coach journey from York to London took 4 days; in 1790 the 'Highflyer' coach was clocking 31 hours. By 1790 mail coaches connected most of the major towns and their combined daily mileage was just under 7000 miles.

1   Why did roads attract less investment than canals?
2   Who was Matt Pickford?
3   Why is his surname important today in the field of heavy transport?
4   How long did it take the 'Highflyer' to travel from London to York?

5   Which of the following was the most damaging to turnpike roads:
(*a*)   the Railways;
(*b*)   the Canals.

CANAL BUILDING

Traditionally, river navigation was the only effective means of trans-
porting heavy goods around Britain. In the 1700s most of the new
coal-mines and virtually all of the textile mills were a long way from
the established transport system. This meant that industrialists and
the owners of coal-mines were willing to invest money in a 'cut' or
'navigation', i.e. a canal. Most famous of the early examples was the
'Duke's Canal' from Worsley to Manchester (1759–61), built by James
Brindley (1716–72).

Brindley's achievement
The Duke of Bridgewater hired James Brindley to build the Worsley–
Manchester Canal in order to cut down his mounting overheads
while getting the coal away from the Worsley collieries. Brindley was
a genius and one of Britain's first civil engineers. A mill-wright by
trade, he could organise men and building works on a grand scale.
His 'navvies' (the name given to the 'navigators' who built the canals)

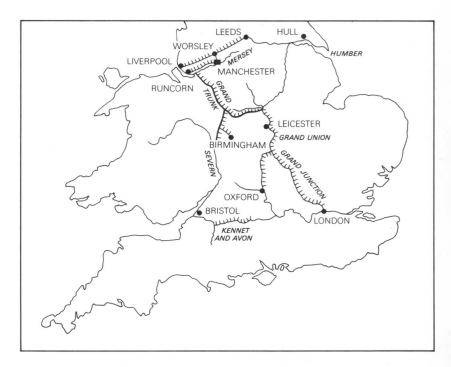

The Great Trunk Canal

took the canal deep into the Worsley mines, crossed the swampy Chat Moss and took the canal over the River Irwell via the Barton aqueduct. Coal prices came tumbling down when the first barges reached Manchester. Soon Brindley was in great demand. He built the Bridgewater cut to Runcorn and began the Great Trunk Canal in 1766 (finished, after his death, in 1788).

Canal mania

The success of the Great Trunk Canal led many people to invest in cuts in the hope of quick profits. Most were to be disappointed especially during 1791–4, the period known as 'canal mania'. Many were started in southern England, away from the main industrial areas.

THE VALUE OF CANALS

Between 1760 and 1840 their value outweighed their defects. Canals linked the major industrial regions and enabled all kinds of industrial products – ranging from Josiah Wedgwood's pottery to James Watt's kits for making steam-engines – to be sold in the growing markets at home and abroad. Unfortunately, the speed of horse-drawn barges on the canals was slow – about two mph. There were lots of ideas to boost the speed of barges (steam power, driving paddles) but the schemes were always rejected. Why do you think this was?

Two other weaknesses were due to the British weather:
1 frost and ice often hindered progress up a canal;
2 drought could sometimes leave barges stranded.

Now attempt this question: A Birmingham industrialist decides to visit Brindley in November 1763 to ask if he is interested in building a canal between Birmingham and the River Trent.
1 Describe the journey by stage-coach from Birmingham to Worsley. Include the following words in your answer: a coachman; a turnpike; a coaching inn; an 'overturning'.
2 Then write a brief description of Brindley's likely response to the idea of connecting Birmingham and the Trent. Look carefully at the map on page 110 before writing this part of the answer.

THE RAILWAY REVOLUTION

THE FIRST STEAM LOCOMOTIVES

Since the Middle Ages miners had used various kinds of wooden tramways to help them transport coal. After 1604 wooden tramways were used for the same purpose especially in the Nottinghamshire and Northumberland and Durham mines. Richard Trevethick was the first to use a high-pressure steam-engine to power a locomotive capable of drawing a heavy load, on the Pen-y-darren Ironworks tramway in 1804. His Catch-me-who-can was the first steam locomotive to transport fare-paying passengers (London 1808).

THE IMPACT OF WAR

Surprisingly, the idea did not catch on immediately. Then, when the price of fodder, horses and pack animals soared in the Napoleonic War (around 1809–14), experiments with locomotives started again. By then it was possible to use a variety of cast-iron rails:

1   the first cast-iron rails were used at Coalbrookdale;
2   the first plate rails were used in Sheffield (1776);
3   the first narow edge rails were used in Leicestershire (1789).

John Blenkinsop devised his 'rack and rail' locomotive and this was used at the Middleton Colliery (Leeds 1812); and in 1813 William Hedley built two remarkable smooth rail engines – Puffing Billy and Wylam Dilly (both still in use in 1862 and now in museums).

George Stephenson 1788–1848 Usually known as the 'father of the railway', George Stephenson completed the construction of the Stockton and Darlington Railway – the first public railway to use a steam locomotive (in this case the famous Locomotion) in 1825.

Robert Stephenson 1805–59 Robert, the son of George Stephenson, designed the Rocket, the locomotive that won the Rainhill competition to choose the engine for use on the Liverpool and Manchester Railway (1830) – 'the first modern railway in the full sense of the term'.

Read this view of the new locomotives by Nicholas Wood, written in 1825:

> It is far from my wish to promulgate to the world the ridiculous expectations . . . that we shall see locomotive engines travelling at the rate of 12, 16, 18 or 20 miles an hour; nothing could do more harm towards their adoption than the promulgation of such nonsense. I think the principle of their action is founded on good grounds; and that they will ultimately reach a state of perfection by facilitating the conveyance of goods at a rate of motion far beyond the power of horses on canals and that they will be of infinite advantage to commerce. Their rails are so durable and the wheel has scarcely any effect on them . . . with horses it is different. The action of their feet alone costs expenditure that is by no means trifling – which is unknown in the use of locomotive engines.

Remember that he was writing in 1825 – five years before the opening of the Liverpool and Manchester Railway:

1   Did he expect engines to travel at 20 mph?
2   Was he in favour of the further development of locomotives?

3   Why did he say they will be 'of infinite value to commerce'?
4   What did he notice about the effect of locomotives on the rails?
5   What did he say about the effect of horses on road surfaces?

The railway builders

Perhaps Nicholas Wood was more optimistic than most. In the first few years after the opening of the Manchester–Liverpool Railway little interest was shown in railway development. Perhaps investors were more cautious about investing money; they wanted to assess the results of the first railways, i.e. would they make a profit? The London to Birmingham line (built by the Stephensons 1833–8) showed that they would and the first period of railway mania began in 1836–7. The second railway mania was 1844–7, dominated by men such as Samuel Peto, Thomas Brassey and – above all – Isambard Kingdom Brunel (1806–59). His navvies had no modern machinery and they built the railways using muscle power and high explosives. They paid a high price: their camps were often plagued by cholera, and casualties due to rockfalls, blasting accidents and similar events were sometimes higher than those the British Army had suffered during battles in the Peninsular War!

Amalgamations

You must remember that Parliament only authorised the railways. It didn't seek to control them, with the result that gauges were different. Brunel used the broad gauge (7 ft 0¼ in); Stephenson used the narrow gauge (4 ft 8½ in). Some of the new railway companies controlled only a few miles of track with perhaps a mere three or four stations. Gradually, amalgamations began – spurred on by the ambitious George Hudson who created the famous LNER (London and North Eastern Railway) based at York. Found guilty of misusing investors' capital, Hudson suffered disgrace in 1849.

Parliament intervenes

Parliament was forced to bring order out of chaos and gradually began to regulate the railway system mushrooming in Britain.

1844 Railway Act

1   The state had the power to buy up (nationalise) all lines after twenty-one years.
2   Each railway company had to run at least one train a day in each direction. This train must stop at each station and must be covered with accommodation for third-class passengers. The charge must not exceed one penny per mile. This was the so-called 'parliamentary train.'

1846 Railway Act stated that all future lines must use the narrow gauge.

1854 Railway Act allowed through trains to use the lines of other companies.

1893 Railway Act limited the maximum fares companies might charge.

THE EFFECTS OF THE RAILWAYS

Read the following account:

> By 1848 the railway was part of the British way of life. Although the existing mail coach services and turnpike trusts suffered from competition, the nation as a whole prospered. Thirty million passengers used the trains each year; industry, the creator of the railways in the first place, derived instant benefits from their construction. There was an ever-increasing demand for iron and steel, bricks and cement, coal and gun-powder; there were new jobs for drivers, guards, porters and firemen. Even new towns sprang out of the railway revolution. Places such as Crewe concentrated on building and servicing the locomotives and rolling stock.

1 How many people were using the railways each year?
2 Name the two transport systems that suffered.
3 What sort of new jobs did the railway provide?
4 What was the specialisation developed at the new town of Crewe?
5 In 1839 George Bradshaw devised something that rail travellers found (and still find) very useful. What was it?
6 In 1841 Thomas Cook provided another sort of railway service. What was it? Does his firm still have a branch in your town?

Two interesting points
The competitive nature of the early railway business led to tremendous progress in the design and technology of locomotives – of great advantage to British manufacturers who would have to keep well ahead of international technology if they were to survive competition in years to come.

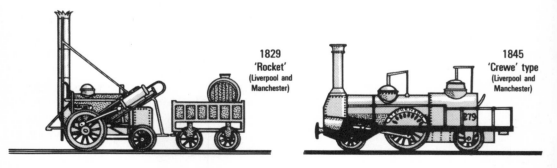

1829
'Rocket'
(Liverpool and Manchester)

1845
'Crewe' type
(Liverpool and Manchester)

The railway revolution. The rapid progress in railway development shown by the changing design of locomotives (both by Stephenson) over the space of sixteen years

2   The railway building programme proved to be the biggest civil

engineering event in nineteenth-century Britain. It employed around a million men during the 1840s. You will remember that this was a time of great social unrest, e.g. the Chartists. Do you think that the 'railway revolution' helped to avert a 'political revolution'? After all, it did siphon off a lot of the unemployment.

Some technical terms

Plate rails these rails had a vertical rim to keep the smooth wheels in position so they would not 'run off the rails'.

Edge rails this type had a rounded head rather like the type used today.

Rack and rail rails with a protruding lug at the side. The engine had a special cog that fitted into each lug as in the drawing:

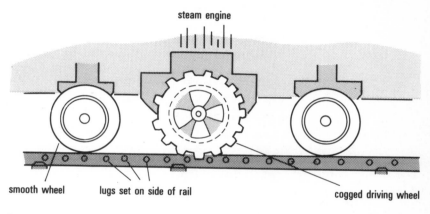

Rack and rail

SHIPPING

THE SAILING CLIPPERS

Sailing ship development peaked during the nineteenth century. Some of the most beautiful ships were the clippers – bringing wool from Australia or tea from China and fighting to clip minutes off the time of each voyage. One of the most famous clipper races was the one between *Ariel* and *Taiping* in 1866. Both reached London after a record voyage of ninety-nine days.

THE FIRST STEAMSHIPS

Long before this, in 1798, William Symington had launched a steamship on the River Clyde. In 1802 he built a steam-powered paddle-steamer, the *Charlotte Dundas*.

Another Scottish engineer, Henry Bell, built the twenty-eight ton

Comet in 1812 and from now on British steamships (some made of iron) plied the rivers, then the seas around the coast and, finally, (in 1838) sailed across the Atlantic.

They had distinct weaknesses:
1   They were costly to build and operate.
2   Their coal bunkers took up a great deal of cargo space.

Technical improvements
Several technical changes revolutionised the vessels of the Royal Navy and the merchant marine:

1 compound engines used exhaust steam to fire an extra cylinder – more power for about the same coal consumption (1856);

2 triple expansion engines reduced coal consumption (1881);

3 steam turbine engines (invented by Charles Parsons in 1884) were then developed and refined – fitted to the *Turbinia*, they enabled this 100-foot vessel to outstrip the Royal Navy's destroyers during the 1897 Spithead Review;

4 diesel engines were fitted to ships in 1912 – so coal was now being challenged by oil as the fuel for modern shipping.

Significance
From 1890 to 1914 Britain built most of the world's merchant shipping. Her own mercantile marine was the biggest in the world.

Effects
1   Many ships had steam operated refrigeration plants and these could bring in all sorts of cheap and exotic foodstuffs for the British people.
2   British seaports grew rapidly and provided more jobs.
3   The coal and steel industries prospered.

PERSONAL TRANSPORTATION

The dramatic changes taking place on land and sea had not particularly helped the individual traveller who wanted to move around inside the rapidly growing towns and cities. The arrival of the electric tramway (the first was in Brighton) helped, as did the increasing availability of bicycles (more comfortable after John Boyd Dunlop began manufacturing pneumatic tyres in 1889).

But the most important change came with the invention of the internal-combustion engine, the development of the petrol-driven bus and the private motor car. Significantly, Britain was not responsible for these inventions – most of the credit goes to German and French inventors.

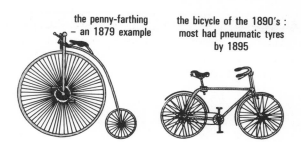

the penny-farthing
– an 1879 example

the bicycle of the 1890's :
most had pneumatic tyres
by 1895

An early motor car

Nicolaus Otto developed the gas-air engine in Deutz, Germany, and Gottlieb Daimler created an efficient power unit by using petrol in the gas-air engine. Carl Benz then used this engine to power a motor car. Wealthy British people imported the new motor cars from France and Germany and today they are highly prized and often seen in rallies and displays.

Many of the new roads built in the Macadam style now received a new surface, using tar. From this came the word 'tarmac' and by 1913 tar-spraying had become widespread with well over 200,000 vehicles on British roads. One of the best-known and highly prized British motor cars was the Rolls-Royce *Silver Ghost*, manufactured in 1907. However, for the majority of people living in the towns and villages, life was changed by the arrival of the motor bus. Even before the First World War these new forms of transportation were widening people's horizons and enabling them to visit relatives and go shopping for the price of a twopenny ticket.

A CONTRAST WITH AMERICA

It is interesting to note the difference between Britain and America as far as the automobile/motor car industries were concerned. In the USA the automobile industry had barely existed before 1896; yet by 1914 there were over 3.5 million cars on American roads. Much credit went to Henry Ford, the Detroit mechanic who applied mass-production techniques to consumer products. Unlike other manufacturers, such as General Motors, he marketed only one type of car – the Model T. His production methods were totally successful. A Model T was $950 in 1909; by 1914 he had brought the price down to $490.

Model T Ford 'flivver', 1914

AVIATION

Man's interest in flight became acute during the eighteenth century – the great ballooning era pioneered by the Montgolfier brothers in France. There was a great deal of experiment in flight without power.

GLIDERS

Sir George Cayley of Scarborough lived from 1773 to 1857 and takes the credit for laying the foundation of modern aeronautical knowledge. He discovered the significance of setting wings at an angle (dihedral) to the body (fuselage). He discovered that a tailplane gave longitudinal stablity. This is a picture of a glider he designed in 1809:

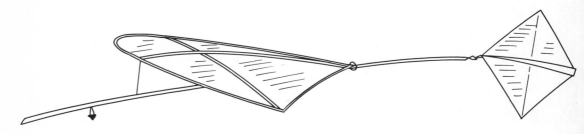

Cayley's glider, 1809 – devised after he weighted the nose of an ordinary paper kite – and flown as a glider.

His later gliders could carry a person – and there was a story that he ordered his coachman to fly one of the new gliders over a valley in Yorkshire. The glider crashed and the coachman gave in his notice.

THE FIRST POWERED FLIGHT

Wilbur Wright (1867–1912) and **Orville Wright (1871–1948)** were the two American aviation pioneers who carried out the first sustained and powered flights at Kitty Hawk, North Carolina, in 1903. Aspiring British aviators soon imitated their designs and men such as Sidney Camm and Edgar Percival built their own gliders and soon added the power of an internal-combustion engine. Louis Blériot (1872–1936) proved its reliability by building and flying a monoplane that crossed the Channel in 1909 (it took thirty-seven minutes and won the *Daily Mail* prize of £1000). By 1910 'air-minded' people were joining the new flying clubs and taking their licences. There were 250 privately owned aeroplanes in Britain (1910–12) – a replica of the Channel-conquering Blériot fitted with a 25 hp Anzani engine could be bought for £480. Significantly, the first military trials of aeroplanes were held on Salisbury Plain in 1912.

Multiple choice questions

1 The following were railway towns specialising in repair and manufac-
   ture of engines and rolling stock:
   ☐   Crewe, Ipswich and Norwich
   ☐   Crewe, Swindon and Rugby
   ☐   Crewe, Swindon and Norwich

2 A British politician, creator of the 'Sliding Scale' to control British
   wheat prices for the benefit of producers was also thought to be the
   first person to be killed by a railway locomotive. His name was:
   ☐   William Huskisson
   ☐   Robert Peel
   ☐   George Hudson
   ☐   Thomas Cook

3 Government standardised wages, prices and working conditions by
   the Railway and Canal Act in:
   ☐   1910
   ☐   1911
   ☐   1912
   ☐   1913

4 Select the statement that is untrue:
   ☐   there were 18,750 miles of railway track by 1914
   ☐   steel rails were general after 1870
   ☐   block signalling was compulsory after 1899
   ☐   pullman cars were not introduced in the nineteenth century

5 Select the statement that is untrue:
   Brunel's *Great Eastern*
   ☐   displaced 19,000 tons
   ☐   had four screw propellers (invented 1836)
   ☐   had four paddle wheels
   ☐   had a wooden hull

6 Britain had the technology to build enormous ships. Two of the most
   famous before 1914 were the
   ☐   *Titanic* and *Mauretania*
   ☐   *Titanic* and *Queen Elizabeth*
   ☐   *Titanic* and *Queen Mary*
   ☐   *Titanic* and *Normandie*

7 In 1914 the British merchant marine was bigger than Germany's. By
   how much?
   ☐   twice as much
   ☐   three times as much
   ☐   four times as much
   ☐   five times as much

8 The first deep tube in London electrified the following line in 1890:
   ☐   City and South London line
   ☐   City and Waterloo
   ☐   City and Bakerloo
   ☐   City and Northern Line

9 Motor taxation began in:
   ☐   1909

☐   1910
☐   1911
☐   1912

10   The Locomotive Act (1865) ruled that the maximum speed on the public highway was 4 mph. It was repealed in:
☐   1893
☐   1894
☐   1895
☐   1896

11   A compound engine:
☐   used exhaust steam to operate two pistons
☐   was used in the *Turbinia*
☐   was very expensive on coal
☐   was a diesel engine

12   Motor buses were allowed on the roads during:
☐   1903–4
☐   1904–5
☐   1905–6
☐   1906–7

SOCIAL CHANGE TO 1914

CONTENTS

PUBLIC HEALTH

THE PROBLEM WORSENS

Remember that the original Board of Health set up by the 1848 Public Health Act (p. 69) could not compel the towns and cities to establish their own local health boards. People were over-conscious of their own rights and liberties and resented government interference in their everyday life. *The Times* actually described the work of the Board of Health as 'a reckless invasion of property and liberty'. A few enlightened areas such as Bristol did try to improve sewage, cleansing services, street paving and lighting but the fact remained that matters were not getting any better:

1 **Death rate** was rising at 23 per 1000 in the 1860s.

2 **Infant mortality** was rising:
      1840 148 per 1000
      1860 151 per 1000

3 **14,000 people** (most of them in London) died of cholera in 1866.
    Yet there was no lack of medical research. Matters could be put right.

MEDICAL ADVANCE

Edward Jenner (1749–1823) had pioneered vaccination. His experiments and observations led him to note that dairymaids who contracted cowpox were immune to smallpox. He inoculated a boy in 1796 and published his results in 1798. His ideas on vaccination were generally accepted and Parliament actually awarded him £30,000 for his work in combatting smallpox.

Joseph Lister (1827–1912) helped to solve the problem of the high death rate common in surgery. Anaesthetics were well-known after the introduction of nitrous oxide (1800); ether (1818 – not used until 1846); chloroform 1847. Lister followed the teaching of Louis Pasteur who showed that micro-organisms (germs) were the cause of so many post-operative deaths. Lister used a spray of carbolic acid to destroy germs and introduced new aseptic techniques (white operating gowns, special surgical instruments and tables, catgut – all of them sterile). The death rate fell dramatically.

Louis Pasteur (1822–95) not only established the germ theory of disease. He developed the process of killing bacteria in milk – pasteurisation (1870); developed vaccines against anthrax in cattle; and vaccines against rabies. He was the founder of the modern science of bacteriology.

Robert Koch (1843–1910) worked along similar lines. He discovered the bacillus that caused tuberculosis (1882) and the cause of cholera (1883).

Florence Nightingale (1820–1910) brought new standards into the nursing profession (before her work the profession had little or no status in British society). Her work at the military hospital in Scutari, Turkey, during the Crimean War (1854–6) and then at Balaclava helped to reduce the shocking death rate among wounded soldiers. She became a legendary figure – the 'Lady with the Lamp' – and founded a nurses' training school at St Thomas's Hospital (1861). Proper nurses' uniforms, professional examinations and a sense of duty and service gave the nurses the status they rightfully enjoy today.

THE 1872 PUBLIC HEALTH ACT

This divided the country into urban and rural sanitary authorities and compulsorily appointed medical officers of health in each of these.

THE 1875 PUBLIC HEALTH ACT

Set minimum standards regarding water supply, sewage removal, the condition of streets and all buildings, rules for burying the dead, rules for the conduct of markets and the control of industries that might cause a public nuisance. Of course, the changes did not come overnight:

Smallpox not eradicated – killed people in the 1870s;

Typhoid still struck, e.g. Maidstone 1897;

Cholera still killed people during the 1890s;

New diseases appeared – influenza epidemic in the winter of 1889–90.

Nevertheless, the Victorians made enormous steps forward as the statistics proved:

Decline in the death rate	1871	1911
England and Wales	22.3 per 1000	13.8 per 1000
Scotland	22.3 per 1000	15.1 per 1000

Completely new techniques added to their efficiency:

1895   Röntgen discovers X-rays;
1896   Mme Curie discovers radium;
1911   vitamins discovered.

So, by combining public health reform with local government reform, for example the *Local Government Act 1871* which combined public health and the poor law under the local government board, the condition of the British people improved, especially during the period 1880–1914.

EDUCATION

Individuals and charitable bodies had provided education during the period 1500–1800 so that by 1870 (the date of the first major Education Act) a wide variety of schools existed:

Grammar schools, many of which dated from the sixteenth century, provided classical education – some free places to clever impoverished children. Flourished in rural England – particularly in the old centres of trade and commerce.

Public schools – usually grew from endowments. There were eight major public schools: Eton, Rugby, Harrow, St Paul's, Westminster, Shrewsbury, Merchant Taylors' and Winchester. Investigated by the Clarendon Commission 1864.

Dame schools – very common in villages.

Day schools – often a crude form of elementary education for a few pence per week. Some were industry schools; others were Sunday schools.

The British and Foreign Schools Society (1814) provided education based on the work of Joseph Lancaster (1778–1838).

The National Society (1811) provided education based on the work of Andrew Bell (1753–1832).

University education was provided mainly by Oxford and Cambridge whose origins dated back to the thirteenth century.

THE BEGINNINGS OF STATE AID

The famous 1833 grant of £20,000 to help the societies listed above expanded in 1839 when the government set up Her Majesty's Inspectors (HMIs) to vet the voluntary schools. Teacher training began in 1840 and the government established its Department of Education in 1856. The first major change (a reprehensible one, in most people's view) came as a result of the Duke of Newcastle's Royal Commission recommendation: that all school grants and teachers' salaries should depend on the children's performance in the classroom. This system of 'payment by results' was begun by Robert Lowe in 1862.

THE 1870 EDUCATION ACT

Introduced by W. E. Forster (often known as the Forster Act), it enabled the State to provide elementary education. The aim was to fill in the gaps left by the voluntary school movement, i.e. the government should provide schools where they were needed. The method was to set up local school-boards elected by ratepayers. The 'board school education' was to be funded from the rates. It was not free to the scholars and not all at first went to school. Then came government legislation:

1880	education compulsory (to the age of 10);
1891	compulsory education free;
1897	the end of payment by results;
1899	compulsory education to age twelve;
	Board of Education established.

THE 1902 EDUCATION ACT

Usually called Balfour's Education Act, it placed the control of eduction in the hands of 330 specially created Local Education Authorities (LEA.) These were responsible for elementary education and had the power to provide secondary education. Many LEAs did this for fee-paying scholars; but after 1907 they offered free places to children who could 'pass the scholarship' examination (developed into the 11+).

So, as a result of government intervention:
(*a*)   elementary education was free and compulsory;
(*b*)   secondary education was neither free nor compulsory. Such was the state of the educational system in 1914.

THE RIGHT TO VOTE

THE 1832 REFORM ACT

This had given the right to vote (the franchise) to a very small number of people:

(a)   the £10 householders in the towns;

(b)   the forty-shilling freeholders, £20 copyholders and £10 lease-holders in the rural areas.

THE 1867 REFORM ACT

This extended the franchise to:

(a)   male householders who paid the rates;

(b)   lodgers who paid £10 a year rent (males only).

This dealt with the largely unfranchised male population in the new industrial towns and cities.

In the countryside, the franchise was given to £12 householders.

Note: this left the farm workers of Britain without the vote.

THE SECRET BALLOT ACT 1872

This ended the traditional 'open' method of voting at local elections and prevented the corruption that was still rife at such events. Note that this was one of the Chartists' aims.

THE 1884 REFORM ACT

This gave the vote to all male householders. Before the 1884 Act there had been 3 million voters; now there were over 5 million voters.

The outstanding omission: women did not have the vote.

THE GRADUAL EMANCIPATION OF WOMEN

LOCAL GOVERNMENT ELECTION RIGHTS

Although women had been denied the franchise, three Acts gave them limited election rights in local affairs:

1   1869 Municipal Franchise Act enabled single women ratepayers to vote in municipal elections.

2   1870 Education Act included a section which enabled women of property to vote for and become members of the new school-boards.

3   In 1894 women were allowed to vote for and sit on parish councils, having already been allowed to vote in county council elections (1888 onwards).

A real breakthrough came in 1907 when women were allowed to become town or county councillors and mayors. So they were by then allowed to play important roles in local affairs; but were denied the right to participate, through any democratic process of election, in national affairs.

Why did women not share equal voting rights?

Women had very little status in Victorian Britain – probably less than they had enjoyed since the seventeenth century. Their role was seen by men as wives and mothers – but they had no legal rights in that capacity. Women were subject to their husbands and lost most of their property when they got married. There was very little education open to single women and there were only two 'respectable' jobs into which they could go – writing and teaching. The vast majority of women found jobs in agriculture – the biggest employer. Next to this came domestic service, in which over a million women worked. Many girls were determined to avoid domestic service and deliberately chose factory work, shop work – or one of the new jobs in a Post Office or as a 'typewriter girl'.

The beginnings of change

Education Girls had received education in many of the voluntary schools and there were even a few girls' boarding schools before 1870. More women went to university* in the 1880s and 1890s. After the Balfour Education Act (1902) girls were able to go to grammar schools; and they flocked to the new special senior elementary schools set up by some LEAs to provide shorthand, typewriting and general office skills.

*Although Queen's and Bedford Colleges for women had been opened in 1848–9 and Girton College had been founded in 1869 only a tiny handful of women had enjoyed 'higher education'.

Changes in the law These gave married women far more rights than they had enjoyed before, e.g.:

(a)   1839 Infants Custody Act;

(b)   1857 Marriage and Divorce Act – through the new civil courts women could divorce husbands for adultery, cruelty and desertion;

(c)   a series of Married Women's Property Acts (1870, 1874, 1882, 1893) allowed women to own, inherit and bequeath property. They were also allowed to enter into legal contracts and establish businesses.

THE SUFFRAGETTE MOVEMENT

Led by Mrs Emmeline Pankhurst (1858–1928), a group of politically conscious women formed the Women's Social and Political Union (WSPU) in 1903. They demanded the suffrage (the vote) and the *Daily Mail* labelled them the suffragettes. They demanded 'votes for women 'and the activities of Annie Kenny (a friend of Christabel Pankhurst) landed her in jail. By 1908 their demonstrations became violent, e.g. breaking shop windows. Many were arrested but they refused to eat and had to endure 'forcible feeding'. Other suffragettes chained themselves to railings or bombarded London with propaganda leaflets dropped from a balloon – the suffragettes used every device to ram home their political point.

The following passage describes their years of violence 1910–14. Certain key words have been omitted. These are:

> King's; greens; Cat and Mouse Act 1913; 'wild women'; suffrage; insurance; Derby Day

Now that other methods had failed, about a thousand _____ turned to violence. They decided to attack private property and hoped that the _____ companies, faced with a deluge of claims, would pressure the government into granting women's _____. So they attacked private houses, slashed pictures in art galleries, set fire to sports pavilions and poured acid on golf course _____. An angry government retaliated with the _____ which allowed them to arrest a suffragette, release her when she was weak from hunger strike and then re-arrest her when she was better. But even this paled in comparison with Emily Davison's sacrifice. On _____ 1913 she killed herself by running in front of the _____ horse.

The suffragette violence ended abruptly in 1914 when war was declared against Germany. The suffragettes poured their immense energy into the war effort and, at the end of the struggle, won (for some women) the right to vote.

Some remarkable Victorian women

Elizabeth Garrett Anderson (1836–1917) She was the first woman to practise medicine in England, passing her finals in 1865. Her great success was founding the London School of Medicine for Women in 1874.

Octavia Hill (1838–1912) She pioneered the movement for open public spaces and better living conditions for the poor. She was one of the founders of the National Trust in 1895.

Dorothea Beale (1831–1906) She was principal of Cheltenham Ladies' College and was a sponsor of St Hilda's, Oxford. She was an active suffragette.

Frances Buss (1827–1894) She worked with Miss Beale to secure higher education for women. She was head of the North London Collegiate School and began the Girls' Public Day School Trust.

Elizabeth Fry (1780–1845) She was a Quaker and notable prison reformer who carried on John Howard's work. She began her work after visiting women prisoners in Newgate Prison and being appalled by their conditions.

THE INDEPENDENT LABOUR PARTY

THE LABOUR REPRESENTATION LEAGUE

Two years after they received the vote, a number of working men founded the Labour Representation League (1869). Their wish was to arrange that predominantly working-class constituencies would have working-class MPs to represent them. The first two were Alexander

Macdonald and Thomas Burt (they sat with the Liberals in 1874 and were nicknamed the 'Lib-Labs'). The Labour Representation League was but one of several completely new political movements.

THE SOCIAL DEMOCRATIC FEDERATION

This was a new socialist movement founded in 1881. It wanted to pay MPs and give women the vote. It wanted a peaceful revolution in Britain – through parliamentary legislation.

THE FABIAN SOCIETY

This was a society formed by intellectual socialists in 1884. Led by George Bernard Shaw (1856–1950), Sidney James Webb (1859–1947) and his wife Beatrice Webb (née Potter, 1858–1943), the Fabians exerted a great deal of influence on parliamentary legislation – and helped to found the London School of Economics (1895) and the *New Statesman* (1913).

THE INDEPENDENT LABOUR PARTY

Founded by Keir Hardie (1856–1915) in 1893, the ILP was dedicated to sending Labour MPs to Parliament. Three went in 1892 (a result that gave Keir Hardie the thrust to found the ILP) and there was every prospect that the number of working-class MPs in Parliament would increase. From his position as a Labour MP, Keir Hardie pushed through the idea of joining forces with the other socialist movements in the country. In 1900 the ILP met the Fabians and the Social Democratic Foundation and decided to form a Labour Representation Committee. Its secretary was Ramsay MacDonald (1866–1937), destined to become the first Labour Prime Minister of Britain in 1924.

THE 1906 ELECTION

The ILP did well in 1906. It put up fifty candidates and won twenty-nine seats in the House of Commons. Note that in this election there were twenty-four Lib-Labs – they joined the Labour Party in 1910, a year in which its numbers grew to fifty-three MPs. They had great influence on the Liberal legislation after 1906.

THE LIBERALS AND THE BEGINNINGS OF THE WELFARE STATE

The nineteenth century had seen many people devote themselves to the needs of the poor and the deprived. They were often called philanthropists – people prepared to dedicate themselves to the good of humanity. Some were physicians such as Dr Thomas Barnardo (1845–1905) who founded the first home for destitute boys at Stepney and a similar home for girls at Barkingside (1876); others were politi cians such as Samuel Plimsoll (1824–1898), 'the merchant seaman's friend', who was devoted to the improvement of conditions on board merchant ships. The 1876 Merchant Shipping Act partly succeeded in this. Its best remembered feature was the introduction of the 'Plimsoll mark' to indicate the maximum load a ship should carry. Businessmen such as Joseph Rowntree (1801–59) and his son Benjamin Seebohm Rowntree (1871–1954) made careful studies of York and laid the foundation of later social surveys designed to discover the nature of poverty and ways of bringing this scourge of a modern industrial society to an end. Poverty and social deprivation were still rife in early twentieth-century Britain – especially among the elderly, the casually employed and the long-term unemployed. Armed with this knowledge, the new Liberal Government began its attack on the numerous social evils it had inherited in 1906.

Help for the sick The Workmen's Compensation Act 1906 made employers pay compensation to workers who suffered injuries in accidents at work. Then in 1911 Part 1 of the National Insurance Act (passed that year) ruled that workers between sixteen and seventy could pay 4d a week into a national scheme for medical attention. The employers would pay 3d and the State would add 2d. This was the famous '9d for 4d' – the beginnings of National Insurance.

Help for the unemployed In 1909 the government set up Board of Trade offices under the terms of the Labour Exchanges Act. These offices (soon called labour exchanges) opened in 1910 to provide details of jobs available. Then, under Part II of the 1911 National Insurance Act, the government brought in compulsory unemployment insurance. Unemployment benefit (7 shillings a week for a maximum of fifteen weeks) was of immense value to those, suddenly thrown out of work, who had no other resources.

Help for the elderly David Lloyd George (1863–1945) made a famous speech in Limehouse in 1909.

> The provision for the aged and the deserving poor – it was time it was done. It is rather a shame for a rich country like ours – probably the richest in the world, if not the richest the world has ever seen – that it should allow those who have toiled all their days to end in penury and possibly starvation.

He had just pushed the 1908 Old Age Pensions Act through Parliament, an Act that meant that on 1 January 1909 old people over seventy could draw a pension of up to 5 shillings a week.

Help for the children The Liberals made many important changes in their concern for children's welfare:

(*a*)   1906 Provision of School Meals Act;
(*b*)   1907 School Medical Services Act;
(*c*)   1907–8 'Children's Charter' – setting up juvenile courts with

powers to put children on probation or to send them to Borstal institutions (the original one was at Borstal in Kent.)

THE 1911 CONSTITUTIONAL CRISIS

All of these remarkable reforms would cost the State a great deal of money and meant an increase in taxation. In 1909 Lloyd George presented his 'People's Budget' in which he was setting out to tax the rich to aid the poor. The House of Lords objected and blocked Lloyd George's budget. This led to two general elections and a threat from the new king, George V, that he would create sufficient peers to outvote Lloyd George's opponents in the House of Lords. This halted the Lords – they withdrew their objections.

Results

1   The House of Commons could now limit the power of the Lords over all money bills.
2   Parliament could last only five years before a general election.
3   MPs would be paid £400 a year.
    'It all added up to a triumph for the forces of democracy and social reform.'

Questions

1   There were three important 'reforming' prime ministers after 1886. Their ministries are listed below:

W. E. Gladstone (1809–98) – the Liberal leader 1868–74; 1880–85; 1886; 1892–4.

Benjamin Disraeli (1804–81) – the Conservative leader 1868; 1874–80.

Lord Salisbury (1830–1903) – led the Conservative Party after 1880; 1885–6; 1886–92; 1895–1902.

Now list the ministries in which the following major reforms appeared:

	Gladstone	Disraeli	Salisbury
1870 Forster's Education Act	☐	☐	☐
1872 Ballot Act	☐	☐	☐
1871 Civil Service Reform	☐	☐	☐
1875 Artisans' Dwelling Act	☐	☐	☐
1875 Public Health Act	☐	☐	☐
1875 Pure Food and Drugs Acts	☐	☐	☐
1876 Merchant Shipping Act	☐	☐	☐

	Gladstone	Disraeli	Salisbury
1875 Climbing Boys' Act	☐	☐	☐
1882 Married Women's Property Act	☐	☐	☐
1897 Workmen's Compensation Act	☐	☐	☐
1888 Local Government Act creating county councils	☐	☐	☐

2   In 1889 a *Medical Congress Report* examined children's diseases that were attributable to poverty and malnutrition. Here is their comment:

> In some areas, such as the Clyde district, almost every child was found to be affected.

(*a*)   Which of the following diseases do you think the Congress had in mind?

cholera; typhoid; influenza; smallpox; rickets

(*b*)   This disease was confined mainly to the industrial districts. Why do you think this was so?

(*c*)   What event in British military history (1899–1902) gave doctors the chance to assess just how fit young men were?

(*d*)   Were the results of this investigation encouraging?

3   In 1906 a distinguished British politician made this statement to give the electorate some idea of what the government intended to do:

> I should like to see the State embark on various novel and adventurous experiments. I am of the opinion that the State should assume the position of the reserve employer of Labour . . . We are all agreed that the State must increasingly and earnestly concern itself with the care of the sick and the aged and, above all, the children. I look forward to the universal establishment of minimum standards of life and labour . . .

He was speaking in Scotland. Was he:
☐   Lord Salisbury
☐   Lord Balfour
☐   Henry Asquith
☐   Winston Churchill (then a Liberal MP)
☐   Lloyd George

4   Old age pensioners fervently uttered 'Thank God for Lloyd George' after 1 January 1909.
(*a*)   Who was Lloyd George?
(*b*)   What position did he hold in the government?
(*c*)   Who was Prime Minister in 1909?
(*d*)   Why were the pensioners so grateful?

CHAPTER NINE

THE FIRST WORLD WAR 1914–18 AND ITS EFFECTS (TO 1931)

CONTENTS

A NEW KIND OF WARFARE

The Germans applied an extraordinary plan in 1914, a plan designed to defeat both France and Russia in a matter of a few months. Their 'Schlieffen Plan' required a surprise sweep through France via Belgium to force a surrender in the west; then the victorious German armies would board troop trains and travel eastwards to defeat the Russians. But when the Kaiser (Emperor) of Germany, Wilhelm II, sent his troops into Belgium the British felt they had a moral obligation to defend that country under the terms of the 1839 Treaty of London. Prime Minister Asquith therefore gave the Germans a few hours to withdraw from Belgium. When they didn't, Britain declared war on Germany. The British Expeditionary Force crossed to France, marched to Mons and there delayed the German advance long enough for the French to prepare for the autumn battles. Huge armies were involved, backed by the might of some of the world's greatest industrial powers. It would not only involve the fighting men; the First World War brought home the reality of modern warfare to the civilians.

A British soldier's view of the early campaigns
The following is extracted from a letter written by a young officer to his mother in September 1914.

> At last I got just a few moments to write you a line . . . Thank you so much for the offer of chocolate. It would be most welcome. Plain 'Mexican' is the best, and good solid lumps, not those little pieces. Another thing we all cry out for is a supply of matches. Wax ones are best, I think. Also candles, good firm wax ones like carriage lamps. If you could find a collapsible lantern with tall sides I should like one awfully, but don't spend much on it, if you think of sending one. When sending parcels make them small. I'm glad B. is getting out here. Every able-bodied man should be on his way out . . . By the way don't you believe half you hear about the atrocities attributed to the Germans. These is little truth in them, I think.
>
> Credit: Brigadier S. N. Floyer Acland

A popular song

This was sung at the beginning of the First World War:

> Oh! We don't want to lose you
> But we think you ought to go;
> For your King and your Country
> Both need you so . . .

Now compare the letter and the popular song:

1 Does the song reflect the belief of the young soldier – that men should go to serve in France?
2 Why do both the letter and the song demand more men in France?
3 Is the letter anti-German?
4 What do soldiers serving in France seem to need most?

The encroachment on civil liberties

Britain passed the Defence of the Realm Act (1914) – usually called 'Dora'. This introduced censorship and encouraged people to give evidence against suspected German nationals and spies. It suspended many civil liberties 'for the duration of hostilities'. For example, once air raids began people who offended against the 'black-out' regulations could be fined; so could people who hoarded food.

PROPAGANDA

It is often said that the first casualty of war is truth. In Britain, the newspapers and magazines didn't need much encouragement to stir up hatred against the Germans. There were terrible stories about atrocities committed by German soldiers against Belgian civilians, rumours of Russian soldiers 'with snow on their boots' arriving at London railway stations to help the British Army fight the Germans, and a barrage of hostility against shopkeepers with German sounding names. Restaurants changed their menus and refused to serve German dishes; even dogs descended from German breeds became suddenly unpopular!

A shortage of manpower

Propaganda certainly succeeded in calling up millions of men in Britain – so many that there was a serious shortage of manpower in coal-mining, the electrical industry, the chemical and high explosive industries. So there was a shortage of workers in vital war industries – and therefore a shortage of war products, particularly shells. In May 1915, after one particularly disastrous attack on German trenches, *The Times* stated that:

> We had not sufficient high explosives to lower the enemy's parapets to the ground . . . a fatal bar to our success.

Government reaction

Asquith reacted quickly. He made Lloyd George the Minister of Munitions and brought a Labour representative, Arthur Henderson, into the Cabinet. Lloyd George, with his customary vigour:

1 put the munitions industry on its feet;
2 prohibited strikes;
3 drafted women into the factories.

Changes in factory production were rapid – sadly, war is often an instrument of rapid technological change. New gun, aeroplane and tank factories sprang up. Their lay-out and manufacturing techniques adopted Henry Ford's system of mass-production. Consequently, the wartime factories looked very different from the typical factories of 1913.

THE ROLE OF WOMEN

Women quickly secured work in munitions factories, acted as railway porters, lift attendants, bus and tram conductresses. One nurse, Edith Cavell, had stayed behind to look after the wounded when the Germans overran Belgium. She helped over 200 Allied soldiers to escape into neutral Holland. Condemned by the Germans, she was shot in 1915. There was great admiration in Britain for women who joined the armed services (strangely, neither the French nor the Germans looked with pleasure on young ladies who wore khaki or blue uniforms):

1 The WRNS (Women's Royal Naval Service);
2 The WAACs (Women's Auxiliary Army Corps);
3 The WRAFs (Women's Royal Air Force).

Of course, all served as non-combatants.

For more women served in the factories or on the land as farm workers. Many paid a heavy price for their efforts. For example, those working 14½-hours shifts in aeroplane factories contracted lung diseases from the poisonous fumes given off by aircraft dope; those who filled shells with high explosive developed skin discoloration and eczema from handling TNT.

AIR RAIDS AND SEA BOMBARDMENTS

December 1914 brought the war home to people living in Dover and on the East Coast. On 16 December two German battlecruisers steamed out of the North Sea mists and shelled towns on the east coast; while on Christmas Eve a Taube monoplane flew over Dover and dropped the first bomb on British soil. Zeppelin and Gotha bomber raids began in 1915. The diagrams overleaf show the first Zeppelin attack on Britain.

RATIONING

In addition to direct action from aeroplanes, Zeppelins and warships,

An early Zeppelin, the L3 – the first Zeppelin to raid Britain

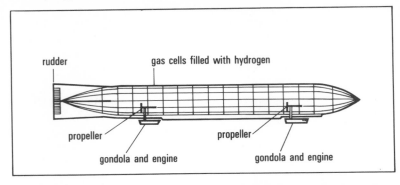

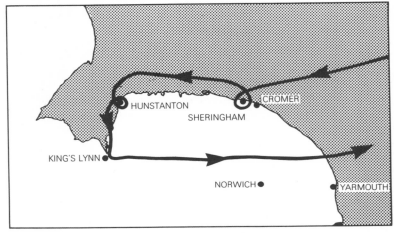

Map showing the raid by L3 and L4 on 19–20 January 1915 from the Zeppelin base at Fuhlsbuttel. Four people died and sixteen were injured

the British people had to endure the effects of the two indiscriminate German U-boat campaigns of 1915 and 1917. The Germans were determined to destroy Britain by starving her into surrender through the U-boat campaigns – they hoped to sink every ship that approached British ports and in 1917 came very near to their ambition. Of course, they ran the risk of America declaring war. This in fact happened on 6 April 1917.

Opposite is a photograph of a German propaganda postcard urging the German people to subscribe to the war loan and help provide a U-boat for use against Britain.

1 Why were the Germans so confident that they could starve the British people?

2 How were the U-boats shown in the photograph finally defeated?

3 Can you name the major towns shown by the artist on his map of Britain?

By the end of 1917 there were very severe food shortages and people had to queue to buy basic foodstuffs. Lloyd George hoped that a newly established Food Ministry could encourage the British people to accept voluntary rationing. This failed, and in 1918 (during February–March) the government imposed food rationing. At the same time there was a virulent outbreak of influenza in the country – it didn't end until 1919 after thousands of people had died.

THE FINAL BATTLES OF THE FIRST WORLD WAR

The campaign on the Western Front (where the bulk of the German army was stationed 1914–18) was marked by the most horrific set piece battles that became etched in people's minds for many years afterwards:

> *Ypres* (1914, 1915, 1917, 1918) – the 1917 battle was 'Passchendaele'; *the Somme* (1916); *the Marne* (1914, 1918) *Loos (1916)*; *Messines, Vimy Ridge, Cambrai* (all 1917); *St Quentin* (1918); *Amiens* (1918).

Some idea of the nature of the fighting can be gained from this description of trench warfare during the Battle of the Somme 1916:

> We had endless clearing and cleaning up to do in that desolation of desolations. We had to construct trenches in an ocean of mud, we had to bail out dug-outs and clear them of their stiff, stark occupants; we had to bury, or attempt to bury, hundreds of the victims of our attacks and many also of our own fellows . . . No one who has not seen and struggled through it can, I am sure, realise a bit what that mud was like. It was a horror quite apart, quite unlike anything else in this war. Imagine a man, wounded on patrol, in front of our own lines, struggling a few yards towards his own people, overcome by the sucking ooze, sinking, sinking inch by inch, in full view of hundreds of willing friends, not one of whom can do a thing to help him: sinking and sinking until, though he calls and calls for help, he realises no help can come – and begs his own people to end his horror with a bullet.
>
> Credit: Brigadier S. N. Floyer Acland

It was difficult for soldiers to convey these scenes to their own families and a great gulf developed between fighting men and their loved ones. Mothers with a husband in the trenches tried to ensure that at least one son survived. Lloyd George was highly conscious of this and kept several divisions of youngsters (they were called 'boy conscripts') in reserve in Britain – right up to the final offensives in 1918. Even then the British spearheaded their attacks with the superb fighting divisions provided by the Commonwealth countries – especially Canada, Australia and New Zealand.

The war ended with the German surrender on 11 November 1918 – Armistice Day. The final Peace Treaty at Versailles was not signed until 1919. By then the full impact of the sacrifices and the many

A boy conscript, 1918

changes that had taken place during the 'Great War' (for that was the title of the First World War before 1939) had become apparent.

About 3 million British and Empire troops had suffered death or injury during the fighting. 1570 British people died from enemy attacks on Britain itself; and 4050 were injured.

Some effects of government control during the war

Agriculture The 1917 Corn Production Act guaranteed farmers minimum prices. This encouraged farmers to increase their acreage under the plough – and the effect was to increase production by 50 per cent.

Industry There was a rapid increase in the number and type of specialist machine tools used in arms factories. Many unskilled workers learnt how to produce very accurate weapons at very high speeds – these were the new turners, millers and capstan lathe operators.

Trade unions The 1915 Shell and Fuses Act allowed skilled workers to work side by side with unskilled workers (this was called 'dilution of labour') – on condition that the government would dismiss the 'dilutees' at the end of the war.

Nationalisation During the war the government had taken over control of the railways and the canals.

VOTES FOR WOMEN

Prime Minister Lloyd George canvassed for the votes of women when he sought re-election in 1918. This was because, in recognition of their immense services during the war, government had passed the 1918 Representation of the People Act. Now all adult males and women over thirty had the vote. Lloyd George won 533 out of the 634 Parliamentary seats – the biggest ever majority.

ECONOMIC UNCERTAINTY 1919–26

THE SHORT-LIVED BOOM 1919–20

There seemed to be plenty of money about at the beginning of 1919. There were several reasons for this:
1. Businessmen had made some big profits out of the war.
2. Demand for consumer goods increased – as did prices.
3. Ex-servicemen had their gratuities to spend.
4. Trade unions tried to keep up their regular wage increases (they had achieved this during the war) and when they couldn't get them they resorted to endless industrial action during the boom year 1919–20. There were over 2000 strikes that year. This was precisely the moment when Britain was desperate to sell her manufactured goods abroad because other countries were putting up trade barriers (tariffs)

against British products. Employers could think of only one way of combating this – cut wages.

UNEMPLOYMENT

Over 10 per cent of British workers lost their jobs in 1921 and the government had to face up to the problem of unemployment. The National Insurance Act of 1911 had to be updated – prices had risen and therefore the cost of living was higher. The new Unemployment Insurance Act (1920) gave people the 'dole'.

Industrial crisis – events leading up to the General Strike. There were many disputes in 1921–2. For example, the Lancashire textile factories shut down for six months, and Midland engineering works shut down for three months. Even worse, the threat of a protracted miners' strike was hanging over the nation. The threat had emerged in 1919 when miners demanded:

1   more pay;
2   a shorter working day;
3   permanent nationalisation of the mines.

Lloyd George forestalled a strike by setting up the Sankey Commission to review the coal industry. Lord Sankey came out in favour of the miners so Lloyd George agreed to lop an hour off the eight hour shift and subsidise miners' wages. But he refused to nationalise the industry. He might have settled the matter – but it wasn't in his power to do so. The miners and employers were happy as long as the price of coal remained steady – and when European coal production declined during 1923 (mainly due to the Ruhr crisis when French and Belgian troops moved into the region after Germany failed to meet her reparation payments) demand for British coal increased.

But during 1924–5 European production picked up and British coal prices dropped. At the same time Prime Minister Stanley Baldwin (in office since November 1924) wanted to withdraw the subsidy on miners' wages. Naturally, the mine-owners then sought to reduce miners' pay. But the miners were adamant: 'Not a penny off the pay, not a second on the day.'

So Baldwin, leader of a Conservative government, asked Sir Samuel Herbert to lead another Royal Commission of enquiry. Throughout the winter of 1925–6 the nation awaited his findings. When the Samuel Report came out in March 1926, its short term solution was to ask the miners to rescue the industry by taking a cut in wages.

THE GENERAL STRIKE MAY 1926

On Sunday 2 May 1926 the General Council of the TUC decided to take 'concerted action' against the government; certain 'trades and undertakings shall cease work as and when required'. Note very carefully: it did not mention a General Strike. Nor did it delegate to anybody the power to settle the miners' dispute with the government. Remember: there were very few formal negotiations. In fact, both sides failed to keep in contact with one another – even by telephone! When the TUC members tried to see Baldwin that evening they were told he had gone to bed!

When the British people woke up on the Monday morning they found that a General Strike backed by 3.65 million workers would begin at midnight.

Baldwin was well prepared.

1   He proclaimed a state of emergency.

2   His OMS (Organisation for the Maintenance of Supplies) swung into action.

3   The government neatly used the BBC and its own newspaper, the *British Gazette*. Deprived of their ordinary newspapers, the people depended on the government for news of the strike's progress.

4   Baldwin appealed to wartime patriotism – and volunteers came forward to drive lorries and buses. A few realised their schoolboy ambitions and became engine drivers! Others helped out at power stations or enrolled as special constables.

It is very important to remember this: very few people had any understanding of the TUC's point of view – that this was a *national* not a *general* strike; that the transport workers and the National Union of Railwaymen had come out in support of the pre-war Triple Alliance as a gesture of solidarity; that this was an industrial dispute and not, as the *British Gazette* described it, 'an organised attempt . . . to starve the people and to wreck the State'.

There was some violence, mainly in London and at big ports such as Liverpool and Hull. There were thousands of police prosecutions for 'incitement to sedition'; and police raided the headquarters of the British Communist Party almost every day!

Was there suppression of news? Undoubtedly, yes. There was also misrepresentation of facts. The BBC had a monopoly and could influence public opinion simply by selecting certain material and deciding to discard other information. It refused to let the Archbishop of Canterbury (on 7 May) broadcast a national appeal for a settlement.

On 10 May the government decided (via the Samuel Memorandum) to re-open negotiations on the miners' demands. But the miners refused to co-operate. At this point the TUC made its own momentous decision – it decided to abandon the miners and leave them to their fate.

Why do you think they did this? One reason may well be that the General Strike was so effective. The TUC leaders could see themselves on the edge of a major confrontation with the country's entire political and social system. They backed away – a deputation went to Downing Street on 12 May and agreed to end the strike. They left the coal dispute – the cause of the strike – unsettled.

Once the strike was over, most people thought the main economic problems were settled and were only too pleased to see Baldwin take tough action against the unions.

THE TRADE DISPUTES ACT 1927

Throughout the summer of 1926 the miners continued their futile resistance – until the threat of starvation forced them to go back to work at reduced wages. In some mining communities schools closed, children suffered from malnutrition, and shops shut for lack of customers. Communities disintegrated in the mining areas. Hundreds of families pulled up their roots and left the mines for work in the light industries of South-East England. They had not taken part in a revolution – simply a protest against the social and economic injustices they were suffering as a result of the decline of the traditional smokestack industries during the post-war years. Baldwin was not sympathetic. He was determined not to have another general strike in Britain. His Trades Union Act:

1 banned sympathetic strikes;
2 banned any strike designed to coerce the government by 'inflicting hardship on the community;
3 made intimidation during strikes illegal;
4 stated that trade union members should 'contract in' if they wished to make payment of a political levy to the Labour Party.
Labour leaders said they would repeal this Act – and managed to do it in 1946 when they had a large majority in the House of Commons.

1 The TUC sensed that the British people were not, in general, sympathetic to the General Strike. Why do you think this was so?
2 Do you think that the TUC wrecked the chances of the mining communities to have good working conditions and a steady job?
3 What advantages do you think Stanley Baldwin had in dealing with the dispute?
4 Could the TUC have put their case better?
5 Can you name one area of light industry to which mining families migrated in large numbers?

THE BRITISH PROBLEM

Before the First World War over 65 per cent of Britain's export trade involved her staple industries – coal-mining, iron and steel products such as ships, steam locomotives, boilers, textiles (especially cotton), cutlery and tools. A quarter of the British people made their living in these staple industries. Tragically, these were not the goods that the world wanted after the war. Other countries now demanded electrical equipment, plastics, chemicals, aeroplanes, motor cars, bicycles and rayon goods. Britain had led the world in the first Industrial Revolution, but in the second (the mass-production of electrically-controlled consumer goods) she had no headstart. Britain faced massive problems in changing from the old ways to the new – problems heavily disguised by the huge emphasis on war production 1914–18.

The most obvious fact was: the numbers of people entering the new light industries did not balance the increase in redundancies. So, as the staple industries declined, unemployment increased at an abnormally high rate. By 1929, about 11 per cent of the work-force had no jobs – though in the staple industries figures were far worse:

coal-mining 28%	iron and steel 33%
shipbuilding 31%	cotton manufacture 45%
woollen manufacture 26%	

Note that these declining industries were grouped into distinct geographical areas; while the new industries grew up in the South and the Midlands. There were two Britains in the 1920s: the poverty stricken North and the relatively prosperous South.

Social improvements

In 1919 Lloyd George's coalition government set up the Ministry of Health and passed the Housing Act – often known as the Addison Act after the new Minister of Health. Government believed it was important for local authorities to build houses subsidised by central grant. Between 1919 and 1923 over 171,000 houses went up.

Read this account:

> Many new council estates often lacked the amenities associated with modern urban life. Medical provision was often scanty though, of course, it was poorly provided throughout the nation as a whole. The Ministry lacked the funds to provide a national health service so the families of insured workers had to pay to go 'on the panel' of a local doctor. Conditions in the new homes – usually fitted with a kitchen, two living rooms and a separate bathroom/toilet – improved once electricity was laid on.

1 Were the poor amenities on new council estates typical of the nation as a whole?
2 Name the 'Ministry' being discussed.
3 What did the expression to go 'on the panel' mean?
4 What generally improved living conditions?

The 1926 Electricity Act created a national supply body, the CEB or Central Electricity Board. The CEB began building the national grid (1927) and the great pylons carrying the high voltage transmission lines began their inexorable tramp across 4000 miles of British countryside.

The 1929 Local Government Act (Neville Chamberlain was Minister of Health) abolished the Poor Law and replaced it with Public Assistance Committees run by county and county borough councils. Fears of being 'driven to the workhouse' (a common expression in the 1920s) vanished. Gradually, these councils became responsible for the provision of social services to:

1 expectant mothers;
2 young children;
3 people generally in need of care and assistance.

THE ECONOMIC BLIZZARD

Baldwin lost the 1929 election and his successor, the Labour Prime Minister Ramsay MacDonald, had to face the effects of the Wall Street Crash on the British economy. Few people realised, on 24 October 1929, that this setback in US financial history would herald an international calamity resulting in poverty for millions of families in Britain – and in the rest of the industrialised world.

Jobs were the great issue in Britain during 1929 – and the Labour Government could do nothing about them. British overseas trade halved between 1929–31 and the unemployment figures topped 1.76 million in January 1930. The government now feared a decline in revenue – there was no rich source of North Sea oil funds in those days! How long could the government pay the dole? By July 1931 there were 2.8 million unemployed – and the Bank of England was losing its gold reserves at over £2 million a day. The Labour Government was in the red – and everybody, said the economists of the day, must make sacrifices.

1 Those in work must pay higher taxes.
2 Those on the dole should take a cut in State benefits.

Eleven members of the Labour Government supported the idea; ten didn't. MacDonald then went to King George V and asked him to call a meeting of all party leaders. All agreed that the best thing to do in the midst of an unprecedented crisis was to sink party differences and form a National Government with Ramsay MacDonald at its head.

So MacDonald called another Cabinet meeting and told his stupefied colleagues that they were out and he was in! He then resigned on behalf of the Labour Government and announced the formation of a National Government with a Cabinet made up of:

4 Conservatives;
2 Liberals;
3 Labour.

It was this government that:

1 raised income tax from 4s 6d (20½p) to 5s (25p) in the £.
2 cut back teachers' salaries;
3 reduced the salaries of MPs, judges, members of the armed forces (this caused a brief mutiny at Invergordon);
4 took Britain 'off the gold standard'.

The exchange rate for the £ sterling fell from $4.86 to $3.40; as was said, 'hardly a leaf stirred'.

Multiple choice questions

1   Women had secured the vote in 1918 provided they were over:
- ☐   21
- ☐   25
- ☐   28
- ☐   30

2   Women over twenty-one secured the vote in 1928. This was called the 'flapper vote' and the Prime Minister in power at the time was:
- ☐   Asquith
- ☐   Lloyd George
- ☐   Ramsay MacDonald
- ☐   Baldwin

3   The government newspaper during the General Strike was the:
- ☐   *British Gazette*
- ☐   *Daily Worker*
- ☐   *Daily Express*
- ☐   *Daily Herald*

4   The Royal Navy mutiny following the wage cuts in 1931 took place at:
- ☐   Devonport
- ☐   Plymouth
- ☐   Holy Loch
- ☐   Invergordon

5   The monarch at the time of the economic blizzard was
- ☐   Edward VII
- ☐   Edward VIII
- ☐   George V
- ☐   George VI

THE DEPRESSION AND ITS EFFECTS 1931–9

CONTENTS

THE CONDITION OF THE BRITISH PEOPLE IN THE 1930S

THE END OF FREE TRADE

Ramsay MacDonald was Prime Minister in name only as his position depended on the support of the Conservative Party led by Stanley Baldwin. One of the first things his government did was to protect British industry against competition from low-priced foreign imports by imposing tariffs (i.e. duties on goods entering the country).

1932 Import Duties Act This imposed tariffs ranging from 10 per cent to 33 per cent on most imported goods. Pending the Imperial Economic Conference to be held in Ottawa that summer, Empire goods were excepted. At Ottawa, the Dominions and Britain agreed on 'Imperial Preference', i.e. they would favour one another's products and not seek to put heavy duties on them. Thus ended the long tradition of free trade in Britain.

The farmers' fears

Though the new tariffs did not raise food prices in Britain there was a very real fear that agriculture might decline, leaving the country dependent on food imports. Between 1928 and 1933 100,000 farm workers left their jobs.

1933 Agricultural Marketing Act This placed every branch of British agriculture under a marketing board. This:
1   limited domestic production to the amount of consumer demand;
2   fixed the price to be paid by the public;
3   imposed a quota on foreign imports.
The diagram overleaf shows how the Milk Marketing Board operated.

GRADUAL TRADE RECOVERY

World trade fell by nearly 30 per cent during the economic blizzard 1929–33. By then, Britain's unemployment figures topped 2.95 million. But as statisticians only counted the number of insured people who were out of a job, the total number of unemployed was well over 3 million. The 'two nations' persisted. The relatively prosperous South made a quick recovery from the depression. In the distressed North mass unemployment persisted right up to the Second World

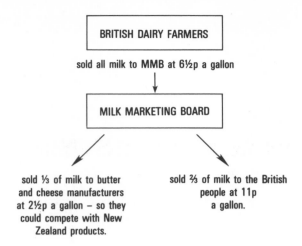

The Milk Marketing Board

War. Yet most people had a higher standard of living in 1939 than they had in 1929; and for those in work that standard increased every year. One reason was that the 1930s saw a period of deflation – a time when prices and consumer goods remain steady or even fall. If that seems incredible in our society, think of it like this:

> A wage-earner bringing home £2 or £3 a week in the mid-1930s had the purchasing power of a worker earning between £2.50 and £3.50 in the mid-1920s.

It was this increase in purchasing power that boosted the consumer industries and enabled families to buy domestic luxuries, afford weekly gambles on the football pools, go to the cinema, make a down payment on a new house and have a week's holiday at the seaside.

The table below, however, shows the reality of the 'two nations' in the mid-1930s.

Prosperous town	% unemployed 1934	Distressed town	% unemployed 1934
Luton	8	Jarrow	68
Watford	7	Merthyr Tydfil	62
Birmingham	6	Maryport	57
Coventry	5	Abertillery	50
High Wycombe	3	Gateshead	44

'The Two Nations'

It was costing £1.00 per week from public funds to keep each Merthyr Tydfil family in basic necessities 1936–7; but the local council had to levy very high rates @ £1.7s.6d (£1.37½) in the £ to help pay for this – and these high rates stopped those firms that wanted to set up new factories from coming to the town.

THE FATE OF THE TRADITIONAL INDUSTRIES

SHIPBUILDING

There were many attempts to draw the nation's attention to the plight of the unemployed. One of the most famous was the 1936 Jarrow Crusade.

Read the following account:

> Organised by the MP Ellen Wilkinson, 200 Jarrow men took part in a march on London. Jarrow was the victim of a situation in which an entire community depended on a single source of employment – in this case shipbuilding. As part of their rationalisation programme the shipbuilders had decided to close down Palmer's Yard in Jarrow. They launched their last ship in 1932 and the yard closed in 1934. This made 73 per cent of the Jarrow work-force unemployed! Residents in Surrey adopted the town, sending it food parcels and organising relief subscriptions. For a time there was a chance that a new steelworks would open – but this came to nothing. So the men of Jarrow made their memorable demonstration. Largely through newsreel films, it won national publicity and in the 1980s its poignancy encouraged other groups of unemployed workers to make their own 'Jarrow Crusades', carrying the famous banner of the Jarrow men. Interestingly, their attempts never made the same impact.

1 Name the MP who helped organise the Crusade.
2 Why were so many men unemployed in Jarrow?
3 What did they hope might happen after the shipyard closed down?
4 Why did they march on London?
5 Why do you think that imitators of the Jarrow crusade made less impact in the 1980s?

After the Crusade, several companies set up companies in Jarrow (1937–8); and in 1939 the new steelworks opened.

Government help

During the years of slump the government tried to help the shipyard workers – 60 per cent of whom became unemployed.

1934 North Atlantic Shipping Act To help the completion of a liner left unfinished on the stocks at Clydebank. She would eventually become the world-famous *Queen Mary*.

1935 Merchant Shipping Assistance Act Provided loans to build more tramp steamers.

THE COAL INDUSTRY

1930 Coal Mines Act
This had set production quotes for all pits and fixed the royalties paid to mine-owners. This did not especially help the mine-workers, 115,000 of whom left South Wales during the slump.

Slight recovery
This unplanned decline in the miners' work-force helped the industry to re-establish itself in South Wales and elsewhere. Miners managed to win a shilling a shift pay increase and by 1937 coal production had almost regained its 1930 figure of 244 million tons.

THE STEEL INDUSTRY

Decline
Many steel plants, including such famous names as Mossend at Coatbridge and the great Welsh ironworks at Dowlais, closed down.

Expansion
At the same time, industry tried to re-locate the plants close to new, unworked materials. Consequently, steel production actually increased by 30 per cent during the decade. Corby in Northamptonshire saw the first big expansion. About 4000 people found jobs at the new plant – operational in 1934 – and many of these were Scots who had migrated from the depressed areas on Clydeside and in Lanarkshire. A new tin-plate mill opened in Ebbw Vale in 1938 while three huge works – at Frodingham in Lincolnshire, Workington and Shotton (in Cheshire) were in production by the end of the 1930s.

THE TEXTILE INDUSTRY

New trading patterns
World consumption of raw cotton recovered and in the late 1920s and early 1930s Japan, India, China and Brazil were all busily installing new machinery and turning out cheap, printed cottons. India's own power looms were feeding 70 per cent of her home market – where British cotton had once reigned supreme. Japan was producing high quality cotton goods by 1935 – cheaper and in greater quantity than Britain could produce.

Effect on Britain
Lancashire's cotton industry suffered most from these changes in the world's manufacturing and trading patterns. By 1938 the British textile industry was in serious decline and there was mass unemployment in the North-West.

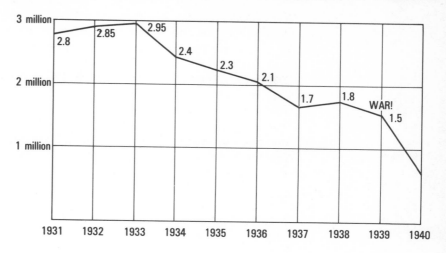

Unemployment in Britain 1931–40

THE GOVERNMENT RESPONSE

What happened?

It is sometimes said that in response to the depression in the 1930s the National Government intervened to rescue Britain from the miseries of shut-down and redundancy; and that it borrowed large sums of money to invest in two programmes to absorb the unemployed: public works and rearmament.

The facts

The government did not noticeably intervene. Yet industrial output increased by 50 per cent 1932–7; unemployment fell from 3 million to 1.7 million. How was this done?

1   A series of prudent budgets, enabling government to resist the temptation to undertake massive spending in areas where there was no direct and immediate profit for the British taxpayers.
2   Even in the matter of defence, significant increases in rearmament expenditure didn't start until 1937.
3   But government did support the generation of electricity for the manufacture of consumer durables – vacuum cleaners, wireless sets, motor cars and motor-cycles.
4   Perhaps the greatest government achievement was the way it encouraged people to buy their own homes – to take out mortgages on privately built houses, millions of which still exist today.
5   Unemployment remained an insoluble problem – true for most of the western industrial democracies. It therefore became accepted practice in a democracy that it was government's duty to pay redundant people from public funds.

The methods of payment

At first this was done through Neville Chamberlain's Public Assistance Committees set up in 1929. Then came new legislation.

1934 Unemployment Act Dole was, typically, £1.50 a week (not in Northern Ireland). This went up to £1.80 in 1936 – provided the man could prove he needed the money.

Proof came via a household *Means Test* – one of the most hated devices introduced by the National Government. Earnings by any member of the family – son, daughter, wife – reduced the dole payment and could even cause the local labour exchange to 'knock you off the dole'. People grew bitter towards the Means Test – it often led to family quarrels. Anonymous letters about people's secret earnings often arrived in the morning mail at labour exchanges. It was a highly insensitive device – and led to a number of 'hunger marches' organised by the communist-controlled National Unemployed Workers' Movement.

THE HOUSING BOOM

The achievement

By 1939 there was no serious shortage of accommodation in England and Wales – due to the work of private builders and local authorities.

The 1935 Housing Act

This obliged local authorities to end over-crowding and to begin slum-clearance projects.

Changes in house-design

'Speculation' building projects by private builders were common in the 1930s. Semi-detached houses with all modern conveniences came on the market at around £400. More expensive houses flanked main roads outside the town (the beginning of 'ribbon development'). Local authorities favoured large estates such as Fishponds in Bristol or blocks of flats such as those at Quarry Hill in Leeds. Scotland faced much greater difficulties because of the overcrowding in the traditional tenements – a way of life in Glasgow and Edinburgh. Over 22 per cent of working-class houses came into the overcrowded category – Scotland lacked a million houses in 1939.

NATIONAL GOVERNMENT RE-ELECTED 1935

Ramsay MacDonald resigned in 1935. Baldwin became Prime Minister. In the 1935 General Election (the last for ten years) the British people gave a vote of confidence of the idea of 'national government' under the leadership offered by Stanley Baldwin – the man who 'had kept his head' during the General Strike and the long years of the depression. These were the election results in 1935:

National Government MPs		Opposition MPs	
Conservatives	387	Labour	154
Liberal Nationals	33	Liberals	21
National Labour	8	Independent Labour	4
Independent	3	Independent	4
		Communist	1
	431		184

The solitary Communist was William Gallacher, MP for West Fife.

Extremist political parties
There were now two extremist political parties – the Fascists and the Communists.

The British Union of Fascists Led by Sir Oswald Mosley, it attracted many extrovert young men who liked to parade in uniform. The movement was largely modelled on Mussolini's Fascisti. The conduct of the British Fascists appalled the British people when Fascist stewards beat up hecklers at the 1934 Olympia mass meeting.

The Communist Party of Great Britain This dated from 1919. After 1924, when its membership stood at 5000, Stalin said it would have to transform the unemployed into a revolutionary movement – an impossible task as leading British communists such as Will Paynter agreed.

The Battle of Cable Street 1936
Whatever criticism you might level against the National Government you certainly couldn't say it was incapable of governing the country. This left the Fascists and Communists with little option but to fight one another – though the police usually managed to prevent serious confrontations. One extraordinary incident in 1936, known as the 'Battle of Cable Street', illustrates this. Mosley led his Blackshirts into the East End to bait the Jewish people living there. Communists had already encouraged the people of Stepney to throw barricades across the streets. This led to a running battle between local residents and the police escorts guarding the Fascist marchers. The Communists and Fascists never managed to get close enough to fight one another.

THE ABDICATION CRISIS 1936

On 20 January 1936 King George V died at Sandringham. His successor was Edward VIII, determined, he said: 'to work for the happiness and welfare of all classes of my subjects'.

In March he visited Scotland to see the *Queen Mary* at Clydebank

Stanley Baldwin

and took the opportunity of seeing for himself what housing conditions were like in the big industrial areas. He went to Knightswood housing estate – a Glasgow showpiece – and then went on to Anderton, one of the city's worst slums. As was noted at the time, the King went to places where his Ministers dared not go.

King Edward VIII's intentions

He intended to marry Mrs Wallis Simpson, an American who had divorced her first husband and who, in October 1936, obtained a decree nisi against her second husband in a petition heard at Ipswich. Prime Minister Baldwin warned the King that marriage with a twice-divorced lady would not be constitutionally acceptable – as it meant that Mrs Simpson would automatically become Queen if the union went ahead. Edward VIII suggested that Parliament should pass a bill enabling Mrs Simpson to become his wife – but not Queen. Baldwin replied that Parliament would refuse. The Church of England and the Dominion Parliaments would certainly object if such a bill were introduced into the House of Commons.

The crisis becomes public

This was the state of the constitutional crisis when the British people first heard of it on 1 December 1936. On the whole, their sympathy was with the King – and they accepted that the final decision was his. On 9 December the King made up his mind. Next day he signed an instrument of abdication – he had ruled for 326 days and now handed over the throne to his brother, King George VI.

Edward went into exile and married Mrs Simpson in 1937. That year Baldwin retired and the new Prime Minister was Neville Chamberlain. A social reformer by inclination, he had to concentrate on defence and the horrifying threat of war.

Edward VIII

Questions

1 Explain the miners' motto in the 1920s:
   'Not a penny off the pay, not a minute on the day'
2 Write a brief account of the conduct of the 1926 General Strike emphasising the following:
   – the TUC called the 'national strike' on behalf of the miners;
   – that it lasted nine days and failed to win the miners' objectives;
   – that the miners stayed out and suffered for it;
   – that it led to the Trades Disputes Act.
3 Now look at the following statistics relating to trade unions 1920–38:

Year	No. of trade unions	No. of members (in millions)	No. of disputes	No of days lost through strikes (in millions
1920	1384	8.3	1607	26.9
1922	1232	5.6	576	19.9
1924	1194	5.5	710	8.4

Year	No. of trade unions	No. of members (in millions)	No. of disputes	No of days lost through strikes (in millions
1926	1164	5.2	323	162.2
1928	1142	4.8	302	1.4
1930	1121	4.8	422	4.4
1932	1081	4.4	389	6.5
1934	1063	4.6	471	0.9
1936	1036	5.3	818	1.8
1938	1024	6.0	875	1.3

(a)   Were the 1920s worse than the 1930s for the number of days lost through strike action?

(b)   Apart from 1926, in which year were the most days lost through strike action?

(c)   Why do you think that 1932 saw the 'low' in trade union membership?

(d)   Why did membership pick up after 1934?

(e)   Is there a correlation between the number of members and the number of disputes?

4   Look at the photo of Stanley Baldwin on page 158. His bowler hat and calm expression were his hallmarks, implying reliability and 'safety first'. What was Neville Chamberlain's hallmark?

5   Why do you think British industrial production managed to increase by 50 per cent and unemployment almost halved 1932–7?

CHANGES IN TRANSPORT AND COMMUNICATIONS

Baldwin had used the radio to keep the British people informed during the General Strike; Sir John Reith had announced to the British people that Prince Edward would speak to the nation by radio (December 1936); Neville Chamberlain (who had never flown before) made his three trips to see Adolf Hitler in 1938 by aeroplane. Yet there were no great technical revolutions in land transport (the internal-combustion engine, the diesel engine, underground electric railways had all been invented in the previous century).

LAND TRANSPORT 1914–39

Road traffic made the greatest social and economic impact after 1918. Many families could afford to buy large motor cars such as the one shown below to go on picnics and trips to the seaside.

Mass-production of lorries and motor cars was typical of the period:

1924   100 workers produced   73 cars per year

1936   100 workers produced 147 cars per year

Vehicle manufacture was probably Britain's most successful industry – brought great prosperity to the manufacturing centres in Oxford,

An old motor car, carrying seven people in comfort

Dagenham and Luton. Small cars became popular partly due to low petrol bills and partly due to tax and insurance differentials that favoured the small motor car. Some people could afford to take their motor cars abroad, such as this little Riley Redwing (1927), on a continental holiday.

1927 Riley Redwing

There were two particularly distinguished British motor manufacturers:

Herbert Austin (1866–1941) He worked with the Wolseley Company before starting up his own firm in 1905. He created the remarkable little 'baby' Austin – a 7 hp motor car – one of the most popular pre-1939 vehicles. Herbert Austin was made Baron of Longbridge in 1936.

William Morris (1877–1963) He ran a bicycle shop – mending students' bikes – in Oxford and then started making the first Morris Cowley and Oxford motor cars. His was the outstanding manufacturing firm in the whole of Europe during the 1920s. He was a modern philanthropist – he endowed Nuffield College, Oxford, in 1937. He became a peer in 1934 and was made Viscount Nuffield in 1938.

New types of vehicles appeared on British roads, designed for specialist duties. Motor buses and trolley buses began to replace the trams; and the first by-passes began to reduce the traffic jams in city centres. Road accidents became serious with nearly 2 million motor cars and almost 1 million lorries on the road by 1939.

1930 Road Traffic Act

This tried to bring order out of chaos:

1 abolished the 20 mph speed limit;
2 required third party insurance for drivers;
3 permitted anyone over eighteen who was physically fit to have a licence.

Note that the 30 mph speed limit was brought in during 1935 when road casualties were as bad as they are today. Traffic lights, roundabouts and Belisha beacons were common by 1939.

AVIATION

Read the following extract:

The evolution of military aircraft during the First World War led directly to the growth of civil aviation. Britain, in common with most air-minded nations, had an unsuccessful flirtation with airships. The idea of linking the British Empire with airship routes was very attractive, especially after 1919 when the R-34 managed a transatlantic crossing. It took 4½ days! In 1928 the R-38 broke up over Hull; in 1930 the R-101 crashed in France. After these tragedies, the British concentrated on fixed wing, piston-engined aircraft. Already De Havilland DH4As had flown a regular service between London and Paris. Imperial Airways, founded in 1924, were flying passengers as far as Switzerland. Their famous Heracles biplanes never had a fatal accident as they made their majestic flights over Europe. When Short Bros built a huge flying boat for the Britain-Australia route it was clear that the dream of worldwide air routes had turned into reality.

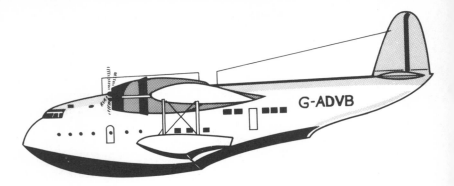

The Short C-class Empire flying boat *Corsair*, operated from Hythe, Hampshire, 1936 onwards

1 Why did airships prove to be unpopular?
2 Name the two British airmen who flew the Atlantic in a Vickers Vimy in 1919.
3 Why do you think that aeroplanes were not developed to take passengers across the Atlantic?
4 Name the British airline founded in 1924 that used the Heracles aeroplanes.
5 Passengers and mail were being flown to Australia in 1938 – in what sort of aeroplanes?

PUBLIC REACTION

Undoubtedly, Britain was an air-minded nation after the First World War. Flying, of course, was the privilege of the rich, but the mass of the people thrilled to the exploits of Amy Johnson (1903–41) – first woman to fly solo to Australia (1930); to Sir Alan Cobham's 'Flying Circus' (1926–36); and to the King's Cup Air Races and the spectacular Empire Air Days held on RAF stations just before the Second World War.

RADIO, CINEMA AND TELEVISION

Sound radio was generally available by 1939 – when there were nearly 9 million licence holders. The BBC (British Broadcasting Company, a private concern, 1922; British Broadcasting Corporation, a public company, 1926) was financed by these licence fees. The cinema was equally popular. Silent films drew mass audiences and cinema visits became even more regular with the introduction of talkies in 1927. Cinema-going was an 'escapist' pleasure and the specially built Roxys, Odeons and Regents were deliberately designed to give an atmosphere of great luxury and comfort, and continuous entertainment (the cinema organ and ice-cream girls during the interval) at a very low price. They were built with an eye to public transport facilities so that they people could get to them easily after they had been home and had their tea. Above all, they were cheap. Television, in contrast, was expensive.

John Logie Baird (1888–1946) was a Scottish inventor who pioneered TV and achieved the following:

1 the first TV image in 1924;
2 developed direction finding techniques using infra-red waves;
3 developed ultra-short wave radio transmissions.

Isaac Schoenberg, Director of EMI (Electrical and Musical Industries) designed the Emitron camera and 405-line definition enabling the BBC to begin its public TV transmissions at Alexandra Palace in 1936.

PACIFISM

Definition
The word 'pacifism' came into use at the beginning of the twentieth century to describe the beliefs and conduct of people who believe war and the use of armed force cannot be justified.

Political application
It became part of the creed (beliefs) of the Liberal and Labour Parties during the 1920s and no man worked harder for peace and international disarmament than Ramsay MacDonald. In 1932 Baldwin had warned the British voter that 'there is no power on earth that can prevent him from being bombed. Whatever people may tell him, the bomber will always get through. The only defence is offence.' However, pacifism had a much greater appeal to articulate people.

The Oxford Union's resolution 9 February 1933
This stated that 'This House will in no circumstances fight for its King or Country'. The resolution was printed in newspapers all over the world and later became widely misinterpreted.

Why?
Many undergraduates who had voted for the resolution said they were expressing 'anti-jingo sentiments' rather than supporting Professor Joad, the main speaker at the debate.

Pacifism – a political issue
When a Tory candidate urged rearmament during the East Fulham by-election (October 1933) he lost to Labour. Canon Dick Sheppard invited anyone who cared for peace to send him a postcard saying:
I renounce war and will never support or sanction another.
During 1933–4 his Oxford Peace Pledge Union mustered 80,000 supporters. They went on Peace Walks and Peace Marches in many parts of the country. In August 1935 they held their Peace Ballot, organised by the League of Nations Union as part of its pacifist propaganda.

The *Daily Express* urged its readers to throw the ballot paper away. So many people favoured disarmament that Prime Minister Baldwin had to choose his statements very carefully and he pledged the National Government to:

1 give full support to the League;
2 abstain from any substantial rearmament.

These are the five questions asked in the Peace Ballot and the number of responses are indicated below each question:

1 Should Britain remain a member of the League?
     Yes: 11,090,387   No: 355,883
2 Are you in favour of all-round reduction in armaments by international agreement?
     Yes: 10,170,387   No: 862,775
3 Are you in favour of all-round abolition of military and naval aircraft by international agreement?
     Yes: 9,553,558   No: 1,689,786
4 Should the manufacture and sale of armaments for private profit be prohibited by international agreements?
     Yes: 10,417,319   No: 775,414
5 Do you consider that, if a nation insists on attacking another, the other nations should compel it to stop
   (a)   by economic and non-military measures?
          Yes: 11,027,608   No: 695,074
   (b)   if necessary, by military force?
          Yes: 6,783,386   No: 2,351,981

Look at the responses carefully. In 1944, when Britain was under attack from V-1 flying bombs and V-2 rocket missiles, the historian J. A. Williamson described the Peace Ballot as 'completely detached from reality'. He also said that it did 'incalculable harm in encouraging the blackguards of Europe and Asia to believe they would meet with no resistance'.

Do you agree with this point of view? You will see that Britain did not neglect rearmament, mainly due to the rise to power of this man. Who was he?

REARMAMENT

During the 1930s newsreels and magazines brought home to the people that war was a reality and that conflicts involving the latest military technology were going on in China, Abyssinia and Spain – and that no country (apart from the Soviet Union who briefly intervened in Spain) was doing anything to stop them.

THE ATTITUDE OF THE NATIONAL GOVERNMENT

Hitler had revealed his rearmament plans in March 1935 but the

National Government wasn't willing to use this as an excuse for Britain to follow suit. Winston Churchill was disgusted. He had been out of office since 1929 but was still an MP. He said:

> I have been told that the reason for the government not having acted before was that public opinion was not ripe for rearmament. I hope that we shall never accept a reason such as this. The government has been in control of overwhelming majorities in both Houses of Parliament. There is no vote they could have proposed for national defence which would not have been acepted with overwhelming strength.

1 Why did Churchill believe the National Government hadn't acted on defence?
2 Why did he refuse to accept this argument?
3 Did he believe the government could have carried a policy of rearmament in the two Houses of Parliament?

Ramsay MacDonald's attitude

He had in fact accepted limited expansion of the RAF in 1934. In 1935 limited rearmament became official policy. One of Ramsay Mac-Donald's last acts had been to produce the White Paper Statement Relating to Defence (1935) and to initial the memorandum authorising limited rearmament – a sad end for this 'apostle of peace'.

Who do you think now said this?

> When you think of the defence of England you no longer think of the chalk cliffs of Dover, you think of the Rhine. That is where our frontier is.

Explain the last sentence.

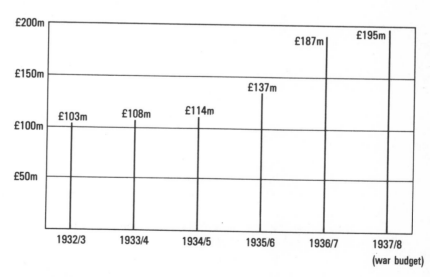

British defence budgets

READINESS FOR WAR

The Royal Navy The best-prepared of the three services for war – though most of its battleships were obsolete by 1939. The new warship building programme stressed the importance of cruisers, destroyers and escort vessels.

The Army was ill-prepared. Only two of its divisions could claim to be partly mobile. Most units still had 'soft-skinned' vehicles and its tanks were either too heavily armoured and under-gunned or lightly armoured and heavily gunned – British tank design left a great deal to be desired.

The Royal Air Force began to re-equip with twin-engined types such as Hampdens, Whitleys, Wellingtons and Blenheims; and had the first of the new interceptors, the Hurricane and Spitfire, in service.

Civil defence

There was no shortage of recruits for the armed forces in 1938 – the year when unemployment figures began to creep upwards and in which the Munich crisis alerted everyone to the danger of war. Civilians became interested in ARP (Air Raid Precautions) first devised in 1935 and put under local authority control in 1937. During 1938 the government issued 38 million gas-masks, including special respirators for babies. Later on, Mickey Mouse designs for babies and very young children could be bought for 15 shillings each. In November 1938 things began to move swiftly. Read the following account:

> Sir John Anderson took overall control of the ARP, prepared plans for the evacuation of children from the main industrial centres and issued the air raid shelters that bore his name. During 1939 over 1.5 million men and women (most of them unpaid) volunteered for Civil Defence duties and began training as rescue workers, ambulance drivers and fire-watchers – jobs that most people thought would be needed in the very near future. In fact, Civil Defence in Britain was very well organised before the outbreak of war. The British people were better prepared, through direct government action, than were the citizens of any other nation that had to face the horrors of aerial bombardment during 1940–41.

1   What was the name of the air raid shelter that was first issued to British families?
2   What was the name of the later shelter that could be used inside one's house?
3   Were most of the Civil Defence volunteers in 1939 paid any money?
4   Does the National Government take the credit for Britain's readiness to resist air attack?

Look at this leaflet issued in 1938:

> Town Hall
> Fulham S.W.6
> 29th September
> 1938
>
> ## ISSUE OF RESPIRATORS
>
> Respirators have now been issued to about 90% of the residents in the Borough. The care of these respirators is of the utmost importance and the following directions should be rigidly adhered to:-
>
> (1) The Respirator should be put in a cardboard box and put in a place of safety so that it is readily accessible if required.
>
> (2) The transparent eyepiece should lie evenly on the top of the container at full length without any deformation under the lid of the box.
>
> ## WHEN THE RESPIRATOR IS REQUIRED FOR USE
>
> (a) Hold Respirator by the straps.
>
> (b) Put on the Respirator by first putting chin into facepiece and then drawing the straps over the head.
>
> (c) Take off the Respirator by pulling the straps over the head from the back.
>
> **DO NOT TAKE RESPIRATOR OFF BY PULLING THE CONTAINER UPWARDS OVER THE FACE**
>
> E. W. Whiteley
> Deputy Town Clerk and A.R.P. Officer

Questions

1 Had most people in Fulham received their gas-masks by September 1938?
2 What name did the leaflet use instead of gas-masks?
3 Why do you think the leaflet avoided that term?
4 What was the facepiece made of?
5 Why did one have to take so much care over the eyepiece?

THE SECOND WORLD WAR 1939–45

CONTENTS

THE HOME FRONT 1939–41

THE DECLARATION OF WAR 3 SEPTEMBER 1939

When the Germans invaded Poland on 1 September 1939, the British government put into operation its evacuation and ARP plans:

1   Evacuation of children from the cities to the countryside and to towns the government expected to be free from German air attack. Expectant mothers and blind people were also offered the chance to be evacuated.

2   Everybody had to obey the new blackout rules – thick curtains, 'blackout paper' and sometimes wooden frames covered in thick paper would be used to seal windows. 'Putting up the blackout' became a common phrase for the rest of the war.

3   Lots of patients were evacuated from hospitals – notably TB patients. This was to make room for the thousands of casualties the authorities expected from gas and bomb attacks.

When war was declared two days later everyone expected these attacks. People had to carry their gas-masks and most were very frightened when the air raid sirens sounded that Sunday lunchtime. It turned out to be a false alarm!

This is an extract from a boy's diary:

> We went to church. The vicar said he would let us go early so we could hear what Mr Chamberlain said. I ran to my grandma's. He said we were at war with Germany. I ran home. We had our dinner and the sirens went. I hid under the table. I liked wearing my gas-mask even though it all fogged up. I couldn't smell the cabbage when I had it on.

1   On what day of the week did Britain declare war?
2   Who was the Prime Minister?
3   What was meant by the gas-mask being 'all fogged up'?

THE PHONEY WAR

In fact, nothing happened. People started to get their Anderson shelters delivered and these were usually put up in the back garden. At the end of September the government issued everyone with an identity card and urged everyone to help with war work. Many soldiers had already been called up under the *Emergency Powers*

Defence Act (1939) and now the government called up all men up to the age of forty-one. Of course, there were lots of reserved occupations in key industries such as gas, electricity and agriculture. But there was no shortage of volunteers, especially for the RAF. Meanwhile, the RAF showered German civilians with leaflets to persuade them that the war was futile; while the German Luftwaffe (Air Force) attacked the Orkneys and the Firth of Forth – Hitler forbade it to attack British cities. U-boats and German surface raiders were very active – and news that three cruisers (*Ajax, Achilles* and *Exeter*) had forced the German pocket battleship *Graf Spee* to scuttle itself was a great morale booster (December 1939). For most people, the blackout caused the greatest danger – car drivers especially found it hard to see with their compulsorily fitted headlamp visors and over 1000 people died on British roads in December 1939.

RATIONING

This began in January 1940 – ham, bacon, sugar, butter were rationed. Over the next few months, meat, tea, margarine and cooking fats were added to the list. Cheese was sometimes 'on' and sometimes 'off' the ration. Meals in restaurants and cafés declined in quality and quantity. Everybody – including the King! – had ration books as well as identity cards. In 1941 clothes-ration books and a 'points scheme' began so that people could buy restricted quantities of tinned foods, sweets and chocolate. The nation became accustomed to shopkeepers' snipping out small parts of the various documents that had to be carried when shopping. Then came the utility scheme for buying consumer goods – furniture in particular became very scarce and was marked with a utility sign that many people regarded as a sign of inferior quality. The word 'utility' was often used as a derogatory term.

The utility mark, seen on clothes and furniture during the Second World War

DUNKIRK 1940

Up to April 1940 the whole atmosphere was unreal. Prime Minister Chamberlain himself said (9 January 1940) that:

> This is the quiet of the calm before the storm. Vast numbers
> of men, armed with the most powerful weapons of
> destruction that science can devise, are watching one another

from behind their defences. From time to time we hear the sound of guns. We do not know how long that will last.

It lasted until 9 April 1940 when Hitler began his blitzkrieg in the west. Tens of thousands of British, Belgian and French troops retreated across the Ardennes towards the coastal ports. The British pulled out of France under a well-prepared scheme called 'Operation Dynamo'. Dunkirk was the main evacuation centre and many British civilians took their small boats across to France to help with the operation. At the end of nine days 330,000 troops had escaped. By then Chamberlain had resigned and the new Prime Minister, **Winston Churchill (1874–1965)** told the House of Commons:

> Wars are not won by evacuations. But there was a victory inside this deliverance which should be noted. It was gained by the Air Force. Many of our soldiers coming back have not seen the Air Force; they only saw the bombers that escaped its protective attack . . .

However, lots of soldiers remained critical of the 'Brylcreem boys' who had fought out a very skilful air battle high above the French coast. The RAF lost 106 aeroplanes – about the same as the Germans lost.

The British people welcomed the returning soldiers home and steeled themselves for a German invasion. Men joined the Local Defence Volunteers (later these became the Home Guard), sea defences went up and fields suitable for landing gliders were scarred with trenches or filled with old farm carts and motor cars.

1 Why do you think that people dug trenches across fields?
2 Many rural areas were defended by 'pill-boxes' – small, concrete strongpoints designed to house riflemen and machine-gunners to stop a German advance. Are there any in your area still?

THE BATTLE OF BRITAIN 1940

Before the Germans could invade Britain they would have to win control of the air. That is why the Luftwaffe tried to destroy the convoy routes in the English Channel, shoot down all the British fighters and destroy the British radar systems and main airfields.

Overleaf is a photograph of the present 'Battle of Britain Memorial Flight'. The two small aeroplanes were fighters. The one banking towards you is the Hawker Hurricane. The other one is even more famous:

1 What is its name?
2 The big bomber is a Lancaster. Was it used in the Battle of Britain?

Hitler failed to win the Battle of Britain and therefore tried to bomb Britain into surrender. This was known as the 'blitz'.

THE BLITZ

Daylight raids on Britain had begun during the Battle of Britain and even after the great victory on 15 September 1940 the fear of invasion remained. Said Churchill:

> Even though large tracts of Europe and many old and famous states have fallen or may fall into the hands of the Gestapo, we shall not flag or fail. We shall go on to the end; we shall fight . . . on the seas and oceans; we shall fight with growing confidence and growing strength in the air; we shall defend our island whatever the cost may be. We shall fight on the beaches; we shall fight on the landing grounds; we shall fight in fields and in the streets; we shall fight in the hills. We shall never surrender.

In fact, during the night blitz (in the winter of 1940–41) most people discovered that it wasn't easy to fight back.

Read the following account:

> It was the night-time blitz, for which the British air defences were ill-prepared, that caused havoc and heavy casualties in most British cities. London was the first to adapt to the new role of being a frontline city, with its people exposed to as many hazards as any infantry soldier. High explosive bombs and landmines demolished rows of houses; incendiary bombs and the even more appalling oil-bombs set fire to office blocks and factories. Newspapers kept up national

morale with stirring stories of 'we can take it' but in fact the blitz led to mass migrations from city centres into the surrounding countryside. Those who 'stayed put', who spent nights in their tough little Anderson shelters or who found accommodation in communal air raid shelters such as the London Tubes and the Manchester Canal Centre, did discover that everyone was sharing a common adversity and did develop a new, caring feeling towards one another. Nevertheless, air raid survivors experienced a great deal of distress. After a heavy raid, a town's gas, electricity and water supplies were usually out of action; shops were boarded up; fires were still burning; and food supplies were suddenly scarce.

Government censorship rigidly controlled press photographs of the effects of air raids; and that is why in your text book you will be unlikely to see those effects save on cars, buses, lorries and buildings. Photographs showing the killed and injured were banned – it was bad for morale.

Questions

1 In Churchill's speech above, what does the word 'Gestapo' mean?
2 In the account of the blitz, how did newspapers try to keep up national morale?
3 What is meant by 'a communal air raid shelter'?
4 Were the British a caring people during the blitz? Why?
5 Why did air raid survivors often have to suffer distress?
   The first city outside London to experience this distress on a large scale was Coventry – bombed for eleven hours during the night of 14–15 November 1940.

WOMEN AT WAR

THE END OF UNEMPLOYMENT

The fact that the National Government led by Churchill was a coalition government helped to heal some of the political differences between the British people. The 'North' versus 'South' conflict was less apparent when workers in the heavy industries of the North-East had so much overtime available that they became the highest paid workers in the country. Unemployment had vanished by the end of 1942 and yet there was still a labour shortage. To meet this, Britain turned to her womenfolk.

MOBILISATION

Britain was far more committed to the mobilisation of women than was either Hitler or Stalin – though no women served in frontline bomber or fighter duties as Soviet women did in 1942–3. But without the Women's Land Army and the Land Clubs (often consisting of bands of women travelling in lorries around the farms) agriculture couldn't have achieved its incredible revival – 50 per cent more land came under cultivation. None of the armed services could have functioned without the help of the Auxiliary Territorial Service (ATS), the Women's Auxiliary Air Force (WAAF), the Women's Royal Naval Service (WRNS), the Voluntary Aid Detachments (VAD) and the Royal Observer Corps (many of these were men). Thousands of women were in first aid posts, worked as fire-spotters or air raid wardens, or ran Salvation Army canteens. Millions worked in the munitions factories as their mothers had in the First World War. Throughout the conflict – and times grew harder during 1942 and 1943 when (despite the victories at El Alamein, Stalingrad and Kursk, Cape Bon and Sicily) the war seemed endless – the British people looked forward to a better world – a world in which women would play a much more significant role than in the past.

NURSERIES AND FOOD SHORTAGES

However, their interests were generally more mundane. Women who wanted to take up war work, but had young children, demonstrated in demand of State-run nurseries. These soon appeared and were rapidly filled. Government didn't encourage marriage in the war. If you were a woman school teacher, you lost your job if you were married (there were a few exceptions as the shortage of teachers grew more acute) while even the General Post Office (GPO) sacked its women switchboard operators if they hinted they were going to get married.

Food remained a constant problem. Certainly, it is true that people were better fed during the war than before – in so far that they had sound diets. But eggs were 'controlled'; white bread disappeared in 1942; dried eggs became a normal part of one's diet; and restaurants couldn't charge more than 5 shillings (25p) for a meal! During July 1943 matters reached their lowest level with food very scarce and a marked shortage of cosmetics for women.

THE AIR WAR 1943–5

GERMAN RAIDERS

German air raids continued against Britain for the rest of the war – the last German bomber to be shot down over Britain was a Ju-88 in March 1945. German bombers now flew in much smaller formations. The Luftwaffe started to use their fast fighter-bombers. The East Coast was particularly vulnerable to Focke-Wulf 190s coming in low under the radar screen and evading most defences. A special air raid siren was used to warn people of their arrival – it was called the 'cuckoo' and when you heard it you took cover immediately.

Here is an extract from a schoolboy's diary describing one such raid in 1943:

> 2nd June 1943
>
> Some FW-190s came over and woke me up early. I heard the scream of a bomb and jumped over the banisters to get downstairs. Something whistled over the house. Then came some more aeroplanes and two huge bangs. I ran outside in my pyjamas but couldn't see any 'planes. There was a lot of smoke rising up from the bottom of Bishop's Hill. The bomb that had come over our house had bounced off the off-licence in Alston Road and exploded in Myrtle Road.

GERMAN V-WEAPONS

In 1944 the Germans began using their reprisal weapons against Britain. Britain was the first country ever to come under sustained missile attack. The first to come were the V-1 pilotless bombs in 1944 (after D-Day, the invasion of Europe, had begun). They could be seen and were often shot down by anti-aircraft guns or very fast fighters. People called these the doodle-bugs or buzz-bombs. Later on Heinkel 111s carried them to Britain under their wings and released them over the coast – that meant the V-1s could fly further inland. Then came the V-2s. These were supersonic rocket missiles and you couldn't hear them coming. People didn't joke about these – except to call them 'gas mains' when they heard one explode.

BRITISH ATTACKS ON GERMANY

British attacks (mainly at night) went on from the end of 1940 to the last days of the war in 1945. The British bombers flew in 'streams'. At first they were twin-engined aircraft – Whitleys, Hampdens, Wellington and the unsuccessful Manchester. Then came the new generation of four-engined bombers – the Stirlings, Halifaxes and, finest of all, the Lancaster. The British people, who were now veterans of night attacks, looked up into the dark skies as the RAF bombers flew out across the North Sea, grateful that they were 'ours'. On 30–31 May 1942 Britain launched the first 1000-bomber raid against Hamburg. Battles were fought over the Ruhr and Berlin in which hundreds of bombers were lost and thousands of air crew killed. It was the only way in which Britain could carry the war to Germany. By 1945 the RAF was the most efficient bombing force in the world – as it demonstrated during the hideously destructive raid on Dresden (13–14 February 1945) when about 60,000 people died.

THE AMERICANS IN BRITAIN

During 1942 170,000 US servicemen arrived in Britain. They were mostly members of the newly created US 8th Army Air Force (USAAF) formed on 28 January 1942. Its mission was to spearhead American daylight raids against Germany and Occupied Europe. Obviously, it would need large airfields to accommodate its B-17 Flying Fortress and B-24 Liberator bombers. Soon the Americans were adding their own labour teams to the British construction workers busily building brand new bases. Eventually, the 8th Air Force had 112 such bases in Britain – and black GIs* played a major role in construction, maintenance and lorry driving work. Black Americans were soon a common sight in East Anglian villages and nearby towns such as Norwich, Cambridge, Ipswich and Colchester.

*GI = Government issue – US slang for any American soldier irrespective of colour.

SOCIAL IMPACT OF AMERICAN TROOPS

The B-17 G Flying Fortress was the most successful US bomber in the European theatre during the Second World War. The men who flew these aircraft – and the pilots of the Thunderbolt, Mustang and Lightning escort fighters – brought with them the American way of life, something that the British people had only experienced through the cinema screen.

American fliers appeared to be affluent, polite and generous. They made an immediate impact on British girls at dances and parties. Americans could easily buy Hershey chocolate bars, Lucky Strike cigarettes and nylon stockings at their PX stores on the bases – no British servicemen could compete with this.

Consequently, there were often fistfights between US and Allied servicemen particularly in the pubs. British people then had to get used to the sight of US 'Snowdrops' (military police who wore a white helmet) patrolling their streets, side by side with British 'Redcaps' and the civilian police.

Black GIs served on most bases where US bombers such as the one shown on page 179 (one of the last flying examples in Europe during the 1980s) were operational. There were about 15,000 – and sometimes they encountered discrimination and racial prejudice. But most people who made direct contact with them welcomed then into their homes and sometimes into their families. British sympathy for black visitors increased when it was discovered that the white Americans had imported their own brand of discrimination into the country. They were amazed to learn that black and white troops lived segre-

A B-17 G Flying Fortress

gated lives on their bases, that they had segregated barracks, segregated hospitals, segregated vehicles and segregated entertainment.

But it was an important experience for the British people – the first time that they had encountered black people in large numbers on British soil.

HOPES FOR THE FUTURE

It is important for you to realise that while the British were waging the toughest war in their history they were also looking forward to peace and a better way of life for everyone.

THE BEVERIDGE REPORT (1 DECEMBER 1942)

Sir William Beveridge (1879–1963) recommended the setting up of a post-war Ministry of Social Security, a National Health Service for everyone, and family allowances for children. His idea of a post-war caring society appealed to everyone during the dark times of 1942–3.

THE BUTLER EDUCATION ACT 1944

R. A. B. ('Rab') Butler was President of the Board of Education during the war and piloted the 1944 Education Act through the House of

Commons – an Act that was destined to change radically the nature of British education after the war. Its main points were:

1   All children to be educated according to their age, aptitude and ability.
2   The school leaving age would rise first to fifteen and then to sixteen as soon as economic conditions allowed.
3   Secondary education would be free.
4   Local Education Authorities would have to provide three progressive stages of education:
    –   primary;
    –   secondary;
    –   further.
5   A new Ministry of Education would replace the old board and schools would be generally divided up in the secondary sector as follows:
    (*a*)   secondary grammar (to enter this school, one had to pass the 11+ scholarship examination);
    (*b*)   secondary modern;
    (*c*)   secondary technical.
    It was also possible for LEAs to set up 'multilateral' schools – the name first used for comprehensives.

VICTORY

The Education Act became effective on 1 April 1945. The British had recovered from their defeat at Arnhem (1944) and were now pushing into Germany alongside American, Commonwealth and other Allied forces. Coming towards them were the mighty Soviet armies who had borne the greatest burden of fighting the land forces of Hitler's Germany on the Eastern Front.

On 30 April 1945 Adolf Hitler committed suicide.

On 4 May 1945 General Montgomery received the surrender of German forces in North-West Europe. Three days later Admiral Doenitz – he succeeded Hitler – formally surrendered. VE-Day (Victory in Europe Day) was on 8 May 1945.

THE DEFEAT OF JAPAN

Many British families had sons and brothers fighting with the 14th Army (sometimes called the 'Forgotten Army') in Burma. Lord Mountbatten was Supreme Commander in South East Asia Command (SEAC) and he ensured that supplies reached the 14th Army, despite the appalling conditions of terrain and climate. The 14th had pushed through Burma in 1944 and were ready to expel the Japanese from Malaya when the two atomic bombs were dropped and Japan eventually surrendered on 15 August 1945.

THE 1945 GENERAL ELECTION

It was ten years since the British people had voted in a Parliamentary General Election. Churchill and his senior advisers anticipated a victory for the Conservative Party on the basis that it was the Prime Minister's brilliant leadership that had done so much to secure victory. However, the memories of many people were long – they recalled the dole, and the means test – and they still blamed Conservatives such as Neville Chamberlain (he had died in 1940) for the appeasement policies that had allowed Hitler to have his own way before the war. The majority – and especially the servicemen – wanted to see the Beveridge Report come true, wanted to see the main industrial sectors such as mining and the railways nationalised for the benefit of the entire people.

Polling day was 5 July 1945 and it resulted in a landslide victory for the Labour Party. Clement Attlee, leader of the Labour Party, became Prime Minister – three weeks before the war against Japan ended.

Multiple choice questions

1 The first great naval victory in the Second World War resulted in the scuttling of the German ship:
   ☐ *Deutschland*
   ☐ *Hipper*
   ☐ *Lützow*
   ☐ *Graf Spee*

2 Clothes rationing began in:
   ☐ 1939
   ☐ 1940
   ☐ 1941
   ☐ 1942

3 The Dunkirk evacuation was called:
   ☐ Operation Market Garden
   ☐ Operation Sunrise
   ☐ Operation Flintlock
   ☐ Operation Dynamo

4 Churchill became Prime Minister in:
   ☐ 1939
   ☐ 1940
   ☐ 1941
   ☐ 1942

5 Outside London, the first major British city to suffer a full-scale blitz was:
   ☐ Hull
   ☐ Coventry
   ☐ Liverpool
   ☐ Glasgow

6 The invasion of Europe, known as Operation Overlord, began on:
   ☐ 6 June 1942
   ☐ 6 June 1943

      □   6 June 1944
      □   6 June 1945

7   The first RAF 1000-bomber raid was against
      □   Cologne
      □   Dusseldorf
      □   Hamburg
      □   Berlin

8   US airmen could buy luxury goods on their bases from a store called
      □   NAAFI
      □   Tesco's
      □   Woolworth's
      □   the PX

9   Sir William Beveridge recommended setting up a new Ministry of:
      □   Transport
      □   Mines
      □   Health
      □   Social Security

10   The Prime Minister who succeeded Churchill was:
      □   Butler
      □   Dalton
      □   Wilson
      □   Attlee

11   One of the following was *not* a famous slogan during the Second World War:
      □   Lend a Hand on the Land!
      □   Plough now by Day and Night!
      □   Dig for Victory!
      □   Food wasted is another ship gained!
    (Only one word is wrong in the incorrect answer; correct it.)

12   One of the following was *not* rationed during the war:
      □   bread
      □   sugar
      □   butter
      □   cheese

ECONOMIC AND SOCIAL CHANGE SINCE 1945

CONTENTS

CREATING THE WELFARE STATE

ATTLEE FORMS A GOVERNMENT

The socialists had clearly gained from a damaging speech by Churchill (4 June 1945) when he had warned the British people of the dangers of voting socialist:

> . . . they were abhorrent to British ideas of freedom . . . they were inseparably interwoven with totalitarianism.

The British people didn't agree and Attlee and his wife went to Buckingham Palace to tell King George VI that he was able to form a government. He drove there in his little Standard 10 motor car. The age of the common man seemed to have arrived!

WINNING THE PEACE

The Labour Government's problem was how to undertake the peaceful process of socialisation for everyone's benefit.

The National Insurance Scheme (1946)

(*a*)   Weekly payments entitled everyone to sickness, unemployment and retirement benefits. Family allowances were paid the same year.

(*b*)   At the same time maternity and death benefits were paid to help families in their times of greatest financial difficulty.

The National Health Service (1948)

Attlee regarded this as his greatest achievement.

(*a*)   It nationalised hospitals and placed them under the control of regional boards.

(*b*)   Doctors agreed to participate provided they would not become civil servants (this had been Aneurin Bevan's biggest problem as Minister of Health).

Housing

Nearly a third of Britain's houses had suffered war damage.

(*a*)   Labour built about a million houses 1945–51 but these were not enough for thousands of families who had to squat in abandoned Nissen huts or crowd inside caravans made mostly of hardboard.

(*b*)   Young couples had to wait for years on council waiting lists.

Some were lucky enough to rent 'pre-fabs' – prefabricated houses designed to last for ten years but still in use in the late 1980s!

(*c*)   The price of houses helped to encourage post-war inflation. Some of the houses built by development corporations in the new towns of Bracknell, Crawley and Hemel Hempstead demanded rents beyond the pockets of most people.

Education

The Labour Government implemented the 1944 Education Act – but secondary education (free to all) was made selective on the basis of the 11+ examination.

(*a*)   Ellen Wilkinson (the only woman in the Labour Cabinet and Minister of Education) did not take the chance of developing a more radical form of education.

(*b*)   Very few secondary technical schools were built – an important omission – though a few LEAs (responsible for the provision of education under the 1944 Act) did begin multilateral projects that developed into the nation's first comprehensive schools.

The main nationalisation programme

The basic socialist belief was that public ownership of the means of production would end unemployment, promote good industrial relations between management and workers, redistribute the wealth of the former factory owners to their employees and boost production. There was nothing new in the idea. The Conservatives had created nationalised corporations in the form of the BBC and the Central Electricity Board twenty years earlier.

Now the pace of nationalisation was rapid:

1946   The Bank of England
1947   Coal and electricity
1948   Gas and public transport
1949   Iron and steel
            Civil aviation (British European Airways and British Overseas Airways Corporation).

Later on Emanuel Shinwell called these three years of nationalisation a 'bloodless revolution'. In fact, they caused very little hostility and there was no determined resistence.

THE CONDITION OF BRITAIN 1945–51

Remember that the two Attlee governments (1945–50, 1950–51) nationalised only about 20 per cent of British industry while embarking on a hugely expensive programme of welfare services.

How had Britain managed this?

1   Through the efforts of her work-force.
2   Through generous US dollar aid ($ 2.4 billion).
      This was crucial.
Britain could begin modernisation (especially in the pits and on the

railways) without cutting back the size of the work-force. This had important results:

(*a*)   full employment in the nationalised industries;

(*b*)   stability and contentment with working conditions;

(*c*)   trade union demands for wage increases always modest;

(*d*)   everyone heeded the pleas of Sir Stafford Cripps (Chancellor of the Exchequer) – Export or Die!

The British people co-operated in accepting:

(*a*)   food shortages – rationing continued and in fact got worse than during the war;

(*b*)   poor quality clothes and furniture and a long wait for a family motor car – though the 'New Look' in women's fashions made a great hit;

(*c*)   the 'Age of Austerity' – in which industrial production went up 175 per cent!

As long as the overseas markets existed, Britain's prospects looked good. Full employment existed because:

(*a*)   Factories and transport systems were so short of workers that they took out advertisements in West Indian newspapers urging people to come to work in Britain.

(*b*)   National Service: young men between the ages of eighteen and twenty were called up into the Armed Services at first for eighteen months and then for two years – this took them off the labour market.

By 1951 people were tired of 'austerity' and of the mounting costs of:

1   the social services;

2   the Korean War (1950–3).

They voted the Conservative Party into power in 1951 – and for the next thirteen years it battled with the problems of the British economy.

THE BRITISH ECONOMY 1951–64

It is not easy to generalise about this period. In 1957 Prime Minister Macmillan made this famous statement:

> Indeed, let us be frank about it; most of our people have never had it so good. Go around the country, go to the industrial towns, go to the farms, and you will see a state of prosperity such as we have never had in my lifetime – nor, indeed, ever in the history of this country.

Certainly, there had been some amazing progress:

1   agricultural production had doubled;

2   there were the beginnings of the electronic revolution in calculators and computers;

3   synthetic fibres such as nylon were widely used;

4   the new petro-chemical industry was booming;

5   the 1954 Television Act set up commercial TV and the new Independent Television Authority began broadcasting in September 1955. By the end of the year over 5 million families had TV; by 1963 over 12 million had TV.

AN IMPROVEMENT IN THE STANDARD OF LIVING

There can be no doubt that there was a marked improvement, especially after Macmillan cut purchase tax on consumer goods:

1   radios, TV sets, refrigerators, washing machines were bought, usually on the 'never-never' (HP payments);
2   60 per cent of the people took their holidays away from home and many ventured abroad;
3   there were 8 million private motor cars;
4   wages rose by over 50 per cent – way ahead of inflation.
     Yet all was not well with the British economy.

Question

Consider the above comments on the British standard of living and consult your textbook.
     Would you agree that the British people 'had never had it so good' as they did 1951–64?

THE PROBLEM OF THE £ STERLING

Government insisted that the £ sterling should be a 'reserve currency'.

What did this mean?

Overseas buyers could do their international trading in sterling. That meant they kept large balances in the Bank of England. But they weren't impressed by Conservative tactics when they deliberately 'manipulated' the economy for political purposes: for example, they reduced taxes just before general elections (they 'reflated' the economy) and they increased taxes in the next budget (they deflated the economy).
     The classic example was in 1955 – and this had the effect of reducing the value of the £ sterling. Foreign traders then withdrew their cash reserves from the Bank and asked for dollars or marks in exchange.
     This was called the 'flight from the £'. It became a feature of the British economy. There was a great danger in this.

1   Britain could run out of reserves to pay for her mounting imports.
2   This could damage the whole fabric of international trade.
     Macmillan (and, in all fairness, the next Labour Prime Minister as well) thought this was something the British economy could bear. Sadly, it wasn't.

1   It encouraged British investment in overseas investment rather than in the less profitable but vital investment at home.

2   It brought the contemptuous charge from Labour MPs that all the Conservatives could offer were 'stop-go' policies.

Question
Explain the problem of 'stop-go' policies during the period of Conservative government 1951–64. What were its dangers for Britain?

TRADE UNION INFLUENCE

Ever since 1945 when the Attlee Government had repealed Baldwin's 1927 Trades Disputes Act the trade unions had ever-increasing political influence. In 1958 they clashed with the Conservative Government over a bitter busman's strike. Though the busmen lost their demand for a £1.25 wage increase, many other unions decided to demand a shorter working week and thus gain wage increases by more overtime. Frank Cousins, TUC leader, asked the government to think in terms of a wages policy.

In 1962 the National Economic Development Council (Neddy) was set up.

TRADE UNIONS AND THE LABOUR GOVERNMENTS 1964–70

Labour won the 1964 election and Harold Wilson became Prime Minister.

The National Board for Prices and Incomes 1965
Wilson set up this to ensure that all wage increases would be related to productivity. However, it proved useless as constant strike action by the unions wrecked Labour policies..
1   1966 Seamen's strike: seriously damaged British exports for a year.
2   Wilson devalued the £ sterling.

Effects
1   Few people believed his amazing TV performance when he calmly told the nation that devaluation 'did not mean, of course, that the pound here in Britain, in your pocket or purse, or in your bank has been devalued . . .
2   Of course, it meant precisely that – and boosted inflation.
3   The trade unions demanded wage increases to cover rising inflation – irrespective of productivity and British sales abroad.
4   Devastating strikes took place in the car industry and, because of poor relations between workers and managers, meant that the newly created British Leyland Motors Corporation could not compete effectively against the attractive foreign motor cars flooding into Britain.
5   Deeply worried by the deteriorating relations between government and the trade unions, Barbara Castle brought in her famous White Paper 'In Place of Strife'.

In Place of Strife

She hoped to persuade the trade unions not to take instant strike action.

1 Take a 'cooling off' period before going on strike.
2 Any striker refusing to do this should be jailed or fined.

The unions were astonished. It seemed a direct attack on cherished Labour beliefs: the right of a worker to withdraw his or her labour; and the right to engage in voluntary wage settlements.

It certainly didn't help Labour's prospects in the 1970 General Election.

THE CONSERVATIVE GOVERNMENT 1970–4

In 1971 Edward Heath's Conservative Government passed the 1971 Industrial Relations Act designed to ban 'unfair' industrial action:

1 strikes aimed at bringing about a 'closed shop';
2 strikes designed to smash a previously agreed wage settlement;
3 strikes by 'unregistered' unions.

This led to widespread industrial protest 1971–2, including a bitter miners' strike. Conflict with the miners did not end in 1972; eventually, the National Coal Board offered the miners a 13 per cent pay increase in 1973. The miners turned it down and imposed an overtime ban – just in time for the cold British winter to bite into the hearts and minds of the British people.

Nobody doubted that the miners had a good case. The people understood the dangers from accidents and the 'dust' (pneumoconiosis). In November 1973 the government imposed the following:

1 cuts in TV broadcasting;
2 cuts in shop-window lights and street lighting.

Suddenly there was a shortage of everyday goods and on 2 January 1974 the Heath Government imposed a three-day working week.

All was not well with the British nation. The people found themselves in a 'state of emergency' uncertain what to do. Then the Prime Minister decided on a General Election (February 1974). It was a confusing affair with several new political parties. Eventually, Labour was returned to power.

The 1974 Election result

	Labour	Conservative	Liberals	Ulster Loyalists	Welsh & Scottish Nationalists	SDLP (Gerry Fitt)
Seats	301	297	14	11	9	1

There were 54 National Front and 44 Communist candidates in 1974

**THE LABOUR
GOVERNMENTS 1974–9**

Wilson made a settlement with the miners. They went back to work, the normal working week for the rest of the nation was restored and the state of emergency ended. It was a time of significant economic change: the first tanker bearing North Sea oil arrived in 1975 (the first gas strikes had been made in 1965) – a new source of revenue. The future seemed assured now that Britain was independent of Middle East oil supplies. Harold Wilson resigned in 1976; James Callaghan replaced him.

Prime Minister Callaghan inherited an unhappy society:

1   unemployment was increasing;
2   inflation was at 20 per cent;
3   British industry was clearly inefficient.

Callaghan therefore introduced his incomes policy, demonstrating that his first priority was the reduction of inflation – the cause of falling living standards. His approach was not so dramatic as Heath's had been; Callaghan did not want a repetition of Heath's three month state of emergency (1973–4).

1   He offered a maximum 5 per cent wage increase annually.
2   This would not be related to productivity.

The unions were furious because they felt it was totally unfair.

Read the following account:

> Farmworkers, sewage workers, water workers and other low paid groups had no chance of a company car, free medical insurance, help with moving house or free petrol. Yet many people described as executives and managers did get these 'perks' and perhaps £10,000 a year or more. Far too many full-time workers received such low wages that they had to apply for FIS – Family Income Supplement. As people said, percentages were a con. They wouldn't mind 5% of Callaghan's wages.

1   Describe three 'perks' commonly given to executive and managers by private companies.
2   Why should they regard 'free medical insurance' so highly?
3   Explain 'FIS'.
4   Explain the statement 'percentages were a con'.
5   Why wouldn't they mind 5% of Callaghan's wages?

THE 1979 GENERAL ELECTION

Prime Minister Callaghan secured a wages standstill in 1977–8 and brought the rate of inflation marginally below 10 per cent. For a time he had the Lib-Lab alliance (from 1977) and he hoped he would have the chance of another term of office to carry out sweeping economic and social reform. However, there were over 1.8 million unemployed and well over 2 million families still lived in sub-standard accommodation. Again, the trade unions let him down in their so-called 'winter of discontent' and completely destroyed Callaghan's plans for a new 'social contract' between government and unions. He therefore prepared for the 1979 election. This was the Labour Party's manifesto 'Into the Eighties':

> This election comes at a time of change unparalleled since 1945. A generation has now grown up in a welfare state that remains the envy of the world in health care and education. We have demonstrated a capacity for skill and involvement which keeps us in the forefront of world technology . . . A Tory government would put all this at risk . . . Their uncaring meanness would mean misery for millions of the most vulnerable since their policy of cutting public services can only mean a drastic reduction in all our social services.

1   If these statements were true, why did the electorate vote Mrs Thatcher's Conservative Party into office?

2   There was a world recession in progress. Did the electorate wonder how the Labour Party would finance its proposed reforms?

3   Did the electorate expect the Conservative Party to introduce more prudent budgets and reduce taxes?

4   Do you think the electorate was worried about Labour's defence policies?

Margaret Thatcher's response was that the Conservative Party offered 'no magic formulas or lavish promises'. Her priority was:

> . . . the restoration of the health of our economic and social life, by controlling inflation and striking a fair balance between the rights and duties of the trade union movement.

The 1979 election result was

Conservatives	339
Labour	268
Liberal	11
Others	16

– an overall Conservative majority of 44.

MONETARISM

Monetarists believe in price stability, secured by preventing people's purchasing power exceeding their productivity. This required a radical change in attitude on the part of the British people. They had come to expect an automatic increase in wages every year, increases usually unrelated to productivity. It was argued that the British people were pricing themselves out of the world's markets. Conservative policies therefore meant cuts in some public spending sectors such as the armed services, the Civil Service and the local authority rate support grants. Industry was encouraged to become efficient by cutting down overstaffed departments and factories. The price of such a policy was serious – prolonged unemployment. Against this had to be balanced the remarkable drop in inflation – well below 10 per cent in 1982, less than 6 per cent in 1983 and falling to 2 per cent in 1986.

Reactions

Thousands of British families experienced for the first time the meaning of redundancy, living on dramatically reduced income and bringing up children who had little prospect of finding a job. This led to new political developments (compare the effect of drastic economic change on people in the 1820s and in the 1930s).

1   Emergence of the Social Democratic Party (25 January 1981): formed by four ex-Labour Cabinet Ministers (David Owen, William Rodgers, Shirley Williams, Roy Jenkins).
2   The Labour Party was in disarray. James Callaghan retired in 1981.
3   Splits in the Labour Party began when extreme left-wing Militant Tendency activists began to dominate local council, trade union and even National Executive affairs.
4   Re-election of Margaret Thatcher's government (partly due to the 'Falklands factor' – the successful British campaign to liberate the Falkland Islands in 1982). Her victory was a landslide – an overall majority of 144 seats.

TRADE UNION LEGISLATION AND THE 1984–5 MINERS' STRIKE

Margaret Thatcher's second government was determined:
1   to continue to limit the control of the State over British industry by encouraging privatisation;
2   to make British industry even more efficient;
3   to limit the power of the trade unions.

Privatisation

This encouraged contracting out of certain 'public sector' services to private firms. For example the National Health Service was encouraged to use private firms for cleaning and catering. It also encouraged the further sales of public enterprises. The government had already sold off part of British Aerospace, Britoil, Cable & Wireless. Now over 50 per cent of British Telecom was sold – a shares 'bonanza' for private investors.

The Conservative Government was determined to convert the British people into a share-owning democracy and British Gas and British Airways were privatised in the late 1980s.

The Prior and Tebbitt Employment Acts 1980, 1982

These acts attempted to deal with the problem of excessive trade union powers such as:

closed shop practices; unfair dismissal; trade union immunities; strike ballots and the election of trade union officers.

The 1984 Act

This provided public money to pay for secret union ballots – designed to ensure that all trade union members were consulted before their leaders decided on a strike. It is interesting, however, to note that these laws were not the ones used to deal with the miners' strike that dominated 1984–5.

THE MINERS' STRIKE 1984–5

This was one of the most dramatic events in British economic and social history since the Second World War. Its origins were in the National Union of Mineworkers' (NUM) objections to pit closures as part of the Coal Board's programme of greater efficiency and modernisation.

The main events

1983: NUM began its overtime ban, without balloting its members. Coal stocks were at their highest – 24 million tons at the power stations and even more at the pits.

1984: The strike began in Yorkshire in protest at plans to close the Cortonwood pit. The NUM expected each district to come out on strike – including the Nottinghamshire miners.

The NUM changed its rules so that it could call a strike if 51 per cent of its members voted so in a national ballot. But there was still no move to ballot the NUM membership.

The TUC offered to support the miners but very few unions (especially the key steeelworkers and transport drivers) were enthusiastic.

NUM pickets arrived in Nottinghamshire to try to deter miners from working. Violence began and soon there was a huge police presence – 8000 officers were drafted in from all over the country.

In October 1984 the NUM was fined £200,000 for 'contempt of court' and sent its cash reserves abroad. The High Court ordered total sequestration of NUM funds and appointed a receiver to take over the union's financial affairs.

These tactics were perfectly legal and they were based on laws that apply generally – not to trade unions in particular. They surprised the NUM – especially when accountants tracked down the NUM's funds in Luxemburg.

1985: Nottinghamshire broke away from the NUM and miners returned to work in many pits.

These events were not regarded with pleasure by any section of the British people. In the House of Lords, Harold Macmillan (now Lord Stockton) made his moving appeal:

> It breaks my heart to see what is happening in this country today: this terrible strike by the best men in the world who

beat the Kaiser's and Hitler's armies. Britain cannot afford this kind of thing.

Many people saw it as a deliberate confrontation between the government's representative, Ian MacGregor, and the NUM leader, Arthur Scargill. They were appalled by the violence, the suffering among miners' families and the prospect of decay in so many mining communities – a repetition of the harsh events of the 1930s.

The strike ended on 4 March 1985, a failure for Arthur Scargill (who now had a divided NUM) and an apparent victory for the Conservative Government.

Reasons for the miners' failure

1 The government was determined not to suffer the same fate as Edward Heath had experienced in 1973–4. It therefore made contingency plans for a possible confrontation with the NUM – building up coal stocks, arranging for coal imports, recruitment of non-union members to drive coal lorries. This was based on the so-called Ridley Plan (worked out by Nicholas Ridley).
2 Arthur Scargill certainly over-estimated the willingness of his NUM members to join a strike that had not been secretly balloted.
3 The loss of the NUM's £6.8 million was a serious blow – Arthur Scargill's 'flying pickets' soon ran out of funds.

Significance

The failure of the miners' strike showed many other unions and political groups the dangers and futility of militancy in British politics.

SCIENCE AND TECHNOLOGY

OIL

NORTH SEA DISCOVERIES

After the Dutch made their first natural gas field discovery at Groningen (1959) geologists discovered that the Permian layer holding the gas stretched under the North Sea. Then the Norwegians found oil at Ekofisk (1970) and the North Sea oil boom began.

The oil rigs

Manufacturing and siting the massive oil rigs took a high level of engineering skill. Philips Petroleum had found oil at Maureen in 1973 – 163 miles (262 km) north-east of Aberdeen. It cost £700 million to develop the rig. The huge sub-sea platform was built on Clydeside; while the complex topdeck was constructed at Kishorn. The completed structure was then towed between the Orkney and Shetland islands to the edge of the UK North Sea sector.

Maureen went into production during 1983, undoubtedly one of the engineering marvels of the twentieth century. Taxation on its production, plus the production of all the other oil wells, brought the British government hundreds of thousands of £s per hour, every day of the week, every week of the year.

Why has government found the new oil revenues so valuable during the 1980s?

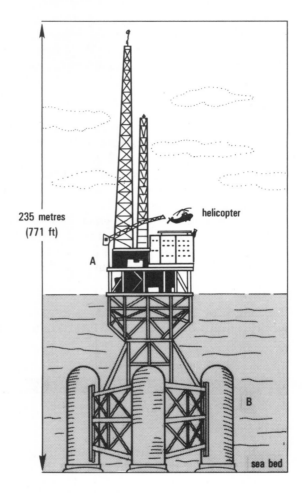

235 metres
(771 ft)

helicopter

A

B

sea bed

The Maureen oil rig. This is really a factory designed to: (i) extract oil from deep below the sea bed, process it at A to remove water and natural gas and then store it in three tanks, B, under the sea; (ii) pump this oil to a distant loading station

INDUSTRIAL CHANGE IN SCOTLAND SINCE 1973

Apart from prosperity during the Second World War, the coal-mines, steelworks and shipyards in Scotland have suffered more than most. Once the world recession after 1973 hit labour-intensive Scottish firms (e.g. Timex, Massey Ferguson, Goodyear) many Scottish workers

(*Opposite*) The exploitation of oil and natural gas in the North Sea

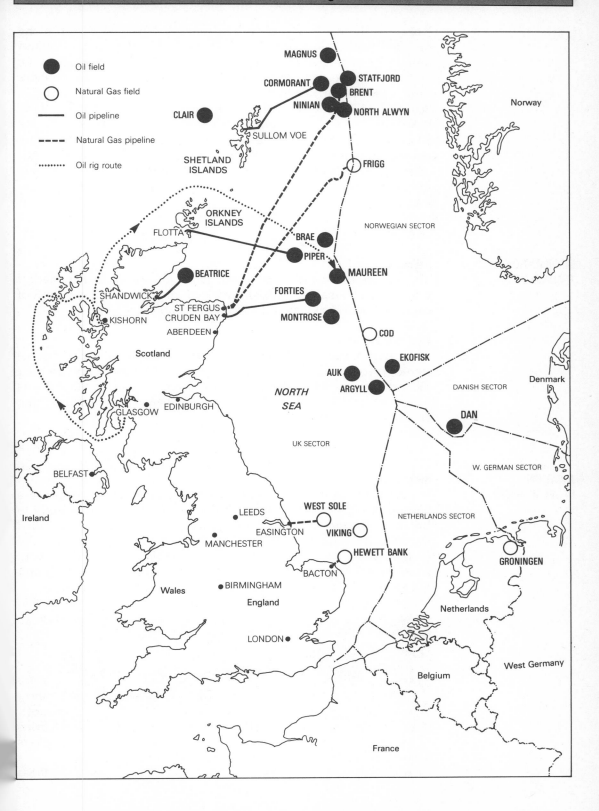

Legend:

- ● Oil field
- ○ Natural Gas field
- —— Oil pipeline
- – – – Natural Gas pipeline
- ·········· Oil rig route

MAGNUS

CORMORANT   STATFJORD
             BRENT
NINIAN   NORTH ALWYN

CLAIR

SULLOM VOE

Norway

SHETLAND
ISLANDS

FRIGG

ORKNEY
ISLANDS
FLOTTA

NORWEGIAN SECTOR

BRAE
PIPER
MAUREEN

BEATRICE

SHANDWICK
KISHORN

ST FERGUS
CRUDEN BAY
ABERDEEN

FORTIES
MONTROSE

COD

Scotland

EKOFISK

AUK

ARGYLL

Denmark

DANISH SECTOR

NORTH
SEA

EDINBURGH

GLASGOW

DAN

W. GERMAN SECTOR

UK SECTOR

BELFAST

Ireland

LEEDS

MANCHESTER

WEST SOLE

EASINGTON   VIKING

HEWETT BANK

BACTON

BIRMINGHAM

Wales

England

LONDON

NETHERLANDS SECTOR

GRONINGEN

Netherlands

Belgium

West Germany

France

looked to the new oil industry that provided 100,000 jobs over the next ten years. Most of these worked in oil-related industries and found jobs in the business organisations that moved in to share in the oil boom. The centre of this was Aberdeen, hailed as the offshore capital of Europe. Nevertheless, of the 5,167,000 people living in Scotland 14.8 per cent of the work-force had lost their jobs. Many looked to the high technology industries for work. Backed by the Scottish Office and the Scottish Development Agency, 40,000 or more people found jobs in the microchip and personal computer industry – often called 'Silicon Glen' – of immense benefit to Scotland's new towns: Irvine, Glenrothes, Cumbernauld, East Kilbride and Livingston.

INFORMATION TECHNOLOGY

Definition

This covers the handling of vocal, pictorial, textual and numerical information by making use of microelectronics-based combinations of computation techniques and telecommunications.

Electronic publishing

The arrival of transistors made computers a vital part of the microelectronics revolution.In 1977 BBC (Ceefax) and ITV (Oracle) began their teletext services and within five years over 0.5 million teletext sets had been sold in Britain. In 1981 Oracle began to sell advertising space to the general public.

AVIATION DEVELOPMENTS

Helicopters

Britain had begun experiments with helicopter design before the Second World War – beginning with the autogiro designs brought to Britain by Spanish-born Juan de la Cierva. A British helicopter (called the Weir W5) flew in 1938. After the war Westland Aircraft Ltd (Yeovil) dominated the helicopter production industry in Britain, adapting US Sikorsky designs and working with the French to produce its own remarkable array of civilian and military helicopters.

A BAC 1–11 – a British design fitted with British engines and part of the British Caledonian fleet

The jet engine

The development of the jet engine went on in several European countries. In Britain, the pioneer was Sir Frank Whittle. Rolls-Royce dominated British jet engine production. Rolls-Royce engines power many British and American airliners.

The most famous jet airliner is the supersonic Concorde, developed by Britain and France. Concorde began carrying passengers in 1976.

THE QUALITY OF LIFE

Living standards reached their peak during the 1980s with the biggest consumer boom in British history.

LEISURE

Though over 3 million people had to experience enforced leisure through unemployment, sport and leisure activities also reached their peak during the 1970s and 1980s. Spectator sports such as motor-racing and air shows were always well attended; football matches tended to see a slip in spectator support due to hooliganism that sadly brought the sport into disrepute. Jogging and keep-fit activities

The attraction of air shows

became highly refined, compared with the cycling clubs and League of Health and Beauty activities of the 1930s. Clothing and equipment for specialised sports such as skiing, wind-surfing, squash and hang-gliding were expensive – but nevertheless eagerly purchased.

RELIGION

Religion played a relatively small part in the material culture of most of the British people. Church of England attendance declined significantly and many priests had to take responsibility for services in two, three or even four parishes. This was less true in the Roman Catholic and Methodist congregations. John Wesley's teachings (he lived from 1703 to 1791) were still very much alive.

Charity and good works

The example set by philanthropists such as William Booth (1829–1912 – the founder of the Salvation Army) was still heeded and numerous charities such as Help the Aged, Oxfam and the Cheshire Homes flourished. The kind of example to which young people responded, however, was a little different – notably the 'Live Aid' and 'Band Aid' concerts and record sales led by Bob Geldof and other pop musicians who gave their services freely to raise money for their 'Feed the World' campaign (1984–5).

THE STATUS OF WOMEN

LEGISLATION

After the Second World War, in which they had made a major contribution to victory, women did not enjoy equal status with men. Yet women were marrying earlier, postponing the time when they had their first child and increasingly going out to work as these figures show:

1951   Women made up 11% of the work-force; 38% married
1964   Women made up 19% of the work-force; 53% married
1976   Women made up 25% of the work-force; 70% married

During those years, the status of women was upgraded by means of legislation, carried out by mainly Labour governments:

1967 Abortion Act (introduced by David Steel);

1968 Divorce Act;

1970 Equal Pay Act;
    Matrimonial Property Act;

1975 Sex Discrimination Act: specially designed to prevent discrimination in work opportunities; education and training;

Employment Protection Act (the maternity provisions).

EQUAL OPPORTUNITIES

Despite the laws, women still suffered discrimination.
1 They did not receive education commensurate with their ability.
2 Few received specialist training to equip them for the modern world.
3 Few made much headway in politics – when Mrs Thatcher became Prime Minister in 1979 there were only eighteen women MPs. In 1951 there had been seventeen. But there was a significant increase after the 1987 General Election.

Feminist movements

These gained strength in the 1960s and 1970s. 'Women's Lib' greatly aided the entry of women into the media industries, especially broadcasting, journalism and publishing. By 1980 there were few obstacles to hinder the progress of able, determined women in the careers of their choice.

Yet in 1980 only 8 per cent were employed as managers – 66 per cent of women found jobs in education and health. In traditional male occupations (e.g. engineering) they were as low as 0.5 per cent of the work-force. The failure in education was emphasised by Sir Keith Joseph (Secretary of State for Education) in 1983:

> The facts are disquieting. At all stages of the education process girls fail to reach their potential.

Simultaneously, the Chairman of the Equal Opportunities Commission (founded in 1975), Lady Platt, emphasised that girls should include information processing in their education so that they would be fitted to participate in the technological changes of the next century.

ETHNIC MINORITIES

POST-WAR IMMIGRANTS

Many Poles came to live in Britain during 1946-7 and the British allowed them to stay permanently as citizen members of the 1947 Polish Resettlement Corps. This arrangement applied to numerous Latvians, Lithuanians, Estonians, Czechs and Ukrainians – most of them displaced persons (DPs) unwilling to return to a homeland now under Soviet rule. The emergence of an independent India and Pakistan (1947) also led to an influx of immigrants from the subcontinent.

Results

The Labour Government passed the **1948 Nationality Act**. This created two classes of citizenship:
1 citizens of the UK and Colonies

2   citizens of independent Commonwealth countries.

At the same time the *Empire Windrush* brought 800 West Indian immigrants, most of them people who had served in the RAF during the war.

Consequence

The *Empire Windrush* contingent began the history of Britain as a multiracial society (though, of course, black people had lived in Britain in small numbers for centuries and, as members of the Roman Army stationed in Britain, were here before the English!)

WHY THE WEST INDIANS CAME

Traditionally, West Indians sought a better way of life by settling in the USA. But the 1952 McCarran-Walter Act severely limited West Indian immigration into the US; at the same time, Britain was crying out for workers. Most West Indians regarded Britain as their natural mother country and knew that increasing mechanisation on the Caribbean plantations would make their job prospects even worse in years to come. Many therefore decided to 'become English', because they valued English ideas and the prospect of a good living wage. That was why they came.

ASIANS ARRIVE

The lure of a booming post-war economy in Britain attracted many Asians during the 1950s. They didn't come because they were poor or out of work. They came to amass capital to send home to their families who would then be able to buy a few more acres of land. Emigration was already an enduring and honourable feature of Asian family life, carefully prepared and funded as a joint enterprise. Since 1945 Indians and Sikhs from Kashmir, Punjab and Gujurat had settled all over the world.

THE CYPRIOTS

In contrast, many Cypriots were refugees. The British had refused to grant Cyprus its independence after 1945 and a bitter civil war between Greek and Turkish Cypriots began (82 per cent of the population then were Greek Cypriots).

Cyprus became a war-torn island and from it no less than one-sixth of the entire population migrated during the 1950s and 1960s. Immigrants arrived as complete families and settled mainly in London. They were adaptable and quick to make their mark in the restaurant business and the textile trade. Before long, they had spread into the service industries at roughly the same time as the Sikhs were doing this.

Control by legislation

The first serious race riots exploded in Nottingham and Notting Hill (1958) – due to poor housing and job shortages in rundown districts. Sadly, it was only too easy to blame some black immigrants for these conditions – when they had in fact inherited them!

1962 Commonwealth Immigration Act This was intended to control immigration. Thousands flooded into the country to 'beat the ban'.

1968 Commonwealth Immigration Act This arose out of the sudden arrival of 66,000 Kenyan Asians who had lost their right of abode in Kenya but had hung on to their UK passports.

Under the Act, these Asians lost their automatic right to settle in Britain. This was discriminatory and the Labour Government hastily allowed Kenyan passport holders to settle in Britain.

1971 Immigration Act (came into force 1973): This gave the right of abode to 'patrials':

(*a*)   Commonwealth citizens whose parents or grandparents were born in Britain;

(*b*)   spouses and fiancé(e)s;

(*c*)   certain dependants of people already living in Britain.

It is interesting to note that as early as 1950 the Attlee Government considered restricting immigration; but once the government had heard that 'only about 5000' had arrived it decided (February 1951) not to introduce an immigration act for the time being.

THE MYTHS ABOUT IMMIGRATION

Almost every one of these was untrue.
1   Immigration has *not* made Britain into a crowded island.
2   Ever since 1964, the peak year in the post-war British birth-rate, more people had been leaving Britain than arriving; and, since 1974, when the British population topped 54.5 million, the birth-rate had been declining.
3   Black families did *not* get priority on council housing lists.
4   Black children did *not* hold back the rate of learning in multiracial classrooms.
5   Black workers were *not* always on the dole drawing social security benefits – or when they were not doing that, taking all the jobs!
6   Black people were *not* becoming the biggest group in the population. There were about 2.25 million black people in Britain by 1980, about 4 per cent of the population.

Race Relations Acts

1965 Act Forbade discrimination on grounds of race, colour, ethnic or national origin in public places.

1968 Act Made discrimination illegal in housing, work, advertisements and public services.

1976 Act Made incitement to racial hatred in public places, by spoken or written word, a criminal offence.

A 1975 government report thought that 'crude, overt forms of racial discrimination' had largely disappeared and that Britain was moving towards the eventual elimination of racial prejudice.

Other Acts

1   1981 – the year of the Brixton and Toxteth Riots and the Scarman Report – also saw the abolition of the 1824 'sus' law (the cause of some police harassment of ethnic minorities). Replaced by the *Criminal Attempts Act*.

2   *1986 Public Order Act*. The first since the 1930s when Mosley's Black-shirts caused difficulties. The Act, among other things, reinforced the law against racial harassment.

Unemployment and poor housing

Exceptionally high unemployment among blacks aged sixteen to twenty-four contributed to the disorder in some British cities (1981); and poor housing – where repairs and maintenance were kept at a low level for decades – was a national disgrace.

CONCERN FOR THE ENVIRONMENT

There were many groups protesting against environmental pollution during the period 1950 onwards. Conservationists are concerned not to upset fragile ecosystems and much improvement took place with regard to for example:
–   the elimination of unnecessary smoke pollution (Clean Air Act 1956);
–   the cleansing of rivers and the ending of the irresponsible dumping of effluent into waterways by manufacturing firms.
Greatest concern has been shown for the effects of civil nuclear power stations and the stockpiling of nuclear weapons.

CND

The Campaign for Nuclear Disarmament had been founded by the philospher Bertrand Russell, and his friends Kingsley Martin (*New Statesman* editor), A. J. P. Taylor (Oxford historian) and Canon Collins of St Paul's (1958). CND's objective was to persuade Britain to adopt unilateral nuclear disarmament and its 'sit-down' protests and Aldermaston marches won international publicity. Most of CND's supporters were in the Labour Party. However, after France and China joined the 'nuclear club' Prime Minister Harold Wilson decided to confirm the Labour Government's faith in the Polaris deterrent. CND's influence dwindled.

The revival

This followed the 1979 NATO decision to instal Pershing II and Tomahawk cruise missiles in NATO countries to deter the Soviet's new triple-headed SS-20 missiles. CND protest grew 1980–81 and a new organisation called END (European Nuclear Disarmament) formed by the British historian E. P. Thompson and others called for the withdrawal of nuclear weapons from Europe. New leaders appeared in CND, all artists in propaganda and skilled debaters: Joan Ruddock, CND's chairman, Monsignor Bruce Kent and the Rev. Paul Oestreicher. Most media coverage focused on the demonstrations by the 'Greenham Common Women' – the first cruise missiles had arrived at Greenham Common on 14 March 1983.

Other movements

Other groups of women, such as Lady Olga Maitland's Women and Families for Defence, opposed the growing 'peace movement', believing that CND and END confused peace with appeasement.

CIVIL NUCLEAR POWER STATIONS

Civil nuclear power stations in Britain, 1986. Nuclear power supplied 16% of Britain's electricity in 1986

The stocks of fossil fuels are finite – they will not be there for ever. Is it prudent to develop civil nuclear power to make up the likely shortfall in fossil fuel – even with the warning of Chernobyl before us?

This map shows the location of civil nuclear stations in Britain.

BRITAIN AND THE EUROPEAN ECONOMIC COMMUNITY (EEC)

Six European countries – France, West Germany, Italy, Belgium, the Netherlands and Luxemburg – founded the EEC in 1957. Its remarkable trading success encouraged Britain to found EFTA (European Free Trade Association) in 1959.

Macmillan's interest in the EEC

Prime Minister Macmillan wanted Britain to join the EEC and he encouraged Edward Heath to open negotiations with the 'Six' 1961–3. General de Gaulle vetoed the British application (1963).

1   He said the 1947 British Agricultural Act subsidised British farmers so that food prices remained low in the UK.
2   Food suppliers such as New Zealand sold their products at preferential rates to the British.

De Gaulle was adamant that British food subsidies and Commonwealth preference must go.

Wilson's conversion

In 1967 Harold Wilson announced his 'historic decision' to join the EEC but once again de Gaulle vetoed the idea.

Heath signs the Treaty of Accession 1972

With Norway, Ireland and Denmark, Britain signed the Treaty of Accession on 22 January 1972. In 1 January 1973 Britain became a full member of the EEC, a decision confirmed in the unique 1975 referendum.

Multiple choice questions

1   The National Health Service began in:
    - ☐   1945
    - ☐   1946
    - ☐   1947
    - ☐   1948
2   The first woman Minister of Education was:
    - ☐   Ellen Wilkinson
    - ☐   Shirley Williams
    - ☐   Margaret Thatcher
    - ☐   Barbara Castle
3   The 'Age of Austerity' is associated with:
    - ☐   Sir Stafford Cripps
    - ☐   Winston Churchill

    ☐   Hugh Dalton

    ☐   Dennis Healey

4   In 1950 the Labour Government decided to send troops to:

    ☐   the Korean War

    ☐   the Suez invasion

    ☐   the confrontation with Indonesia

    ☐   the Falklands War

5   Commercial TV began broadcasting in:

    ☐   1955

    ☐   1956

    ☐   1957

    ☐   1958

6   The sentence 'You've never had it so good' is associated with Prime Minister:

    ☐   Heath

    ☐   Churchill

    ☐   Thatcher

    ☐   Macmillan

7   The Employment Acts of 1980 and 1982 are associated with:

    ☐   Prior and Tebbit

    ☐   Prior and Heseltine

    ☐   Prior and Ridley

    ☐   Prior and Baker

8   After Callaghan resigned as Labour Party leader he was succeeded by:

    ☐   Dennis Healey

    ☐   Michael Foot

    ☐   Harold Wilson

    ☐   Neil Kinnock

9   'Silicon Glen' is to be found in

    ☐   Wales

    ☐   Ireland

    ☐   The Channel Islands

    ☐   Scotland

10 Britain became a full member of the EEC in

    ☐   1953

    ☐   1963

    ☐   1973

    ☐   1983

BRITAIN AND IRELAND

CONTENTS

THE EARLY HISTORY OF 'JOHN BULL'S OTHER ISLAND'

FIRST LINKS

In 1167 Norman warriors sailed across the Irish Sea to help Dermot MacMurrough, King of Leinster. So began the long history of the 'English colony in Ireland', ruled by Anglo-Irish nobles on behalf of the English monarch. Under Queen Elizabeth I the settlement increased. She approved the Protestant Plantation of Munster in 1586. The native Irish chieftains constantly rebelled – the last was Hugh O'Neill, defeated at the Battle of Kinsale (1601).

Significance

Resistance now passed to the Anglo-Irish nobility. They did not deny the right of the King to rule Ireland; but they did want
1 religious toleration;
2 security of land tenure;
3 the right of Catholics to take part in political life in Ireland.

The Great Rebellion 1641

This was a rising of the Irish against the Protestant settlers, who feared they would all be massacred. In fact, the massacres were carried out by the English for, once Cromwell appeared, 1649–50, life became cheap in Ireland. Dreadful massacres at Wexford and Drogheda have never been forgotten by the Irish.

THE WILLIAMITE SETTLEMENT

This refers to the changes that took place during the rule of William III of Orange after the Catholic James II failed to subdue the Protestant Irish. Derry resisted all Catholic attacks; the forces of William of Orange (he was King of England 1689–1702) won the Battle of the Boyne and Limerick surrendered (1691).
1 Ireland lost another million acres in the Plantation of 1691 – this cemented a sense of injustice against the English.
2 The Lord-Lieutenant ruled Ireland. The Irish Parliament (Protestant) met about once every two years and could always be over-ruled by the Lord-Lieutenant.
3 1692 Act excluded 'Papists' (Catholics) from holding any position of authority under the Crown. Papists couldn't own guns or a horse worth more than £5.

4   Catholics could not go abroad for their education; and they couldn't set up schools in Ireland.
5   Bishops were banned; priests could say Mass only if they first took an oath of allegiance to the Crown.

These were the Penal Laws – never fully applied. But they had two very important and unintended results:
1   They ensured that the Irish would cherish their Roman Catholic beliefs – despite the lack of English toleration.
2   They created a link between Catholicism and the idea of an independent Ireland.

1782–1800

Though the ruling Anglo-Irish totally rejected the ideas of the 1789 French Revolution, they did try to create a prosperous Ireland.

1784 Foster's Corn Law Ireland to become a corn-growing land with England as its market for wheat surpluses.

Irish industry (particularly textiles) to have preferential trade treatment.
    However, the Anglo-Irish neglected to improve the appalling living conditions on the farms where people paid their rents with corn and subsisted on potatoes and salads.

THE 1800 ACT OF UNION

This followed the Irish Rebellion of 1798 that sprang out of the Society of United Irishmen formed by Wolfe Tone (1791). Tone was an Irish politician who believed that an independent Ireland could come about only by an uprising of the poor and oppressed. The rebellion was a total failure and the English government decided to unite the two kingdoms in an Act of Union:
1   Ireland to have a hundred MPs in the House of Commons;
2   Ireland to have thirty-two peers in the House of Lords.
    Ireland was now governed as a part of Britain.

Economic advantages
1   Ireland was a food-exporting country and the rest of Britain was its most obvious market.
2   There was a chance of prosperity for Ireland – but the problem quickly became one of redistributing the wealth gained from increased trade.

Population increase
In the forty years after the Act of Union the population of Ireland increased at an unprecedented rate:

1800   5 million   *1841*   8.9 million

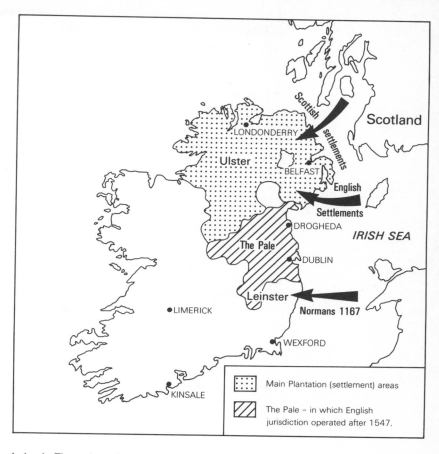

Ireland – The early settlements

The Siege of Londonderry 1688–9

In 1688 William of Orange, married to King James's Protestant niece, Mary, was invited by the English government to become King of England in place of the Catholic James II. King James II fled to France and then went to Dublin determined to use Ireland as a base from which to invade England. Ulster decided to resist him and when a Catholic regiment arrived outside Londonderry thirteen apprentices shut the city gates in the face of the enemy. In this way the Apprentice Boys of Londonderry passed into Protestant legend and symbolise resistance to Catholicism. The motto of besieged Londonderry was 'No surrender!' (the city was under siege for seven months and the defenders were on the verge of starvation) and this too is a motto that has come down to the twentieth century. Remember that the Irish memory is long and that the past is always recalled to inspire the present.

The Irish people were quite unable to maintain living standards. Most people had to depend on their staple crop, the potato. If there was a crop failure, starvation threatened almost the entire population. This danger meant that the Irish were desperate to secure more land. As numbers grew, the amount of land available decreased – because the land-owning class refused to cut up their huge estates. Consequently, Irish farmers were tenant farmers most of whom paid their rent in kind (wheat).

Rapid change

During the Napoleonic Wars, the price of corn rose and Irish farmers were relatively prosperous. Then came the decline after 1815. Estate owners were keen to clear their estates and increase their pastoral acreage. Beef cattle became an important export and the estate owners were perfectly willing to evict their tenant farmers so that they could grow more grass. Soon there was a surplus of labour. If an Irish labourer could not work on the land three options faced him:

1   starvation;
2   beggary;
3   emigration.

Conclusions

1   There seems little doubt that the British government was responsible for the social and economic distress that characterised Ireland 1800–45.
  (*a*)   No attempt to change the system of landlord-tenant farming.
  (*b*)   No attempt to end evictions.
  (*c*)   No attempt to deal with social results.
  This determined display of *laissez-faire* was probably worse than its equivalent in England during the period up to 1846.
2   The British government regarded natural Irish reaction to this state of affairs (secret societies, robberies) as sheer terrorism – and acted accordingly.

THE IRISH FAMINE 1846–7

Daniel O'Connell

Most Irish politicians could see no way to remedy the social and economic injustices in Ireland; so they tried to find a political solution, i.e. by repealing the 1800 Act of Union. Most famous was Daniel O'Connell (1775–1847). He succeeded in:

1   repealing the old Test and Corporation Acts (1828);
2   pushing through the 1829 Catholic Relief Act giving the vote to £10 freeholders (there were very few of these!)
  He then tried to secure 'self-rule' for Ireland (with Queen Victoria remaining as monarch) – and finished up in jail. There were no political answers to the Irish problems at this time.

THE POTATO BLIGHT

Read the following account:

> Potato blight is caused by the fungus *Phytophthora infestans*. It flourishes in warm, wet conditions – as in Ireland. The fungus spores devour potato leaves and invade the potato tubers underground. Nowadays, we can control this with a Bordeaux mixture (copper compounds) – sprayed on the crops. Nobody knew this in 1845. The blight destroyed most of the potato crop that year.

1 What conditions in Ireland encouraged the spread of the potato blight?
2 From which country did the blight come?
3 Who was the British Prime Minister at that time?
4 There was a saying in Ireland: 'You can't eat the rent'. What was the 'rent' and why didn't the Irish eat it when the potato crop failed in 1845?

Conditions were terrible in the winter of 1845–6 and Peel decided that:

1 he must repeal the Corn Laws (he did this in 1846);
2 he must import cheap corn (maize) to help the Irish – and he arranged for these imports.

However, events overtook Peel's plans. The 1846 crop failed.

Results

This began the 'flight of the Irish'. *Read this account*:

> The crop failure led to the 'great hunger' which forced thousands of starving peasants to wander in search of food. Gifts of money poured in from England, the USA and India. Wealthy families such as the Barings headed subscription lists and Queen Victoria donated £2000. But it wasn't enough to buy the food so desperately needed by the Irish people. And it certainly wasn't enough to deal with the results of famine – typhus, cholera and scurvy. In terror, thousands of starving Irish, many of them diseased, abandoned their mud cabins and set sail for either England or America. This mass exodus went on until the end of 1847 and spread disease in cities as far apart as Manchester and New York. Then came yet another crop failure. By the end of 1848 starvation was worse than ever before and within a couple of months the Irish were swearing that 'the land is cursed'.

It is important to understand that this appalling famine took place at a time when State intervention in human affairs was only just beginning. In 1846–9, the mechanism of State relief organisations was totally unable to cope with the Irish problem. The statistics are horrific. At the time of increasing English prosperity and political stability, at the time of the Great Exhibition:

1   over one million Irish died of starvation and disease;

2   well over 2 million emigrated.

'This was the greatest disease in modern British history.' Do you agree?

Consider the following two points:

1   The failure to deal with the potato blight led to a legacy of permanent Irish hatred for the English – still apparent in Ireland and the USA today.

2   The results (paralysis of agriculture, social disaster through death or emigration) led to economic stagnation in Ireland for a century.

Where did the responsibility rest?

The failure to develop a constructive, humane policy towards Ireland was due:

1   *To the ignorance of the British ruling class about Irish conditions.* Many were absentee landlords, controlling the affairs of their Irish estates through 'middlemen'. They were always keen to find out facts about Ireland – there were scores of parliamentary inquiries into Irish affairs during 1800–40. But they revealed little about the Irish people.

2   *To their ignorance of Irish psychology.* There was no attempt to present the suffering of the Irish people to the British (as was done, for example, by Select Committees into the suffering of children in the coal mines and factories). Consequently, there was no fund of sympathy among the English for the suffering of the Irish.

THE LIBERAL ATTEMPT TO SOLVE THE IRISH PROBLEMS

'My mission is to pacify Ireland'

One of the most remarkable prime ministers of the nineteenth century, Gladstone devoted a great deal of effort to solving the 'Irish question'.

The problem was made up of three parts:

1   religious grievances;

2   economic problems – the ownership of the land;

3   political problems – how should Ireland be governed?

RELIGION

Once the British had granted 'Catholic emancipation' it was reasonable to conciliate the majority Catholic population as much as possible:

1837   Collection of tithe ended.

1845   Roman Catholic college at Maynooth given a major grant for training priests.

Gladstone's view was that the Protestant Church in Ireland should no longer be the official church – it must be disestablished now that so many more Irish had the vote (following the 1867 Reform Act). He therefore disestablished the Church in Ireland (1869).

LAND TENURE

Despite the emigration and the deaths through famine and disease, conditions for the Irish peasant did not improve. Gladstone wanted all people to have the same privileges as those enjoyed in Ulster where a tenant could secure compensation for any improvements he had carried out when he left his rented property.

1870 Land Act extended this area to the whole of Ireland.

1881 Land Act gave the Irish peasant the 'Three Fs'
1 fair rents;
2 free sale;
3 fixity of tenure.

GOVERNING IRELAND

Catholic Irish opinion was, generally speaking, in favour of repeal of the 1800 Act of Union with Britain. How this was to be done caused disagreement.

By force – the view of the Fenians and the 'Young Ireland Movement'.

By constitutional change – the view of Charles Stewart Parnell (1846–91) who took over the leadership of the Home Rule Association (founded by Isaac Butt in 1870).
     Parnell soon had a great deal of support – especially in the House of Commons where eighty-six of the Irish MPs (in 1886) were for Home Rule. Gladstone was converted to this also – but the majority of the British people were not, especially after they read in their newspapers of:
1 Mounting crime in the Irish countryside.
2 The Phoenix Park murders (1882) – Lord Cavendish (the newly appointed Chief Secretary of Ireland) was hacked to death with surgical knives by a terrorist group called the Invincibles.
Parnell was appalled – he called the murders a 'stab in the back'.

The First Home Rule Bill 1886 Gladstone defeated by 343 votes to 313 and defeated in the following General Election.

The Second Home Rule Bill 1892 Passed by the Commons but thrown out by the Lords.
     So Gladstone, 'the old man in a hurry', had failed.
     The Conservatives had always opposed the Liberal notion of Home Rule and tried to bring about reforms without granting the Irish their ultimate hopes.

The 1903 Land Act This redistributed the land and at last made Ireland into a nation of peasant proprietors.

The last Liberal attempt to grant Ireland Home Rule came in April 1912 when Asquith brought in the **Third Home Rule Bill**. By then it was impossible to reconcile the differences that existed in Ireland:

1   the Ulster Protestants, now living in the most industrially developed part of Ireland and in the majority within their region;

2   the majority Catholic Nationalists (75 per cent of the population), mostly in agriculture.

Ulster's 'Orangemen' formed the Ulster Volunteers; the Nationalists created their Irish Volunteers. Both sides acquired arms from abroad.

IRELAND DURING THE FIRST WORLD WAR 1914–18

Irish Nationalist leaders such as John Redmond (1856–1918) and James Connolly (1870–1916) disagreed on their attitude towards Germany. Redmond urged members of his own 'National Volunteers' to join the British Army; Connolly's own Citizen Army, joined by the Sinn Fein (Ourselves Alone) movement, plotted rebellion. So in 1916 some Irishmen were fighting the British, while others were going over the top with the British Army at the Battle of the Somme.

THE EASTER REBELLION IN IRELAND 1916

Sinn Fein and Connolly depended on German help to ensure the success of their rebellion against the British – and on the assistance of a renegade British diplomat, Sir Roger Casement. Casement landed by U-boat at Banna (April 1916) to warn the rebels they could expect no help from Germany at that stage of the war. The British captured Casement and executed him. In Galway, Wexford and Dublin the Irish Nationalists attempted their uprising at Easter.

Said Connolly in Dublin: 'The chances against us are a thousand to one.' He was right. During Easter week he occupied the General Post Office in Dublin and proclaimed the Irish Republic. 5000 British troops attacked the main rebel defence points and when the rebel surrendered they were tried by court martial.

Fifteen were shot. Eamon de Valera, a Nationalist battalion commander, was to have been shot but his US passport saved him from execution.

Results

1   British military might failed to crush the spirit of Ireland's nationalist population.

2   They had no more time for Home Rule – they didn't intend to remain as second-class members of the British Empire.

3   They now wanted their natural right of self-determination, an independent Republic of Ireland.

Look at this poster. Its contents were read out by Patrick Pearse when he was standing on the steps of the GPO – the start of the Easter Rebellion 1916:

**POBLACHT NA H EIREANN
THE PROVISIONAL GOVERNMENT
OF THE
IRISH REPUBLIC to THE PEOPLE OF
IRELAND**

IRISHMEN AND IRISHWOMEN: In the name of God and of the dead generations from which she receives her old tradition of nationhood, Ireland, through us, summons her children to her flag and strikes for her freedom.

Having organised and trained her manhood through her secret revolutionary organisation, the Irish Republican Brotherhood, and through her open military organisations, the Irish Volunteers and the Irish Citizen Army, having patiently perfected her discipline, having resolutely waited for the right moment to reveal itself, she now seizes that moment, and, supported by her exiled children in America and by gallant allies in Europe, but relying in the first on her own strength, she strikes in full confidence of victory . . . In this supreme hour the Irish nation must, by its valour and discipline, and by the readiness of its children to sacrifice themselves for the common good, prove itself worthy of the august destiny to which it is called.

Signed on behalf of the Provisional Government
Thomas J. Clarke, Sean Mac Diarmada,
Thomas MacDonagh, P. H. Pearse, Eammon Ceannt,
James Connolly, Joseph Plunkett.

---

1   What were the colours of the Irish flag?
2   What was the name of the secret revolutionary organisation?
3   What was 'the right moment'?
4   Who were her 'gallant allies in Europe'?
5   What is meant by 'exiled children in America'?

THE CREATION OF THE IRISH FREE STATE

THE IRISH NATIONALISTS The 1918 Election had given Sinn Fein seventy-three seats and the Irish Nationalists ten seats in Parliament at Westminster. Some of these MPs met in Dublin and on 21 January 1919 set up the Dáil – the national assembly of the 'Republic of Ireland'.

The Dáil

1 It elected Eamon de Valera as President of the new 'Republic'.
2 It tried and failed to secure representation at the Paris Peace Conference.
3 It encouraged people to use 'Republican courts' instead of British justice.
4 It persuaded expatriate Irish (in the USA, Dominions and in Britain) to contribute to an 'Irish Nationalist Loan'. With the money the Dáil created the Irish Republican Army (the IRA).

Reaction

A very worried British government banned the Dáil; and began to ready itself for a fight against Irish nationalists officered by men who regarded British troops as aliens, as members of an enemy occupation force.

WAR IN IRELAND 1919–21

As early as January 1919 the IRA newspaper, *An t'Oglach*, had proclaimed that a state of war existed between Britain and Ireland. Led by Michael Collins and Arthur Griffiths, the IRA formed its brigades across the entire country and began infiltrating British security and intelligence organisations.

Read this account of the conflict

Recruits from Britain arrived to reinforce the armed RIC, the Royal Irish Constabulary. Most notorious were the Black and Tans, issued with khaki uniforms and the black belts and dark green caps of the RIC; and the Auxis, ex-officers of the Auxiliary Division recruited as military leaders of the RIC. By 1920 the IRA had a maximum strength of 15,000; while the British stationed 45,000 troops and armed police in the turbulent island. Both sides then committed atrocities. 'Bloody Sunday' was 21 November 1920 when the IRA hauled fourteen British officers and civilians out of their beds and murdered them; in the afternoon the Black and Tans drove into Croke Park football ground in Dublin and shot up the crowd. They killed twelve and wounded sixty. On 11 December the Tans and Auxis set fire to Cork and then on 25 May 1921 the IRA burnt Dublin Customs House, only to lose six dead and seventy captured in the battle that followed. Each incident was deplorable. But it was the general picture of the complete breakdown of British rule and the spectre of armed bands roaming Ireland at will that forced the government to seek a political solution for all Ireland's troubles.

1 Explain the meaning of RIC, IRA, Auxis and Black and Tans.
2 What uniform did the Black and Tans wear?
3 What side do you think uttered the following:
'Are we to lie down while our comrades are being shot in cold blood? We say: Never! Stop the shooting of police or we will lay low every house that smells of Sinn Fein.'
4 What does the expression 'Sinn Fein' mean?
5 What kind of solution could the British government recommend for Ireland?

The 1920 Act

The 1920 Government of Ireland Act proposed the partition of Ireland into the North (six counties) and the South (twenty six counties). There would be a northern parliament at Belfast and a southern parliament at Dublin.

Note This was not seen as a permanent arrangement. One day, it was said, there would be 'harmonious action' – a parliament for the whole of Ireland. But, at the time, this Act allowed the Ulster counties to remain part of the UK and for the South to have some measure of freedom.

Reaction of the IRA

They wanted an independent Ireland and no division between North and South. They agreed to a truce (July 1921) and began negotiations for a peace treaty.

The 1921 Treaty

1 The South became the Irish Free State. It had full dominion status.
2 The Irish Free State would allow the Royal Navy to use the harbours at Queenstown, Berehaven, Lough Swilly and Belfast Lough.
Prime Minister Lloyd George signed the treaty in London on 6 December 1921.

Reaction in the South

Civil war flared. De Valera resigned. He opposed the Irish Free State leadership. The Irish government now had to deal with its own insurgents. Internment camps and mass executions became common. Order was restored in 1923 – by then Northern Ireland had opted out of the Irish Free State and the last British forces had sailed from Dublin. After centuries of conflict, Ireland was free, but partitioned.

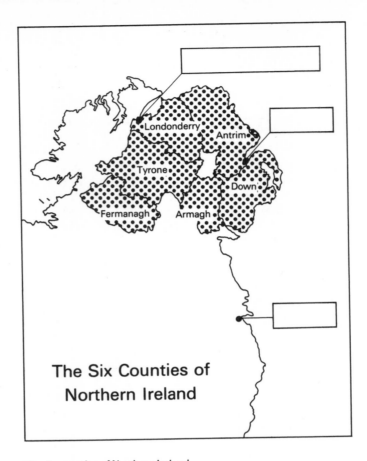

The six counties of Northern Ireland

1   Mark Londonderry in the correct box.
2   Indicate the capital of Northern Ireland.
3   Mark the capital of Ireland in the correct box.
     A note on the 1937 Constitution of Eire
     It stated that the national territory included the whole of Ireland but that, pending
     integration of North and South Irish law would not operate in the Six Counties (of course,
     there was no way that it could!)
         De Valera also ruled that the first language of Ireland would be Irish; English would be
     the second language.
         De Valera (1882–1975) was of half-Spanish decent and was born in New York. He
     joined the National Irish Volunteers before the First World War and after he was released
     (he had been imprisoned for his part in the 1916 Easter Rebellion), he formed his new
     party (Fianna Fail – soldiers of destiny).

Consider Collins' view of the treaty:

         Think what I have got for Ireland – something which she has

wanted this past 700 years. This treaty is the first step for Ireland. If people will only remember that, the first real step.

What do you think was in Collins' mind when he said that?

CONDITIONS IN NORTHERN IRELAND 1923–39

These were the worst in the UK during the 1920s and 1930s – especially housing conditions.

1   There was a chronic shortage of cash.
2   Ulster suffered mass unemployment.
3   There was constant violence.
4   The housing stock was largely sub-standard.

Note that unemployment payments in Belfast were lower than in any other British city. They averaged about £0.80 a week for a family of four. The local authority levied minuscule rates – incapable of providing even basic services to Protestant and Catholic families huddled in a warren of streets around Belfast Docks.

> House-burning was always a feature of sectarian riots and during 1934–5 Northern Ireland actually had its own refugee problem when homeless people had to have temporary housing on the Falls Road and in the Ardoyne.
>
> (British textbook)

Why was there such a serious house shortage in Belfast during this period?

EFFECT OF THE CREATION OF EIRE 1937

De Valera returned to power and began to break all links with Britain. He wanted, he said, to stop Ireland being 'the kitchen garden for supplying the British with cheap food'. Yet in 1938 Ireland was selling 90 per cent of its exports to Britain; and Britain was supplying Ireland with 80 per cent of its imports. The creation of Eire as a 'sovereign and independent democratic state' made little impact, although De Valera managed to regain Lough Swilly and Berehaven (Anglo-Irish Agreement 1938). De Valera claimed the Six Counties of Ulster as part of Eire and it was therefore up to the IRA to keep the Republican spirit alive in the northern province by means of violence and strike action.

1   Lord Craigavon (Prime Minister of Northern Ireland 1921 – 1940) managed to suppress most of the IRA units operating in the province.
2   The Royal Ulster Constabulary and the B-Specials arrested most of the top IRA leaders and prevented a major bombing campaign in the province (1938).
3   The IRA formally declared war on Britain (16 January 1939) and stepped up its bombing campaign.
4   The British passed the **1939 Prevention of Violence Act** to enable the government to expel IRA suspects from Britain.

5   In August 1939 (just before the outbreak of war) IRA terrorists exploded a bomb in a Coventry shopping centre, killing five people and wounding over fifty.

NORTHERN IRELAND SINCE 1945

During the Second World War many Irishmen – North and South – served with distinction in the armed forces. Ireland suffered air attack – on Belfast and (accidentally) Dublin. Eire was not at war with Germany and in 1949 it left the Commonwealth and set itself up as the independent Republic of Ireland. Northern Ireland (variously known as the Province, Ulster, the Six Counties) remained firmly a part of the UK.

In 1949 the Attlee Government defined its status thus:

> Parliament hereby declares that Northern Ireland remains part of her Majesty's Dominions and of the United Kingdom and affirms that in no event will Northern Ireland or any part thereof cease to be part of His Majesty's Dominions and of the United Kingdom without the consent of the Parliament of Northern Ireland.

THE STORMONT GOVERNMENT

The Northern Ireland Parliament was at Stormont and stood for the rule of the Unionist Party to the disadvantage of the substantial Catholic minority left in the North after the 1920 partition.
Discrimination against the Catholics was intense:
1   in the Belfast shipyards;
2   in housing.
Hatred between the two communities was fanned by:
1   the divisive teaching given in sectarian schools.
2   the activities of the Ulster Special Constabulary. Recruited entirely from Protestants, the Ulster B-Specials were part-time policemen who carried out patrols, searches and 'snatches', manned checkpoints and generally harassed the Catholic civilian population at times of IRA activity.

THE IRA

Up to 1962 it put most of its efforts into bombing campaigns. In the mid-1960s it became linked with the Catholic 'Civil Rights' movements in Ulster. The Northern Ireland Civil Rights Association (1967) persuaded Stormont to promise the end of discrimination and to satisfy the basic demand of 'one man, one vote' in local elections. Stormont did nothing and when the Apprentice Boys carried out their provocative march in Londonderry (1968) there was widespread disorder. Two significant events took place:

1   The IRA split into the 'Official' and 'Provisional' wings. The Provisionals (Provos) launched a military campaign to destroy Northern Ireland and eliminate the Ulster government at Stormont.
2   The British Army arrived to reinforce the UDR (Ulster Defence Regiment) and to replace the B-Specials – disbanded in 1969.

THE VIOLENCE

Civil law and order began to collapse in Ulster.
1   11,000 soldiers were on duty in Londonderry, Belfast and along the border with Ireland.
2   New political parties emerged 1970–1:
(a)   middle-class Catholic Social Democratic and Labour Party (SDLP).
(b)   Democratic Unionist Party (DUP) led by the Rev. Ian Paisley.
Stormont Prime Minister Faulkner made matters worse in 1971 when he brought in internment as a means of imprisoning political suspects without trial – it appeared that Stormont was prepared to abolish all civil rights in Ulster just to stay in power.
    Then came another 'Bloody Sunday' (30 January 1972) when British soldiers killed thirteen men in Londonderry. By March the disorder was so widespread that Edward Heath, British Prime Minister, decided to abolish Stormont and rule Ulster directly from Westminster. Still the Provos kept up their offensive. By October 1972 they were demanding:
1   An amnesty for all the newly imprisoned political prisoners.
2   A fixed date for the withdrawal of all British soldiers.
3   A referendum on the future of Ulster in which all Irish people, north and south of the border, could take part.

THE BRITISH RESPONSE

1   Local elections based on universal suffrage.
2   A new constitution in which Catholics and Protestants would engage in 'power-sharing'.
3   A new Northern Ireland Assembly and Northern Ireland Executive that would bring peace to the province.
However, a general strike called by the Protestant Ulster Workers' Council brought down the new executive and assembly and forced Britain to resume direct rule.

THE URBAN GUERRILLAS

By then the Provos were highly organised guerrilla fighters equipped with:
–   car bombs and letter bombs;
–   radio-controlled explosives and wire-controlled land-mines;
–   Armalite rifles and Soviet rocket launchers.

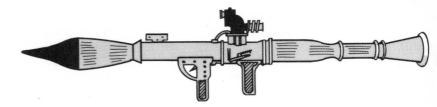

Soviet rocket launchers, as used by the IRA. The RPG–7V anti-tank rocket launcher fires a warhead capable of penetrating armour over 12 in (300 mm) thick. An example was captured 26 May 1981

They had plenty of money – dollars from the USA and profits from the shebeens (illegal drinking clubs run by the IRA). Hunger strikes and assassinations kept the IRA – and others such as the Irish National Liberation Army (INLA) – in the news. Men convicted of murder and bombing attacks went on hunger-strike in H-block, the most publicised part of Belfast's Maze Prison. They demanded to be treated as political prisoners, not as criminals; and their hunger-strike culminated on 5 May 1981 with the death of Bobby Sands. By then, well over 2000 other people had died – including, on one horrific day in August 1979, eighteen British soldiers at Warren Point and Lord Louis Mountbatten, murdered with members of his family while on a boating holiday in Sligo Bay.

SOCIAL EFFECTS OF VIOLENCE

Ulster's social services struggled to survive.
1   Most schools and colleges remained open.
2   Hospital surgeons became expert in the treatment of blast and firearms injuries.
3   The Emergency Housing Scheme operated efficiently in the worst hit parts of Belfast.
4   People were under stress. If they went shopping they ran the risk of being hit by a rubber bullet or suffering from CS gas. Yet there was virtually no increase in the number of psychiatric patients (compare the similar experience of the British people under air attack 1940–45).
5   Nevertheless, violence made a great impact on people's lives and prospects: destruction of shops, warehouses, buses and factories caused unemployment and short time; while unstable environment didn't encourage private firms to invest in Ulster's industry.
Overall, the social and economic life of the province suffered.

THE ANGLO-IRISH AGREEMENT 1985

During the Conservative Party's Conference at Brighton (October 1984) a bomb exploded at the Grand Hotel where most of the government ministers were staying. Margaret Thatcher had a narrow escape. Norman Tebbit was badly injured. This did not lead to a massive campaign against the IRA. Instead, Margaret Thatcher negotiated with the Dublin government. The 1985 Anglo-Irish Agreement resulted, giving Dublin a voice in the administration of Northern Ireland, especially with regard to counter-terrorist policies and the rights of the Catholic minority. Ulster's reaction as far as the Protestant Unionists were concerned was predictable. They saw the 1985 Anglo-Irish Agreement as something they had always feared – the first step towards the eventual reunification of Ireland.

1 RUC officers were attacked by members of their own community.
2 Widespread intimidation and violence along the border after the signing of the Agreement.
3 Catholic families, tolerated up to then, were displaced. As one Catholic said about his Protestant neighbours:
'Because I was a Catholic they now think I'm in the Provos.'
4 There was a sudden rise in sectarian killings – over 600 attacks in the first year after the Agreement was signed.
Why were so many Ulster people hostile to the Anglo-Irish Agreement?
Now examine these materials taken from Irish newspapers published during the 1960s.

1 'In 1914 John Redmond sought to purchase a measure of Home Rule from Britain by offering a gift of Irish youth to the British war machine.'
Explain in detail the meaning of this sentence.
2 'Sinn Fein in the years from 1914 to 1918 gave the Irish people an opportunity of demonstrating their opposition to, and detestation of, the Redmond policy.'
What precisely did the Sinn Fein do?
3 These words and the map of Ireland appeared on a banner carried in a demonstration during the 1960s. Who do you think was carrying it – a Unionist or an Irish Nationalist?

BRITAIN AND EUROPE SINCE 1789

THE FRENCH WARS
1793–1815

CONTENTS

THE FRENCH DECLARATION OF WAR ON BRITAIN 1793

William Pitt the Younger (1759–1806) had been Prime Minister since 1783. He had no wish to fight the French and was forced into hostilities when Revolutionary France (then governed by the Revolutionary Convention) declared war on Britain, Holland and Spain in February 1793.

Why did France declare war?

France had been in a state of near financial and economic collapse during the 1780s and King Louis XVI had taken the unprecedented step of calling a meeting of the States-General (roughly the French equivalent of the English Parliament) in the hope of raising extra money through direct taxation. Within the States-General, the Third Estate (dominated by the rising French middle-class) opposed the King's ideas. Their opposition led to the capture of the Bastille on 14 July 1789 (Quatorze Juillet) by workers from the Parisian suburb of St Antoine, to the *Declaration of the Rights of Man* (26 August 1789) and to the virtual imprisonment of King Louis XVI and Marie Antoinette. Many French nobles had tried to escape the avenging French revolutionaries and had gathered along the French frontier. It was to these that King Louis made his dramatic and unsuccessful 'Flight to Varennes' (1791) and from this moment there was a danger of war in Europe. The rulers of Prussia, Spain, Austria and Britain all feared that the ideas of the French Revolution would infiltrate their own countries.

War began in 1792 between France and Austria and the French armies won important victories at Valmy and Jemappes. French confidence was never higher: the Convention now issued its *Edict of Fraternity and Assistance*, promising help to all peoples who wanted to throw off tyrannical rule (such as had existed in France under the *Ancien Régime*) and win their liberty. Clearly, France was inviting trouble from the rest of Europe, but the radical leaders of France (Georges Danton 1759–94; Maximilien de Robespierre 1758–94) were quite ruthless in their determination to win military victory abroad and eliminate all opponents, inside and outside France. They did not hesitate to declare war on three major maritime powers, Britain, Holland and Spain, in 1793.

Pitt's reactions

Automatically, he adopted the traditional British policy towards an enemy on the Continent of Europe:

1 offer gold to European allies in return for military help;
2 attack any colonial possessions (France had many), raid her trade routes and blockade the enemy ports.

These tactics proved futile.

Pitt therefore sought to build up great coalitions of nations to defeat France by sheer weight of numbers. In 1793 he formed the First Coalition – Austria, Spain, Prussia, Holland and Britain.

The British contribution

1 The Royal Navy continued its blockading tactics and was notably unsuccessful at the Glorious First of June battle (1794) in preventing the French grainships from reaching port.
2 Their attempts to crush the French in the West Indies failed because of the epidemic of yellow fever among British servicemen.

Britain's difficulties

Although Britain managed to keep apart from the complicated land campaigns on the Continent she faced two very real dangers at home

Mutinies in the Royal Navy The Spithead Mutiny was a revolt against poor pay and conditions; but the Nore Mutiny was a direct threat to naval authority and was dealt with ruthlessly. Its leader, Richard Parker and twenty-eight supporters were hanged.

The threat from Ireland The many ports scattered along the west coast of Ireland could provide a useful springboard for an invasion of Britain Wolfe Tone (1763–98) led an abortive Irish rebellion – and when a small French army arrived to help, it was too late.

So Pitt survived the early problems caused by the French Revolutionary War and concentrated on forming his Second Coalition (1799) Turkey, Austria, Russia, Britain.

1 Why were Holland, Spain, Prussia and Austria not members of the Second Coalition?
2 What had happened to King Louis XVI in 1793?
3 What happened to Danton and Robespierre in 1794?
4 Look at the map opposite and insert in the correct boxes:

> The Revolt of the United Irishmen 1798
> The Glorious First of June 1794
> The Spithead Mutiny 1797
> The Nore Mutiny 1797

THE THREAT FROM NAPOLEON

In May 1798 Napoleon Bonaparte (1769–1821) set sail from Toulon in command of a fleet carrying 36,000 French soldiers. Their objective was Egypt – Napoleon hoped to occupy the whole of the Middle East

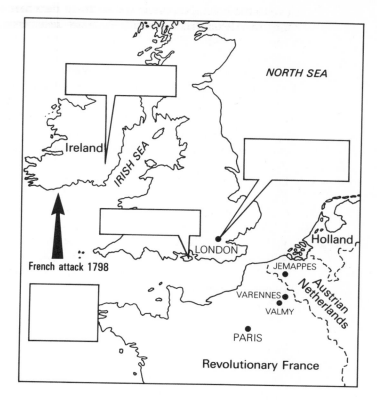

NORTH SEA

Ireland

IRISH SEA

French attack 1798

LONDON

Holland

JEMAPPES

VARENNES

VALMY

PARIS

Austrian Netherlands

Revolutionary France

Some British difficulties 1794–8

and wreck British trade in the region. As he put it to the five Directors (the Revolutionary Directorate now governed France), the best way of attacking England, apart from an invasion, was to take over *le commerce des Indes*. He had urged the Directorate to do something – otherwise France would have to make peace with the English. The British Admiralty knew nothing of Napoleon's plans until he was near Malta – they were more worried about another French invasion of Ireland. Now they ordered Admiral Nelson (1758–1805) into the Mediterranean to discover the intentions of the French.

The Battle of the Nile 1798

The British fleet had had a chequered career up to 1798.

1 The Glorious First of June (1794) had failed in its main objective.
2 The fleet had managed to beat the Spanish at the Battle of Cape St Vincent (1797).
3 Despite the naval mutinies (1797) it had beaten the Dutch at the Battle of Camperdown (where Nelson had been second in command) in 1797.

Now Nelson was determined to defeat the French fleet in the Mediterranean – wherever they were. He found them at Aboukir Bay –

close to the Nile. (Napoleon had anchored them there as there was no room in Alexandria harbour.) *Audacious* broke through the French line while other British warships sailed behind the French to take them on their 'blind' side. There were thirteen French ships of the line – eleven were destroyed. It was a great victory for Nelson on a day that would bring him, he said, 'a peerage or Westminster'.

Napoleon then began a somewhat futile invasion of Syria, with his main forces left in Egypt to oppose Nelson's blockade. He returned to Egypt and slipped away from the Nile in a frigate (the *Muiron*), evaded the British fleet and returned to France. There he overthrew the Directorate and became First Consul of France (the event is known as the Revolution of Brumaire). In 1802, despite his failure in Egypt, Napoleon became Consul for life; in 1804 he became Emperor of the French.

1　Why did Napoleon undertake the conquest of Egypt?
2　Why were the British surprised by this move?
3　When did Napoleon become Consul for life?
　　What did Nelson mean when he said the day would bring him 'a peerage or Westminster'?
5　What reward did Nelson receive after his victory at the Battle of the Nile?

The Peace of Amiens 1802

At first, Napoleon sought peace at home and abroad. He intended to carry out many reforms inside France. He said: 'My policy is to govern men as the great majority wish to be governed.'

Two major areas of change would be in

1　the French system of taxation;
2　the French system of local government.

Napoleon therefore negotiated the Peace of Amiens, signed by Britain, France, Spain and Holland on 27 March 1802. This gave Britain a fourteen month breathing space to reorganise her fighting forces. One significant term in the treaty was Napoleon's willingness to agree to the independence of Portugal, Britain's oldest ally.

Note: the British government signed the treaty with reluctance – it distrusted Napoleon's military intentions. However, Napoleon enjoyed a brief popularity among the British people as the man who made the peace. Normally, mothers frightened their children by saying: 'If you don't do what I tell you, old Boney will get you!'

War resumed in May 1803 and it is usual to date the 'Napoleonic Wars' from then.

THE NAPOLEONIC WARS 1803–15

THE GRAND DESIGN

Having declared war on England, Napoleon began to prepare for a cross-Channel invasion.

1   He closed all French ports to British trade.
2   He ordered the building of more ships of the line – his ambition was to have at least a hundred!
In 1804 Britain reacted by declaring a blockade of all French ports in the Channel and the North Sea.

The Royal Navy was much bigger than the French fleet and Napoleon knew he would have to trick the English into believing that his main attack would come somewhere else in the world – in Africa or in the West Indies. Though the Royal Navy could actually see Napoleon's invasion camp being built at Boulogne, it had to take the possibility of a French naval diversion very seriously.

Napoleon believed that if he could win control of the Channel – just for a week or so – while the Royal Navy was desperately searching for his missing fleet in the Atlantic or the Mediterranean, he could transport an army to England. 'We must have a model of a flat-bottomed boat, able to transport a hundred men across the Channel.' Such boats, of course, would be at the mercy of any warship of the Royal Navy.

The Battle of Trafalgar 21 October 1805

In 1805 the French fleet broke out of Toulon and sailed westwards across the Atlantic. Nelson sailed after it, in hot pursuit. Then the French evaded the British, changed course and headed back to Europe. Said Napoleon: 'With God's help, I will put an end to the future and the very existence of England.'

The French admiral, Villeneuve, was now supposed to link up with the Spanish fleet, set sail to Boulogne, and then cover the invasion of England. But Admiral Nelson caught the Franco–Spanish fleet off Cape Trafalgar and won the greatest victory in the history of sea-warfare.

1   It gave Britain the monopoly of the high seas.
2   It forced the remnants of the French fleet to spend the rest of the war rotting away in Napoleon's ports.
3   It forced Napoleon to abandon his 'Great Design'.
4   It compelled him to undertake a form of economic warfare against Britain that tried to compensate for his lack of seapower – he decided to blockade Britain by refusing to allow any European port to accept British goods.

Read this extract from a British textbook

Unchallenged on the Continent, Napoleon devised a scheme to counter British naval supremacy *par la puissance de terre* – by defeating seapower with land power. He would forbid all open commerce between European seaports and the English, but he would condone smuggling. This would force the English to pay high prices for smuggled goods; and this would mean their gold reserves would dwindle. And if they tried to pay by smuggling their own manufactured goods into

Europe, Napoleon would confiscate them and use them for his own war effort. Such was the substance of Napoleon's Continental System announced in the Berlin Decrees (1806). Britain retaliated with her Orders in Council (1807) and prohibited all trade between one French-occupied port and another. Quite deliberately, the two warring nations upset the whole economy of Western Europe and unwittingly escalated the war throughout the Western Hemisphere.

1 Explain Napoleon's phrase *'par la puissance de terre'*.
2 Why was Napoleon ready to accept smuggling?
3 What did he call his plan?
4 When did he announce his Berlin decrees?
5 How did Britain respond?
   Now look at the map below showing Napoleon's conquest of Europe. Which important part of Europe still stayed outside Napoleon's control?

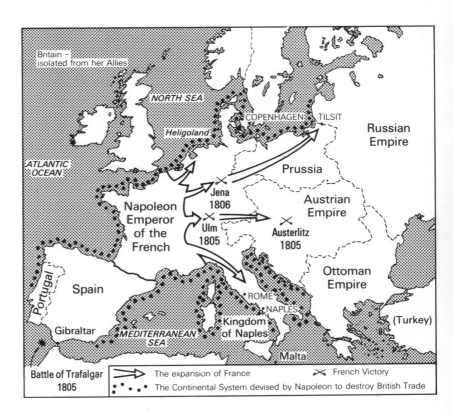

The expansion of France and the Continental System

The death of Pitt the Younger
Nelson's death at Trafalgar caused the British people to shower praise on Pitt the Younger. A very ill man, Pitt said, 'England has saved

herself by her exertions and will, I trust, save Europe by her example.' But he was not to be England's leader. He died on 23 January 1806.

Document 1

> Start, without losing a moment, and sail up the Channel with all the ships you have. England is ours. We are all ready: every man is on board. Appear for 24 hours and the thing is done.
>
> (letter written by Napoleon, 1805)

1   To whom was he writing?
2   'and the thing is done': explain.

Document 2

Sketch of Nelson's flagship at the Battle of Trafalgar, 1805. She was built in 1765, the cost then being £54,748, and was one of the fastest ships in the Royal Navy

1   This is Nelson's flagship at Trafalgar. What was its name?
2   Name the captain of the ship.
3   How was Nelson killed?

THE PENINSULAR WAR 1808–14

The Royal Navy now began searching out weak links in Napoleon's Continental system, capturing Heligoland and smashing the Danish Navy at the Battle of Copenhagen (1807). Napoleon tried to plug the gaps in his system and sent troops into the Iberian Peninsula (Spain and Portugal). British troops landed in the Peninsula at Lisbon (1808) under the command of Sir Arthur Wellesley (1769–1852), created the Duke of Wellington in 1810.

Wellington's task was to aid the Spanish guerrillas fighting the French occupation forces, to build up a strong base at the Lines of Torres Vedra outside Lisbon, and then move inland to drive the French out of the Iberian Peninsula. However, the British government had little confidence in Wellington's ability to win the war against Napoleon by means of a 'sideshow' called the Peninsular War. It therefore kept him short of men and supplies. Nevertheless, Wellington won a string of battles:

> *Talavera* (1809); *Fuentes de Onoro* (1811); *Salamanca* (1812); *Vittoria* (1813)

What was it like in the Peninsular War?

This is part of a letter written by Cpl Emmott, Royal Regiment of Horse Guards (The Blues). He went through the Peninsular War and wrote this letter during 1813, at the time of the Battle of Vittoria.

> I began to hear a rumbling in the air, which was ours, and the enemy was skirmishing and cannonading at this time. We advanced a little further. We met three or four hundred prisoners so we began to think it was time for us to look about us. By this time, the balls came whistling over us and about our ears. Presently falls two horses in front of me by a cannon ball going through them, but the men who rode them were not hurt at all. Now by this time we were in the very hottest of the battle, our Colonel being so fierce. But little could be seen or heard but dust, rattling of cannon, small arms and swords, shrieks and cries and moanings. Heads, hands, arms and legs and bodies falling in all directions . . . How shocking to the eye all this and other unmentionable scenes must be. I am a surety most unable to inform you of much that happened that day at or near Vittoria.
>
> Tell Mrs Heartly that I never had heard of her son John yet. My address is William Emmott, Corporal in Captain Parker's troops, Royal Regiment of Horse Guards, British Army, Spain or France.
>
> Credit: Major Hearson, Household Cavalry Training Cadre (1952)

1   Why did the appearance of several hundred prisoners jerk Cpl. Emmott's troop into action?
2   Why did the Corporal believe he was in the hottest part of the action?
3   Mark Vittoria on the map opposite.

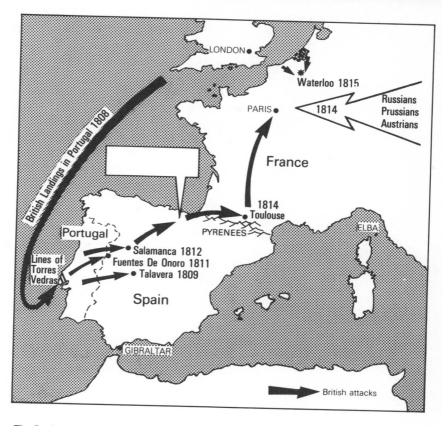

The Peninsular War, 1808–14, and the defeat of Napoleon, 1815

4 Why was the Corporal unable to give much detail about the battle?
5 Why do you think he gave the address of the British Army as 'Spain or France'?

By the time Wellington had crossed the Pyrenees and defeated the French at the Battle of Toulouse (1814), Napoleon had already abdicated. His long succession of victories had come to an end – he had been forced to evacuate Russian and German soil.

Napoleon's disastrous Russian campaign 1812

His *Grande Armée* had crossed the River Niemen on 24 June 1812. 250,000 men marched in search of the Russian army but the Russians skilfully retreated, adopting scorched-earth tactics to slow down the French advance. The first major obstacle was at Borodino – and here the Russian General Kutusov killed 30,000 of Napoleon's troops for the loss of 60,000 of his own men. After 'the bloodbath of Borodino' the Russians retreated east of Moscow and allowed the French to occupy the city. The day after Napoleon rode into the Kremlin, fires broke out all over Moscow and the French had to pull out of the city. He waited, expecting to hear that the Tsar of Russia would surrender.

But the Russians intended to fight on – especially as the weather was breaking. With 100,000 troops Napoleon left Moscow – at the mercy of frostbite, disease, starvation and Russian partisans.

In January 1813 about 13,000 survivors managed to escape from Russia.

Consider these two comments:

1 *Napoleon:* 'We fell a prey to the climate.'
2 *The Russians:* 'Not frost, not lack of provisions, but the counter-attacks under Kutusov, a patriotic effort embracing wide sections of the population, were the main causes of this cruel rout.'
Which of these two explanations for the defeat of Napoleon do you agree with, and why?

The Battle of the Nations 1813 and its results

Russian troops advanced through Prussia and helped to defeat the French at the Battle of the Nations (1813). In 1814 they were in Paris where they joined with Britain, Austria and Prussia in settling the First Treaty of Paris (1814). Napoleon was confined to the island of Elba, off Italy. The Great Powers then settled down to redrawing the map of Europe at the Congress of Vienna (1815). Wellington was actually in Vienna when the news that Napoleon had escaped came through. Wellington was immediately given command of the Allied Army of the Netherlands and moved to engage Napoleon on the field of Waterloo.

The Battle of Waterloo 1815

This was Napoleon's final defeat. He had more troops and guns than Wellington could put together and he attacked with the intention of capturing Brussels, the Allied HQ. The famous fighting squares of the British Army repelled Napoleon's attacks and advanced on the French. The final blow came with the arrival of Prussian reinforcements under Gebhard von Blücher (1742–1819). The Royal Navy took Napoleon into exile on St Helena where he died in 1821.

No 'Napoleon II' ever ruled France – though people who remained loyal to the memory of Napoleon Bonaparte always called his son, the Duke of Reichstadt, 'Napoleon II'. The Duke died in 1832.

The significance of the second defeat of Napoleon

After his first abdication (1814) the Allied Nations had signed the First Treaty of Paris (1814). This:

1 reduced France to her territorial limits of 1792;
2 made Louis XVIII King of France.
After Waterloo, the Allied Nations signed the Second Treaty of Paris (1815). This:
1 pushed France back to her 1790 frontiers;
2 forced France to pay an indemnity;
3 forced France to accept an Army of Occupation – Wellington stayed on as Commander-in-Chief until 1818.

Now the Great Powers could resume their diplomatic discussions in Vienna and devise the 'Congress Experiment' – the idea that the leading nations should always 'act in concert' to put down rebellions that might challenge the legality of the kings and emperors of Europe.

This became known as the 'Concert System'.

THE CONCERT
OF EUROPE

CONTENTS

Leading British ministers

Three remarkable foreign secretaries represented Britain's point of view and had a profound effect on international affairs during the period of the Concert of Europe.

Lord Castlereagh (1769–1822) was in office 1812–22. Castlereagh (his name is pronounced 'Castle-ray') was primarily interested in restoring the peace and balance of power in Europe. He wanted the Great Powers to stand by their treaty obligations and only intervene in the affairs of other countries when peace was threatened. Otherwise, the Great Powers would always be involved in the internal affairs of small states.

George Canning (1770–1827) was in office 1822–27. He realised that liberal, revolutionary movements all over the world could not be ignored and that changes in government must be recognised. While Castlereagh wanted to preserve the status quo as far as possible, Canning was willing to support certain revolutionary situations when they were seen to be beneficial to British interests. He identified the two main threats to international peace as France and Russia.

Lord Palmerston (1784–1865) broke with the Tory party in 1828 and served as a Whig Foreign Secretary as follows:

1830–4   under Earl Grey
1834   under Lord Melbourne
1835–41   under Lord Melbourne
1846–51   under Lord John Russell

He also served as Home Secretary (1852–5) under Lord Aberdeen and was twice Prime Minister (1855–8; 1859–65). He actively faced up to French and Russian attempts to extend their 'spheres of interest' in Europe and the Middle East and was in office during the Crimean War (1853–6) that saw the disintegration of the ideas behind the 'Concert of Europe'.

The leading European statesman

Prince Metternich (1773–1859) was an outstanding Austrian statesmen who had the most powerful influence over Europe's affairs from 1815 to 1848. He was committed to the preservation of the 'old order' in Europe, i.e. the idea that the aristocratic classes were best fitted to govern human affairs. He was opposed to any form of revolutionary change and he defined Europe's problems in the following way.

1   That all over the Continent there were 'partisans of revolution' plotting to overthrow existing governments. This was certainly true. German professors and their students were political activists and there was a great deal of disorder in the German states after 1815; there were several secret societies operating in Northern Italy; army officers were behind several plots in Spain and Russia; and there were plenty of radicals operating in Britain.

2   These conspiracies were being masterminded by some international organisation. He believed that Russia was the source of some sort of 'Eastern Jacobinism' and that Tsar Alexander I was unbalanced and probably the ringleader. Metternich was completely wrong in this analysis of the European situation after 1815. Read this account of Tsar Alexander I, who saw his role as 'the Russian policeman':

> Alexander had played an important part in the overthrow of Napoleon and it was natural that he would wish to see a world emerge in which there would be no more French Revolutions and no more Napoleons. Finland, 'Congress Poland' and Bessarabia gave him a bulwark in the west but he was anxious to prop up Austria and Prussia against any subversion. Yet he did not seem to understand that there was an increasing threat of revolution inside the Russian Empire. He had dragged millions of Poles, Caucasians and Aleuts under Russian imperial rule and they were bound to cause trouble in the future.

Do you think that Metternich misjudged Tsar Alexander's intentions?

THE CONCERT OF EUROPE AT WORK

THE CONGRESS OF VIENNA 1814–15

This had been interrupted by the reappearance of Napoleon and the Waterloo campaign. It had made the following decisions:

1   A new 'small' Poland (Congress Poland), placed under Russian control, together with Finland.

2   Denmark ceded Norway to Sweden.

3   The Low Countries (Beligum and Holland) were united into a single state.

4   Switzerland, the Prussian Rhineland and the Bavarian Palatinate were reconstituted so that they formed a barrier against possible French expansion.

There was no real attempt to settle the German problem (i.e. how to unify the numerous German states) or the Italian problem (Metternich described Italy as a 'geographical expression'). Everyone agreed that international rivers should be free from tolls and everyone promised to end the slave trade as quickly as possible. The peace settlement did seem to be a tidy and authoritative arrangement for Europe in 1815. The problem was: how could it be preserved?

THE HOLY ALLIANCE 1815

This was Tsar Alexander's idea. Everyone should sign a treaty acknowledging themselves as Christian brothers with their subjects as Christian children. They would all then be responsible to God for the proper government of their peoples, etc. Britain had no time for this – there were far too many radicals in Britain for the government to take anything but repressive action. No one asked the Sultan of Turkey for his views! But at least the idea gave a semblance of unity to Europe.

THE QUADRUPLE ALLIANCE 1815

This was to deal with the danger of revolutionary Jacobinism that might still linger on in France. So the signatories to this Alliance (Britain, Prussia, Austria and Russia) excluded the Napoleon dynasty for ever and stated that revolutionary ideas must never be allowed to menace the peace of Europe. Article 3 of the Alliance stated:

> The signatories would meet at another time to devise provisions for the maintenance of peace in Europe.

The processes that followed are called 'the Congress system'. It tried to deal with problems as they arose.

THE CONGRESS OF AIX-LA-CHAPELLE 1818

Metternich argued that members of the Qudruple Alliance should deal at once with any revolutionary outbreak, especially in France. Tsar Alexander disagreed – he said that it might be possible to provide 'liberal governments' in certain countries and thus undermine any revolutionary movement. Castlereagh also disagreed but for completely different reasons. His famous Memorandum stressed the following points:

1 Act in unison when peace is at risk.
2 The internal affairs of European states were not the concern of the Great Powers – unless peace was actually threatened.

A WAVE OF REVOLUTIONS

Europe 1819–21 saw widespread revolutionary movements and Metternich was anxious to crush them before they did 'harm'. He was worried that certain states (Saxe-Weimar, Baden, Bavaria and Wurtemberg) might give in to the revolutionaries. He was secretly delighted when the poet Kotzebue was stabbed to death at Weimar (1819) by students; this gave him a chance to instruct the German princes to crack down on student movements – the 1819 Karlsbad

Decrees. Castlereagh – very conscious of events in Britain – thoroughly approved! Tsar Alexander had his doubts – until revolutions began in Naples, Spain, Portugal and spread to the Spanish colonies in South America. The heir to the French throne, the Duc de Berry, was murdered.

THE CONGRESS OF TROPPAU 1820

Prussia and Russia supported Metternich's view that force must be used to bring back law and order. Castlereagh said no and explained:

1   A revolution was not necessarily a threat to international peace if it simply transformed the way in which one country was governed.
2   He argued that Metternich had no right to suggest concerted European action in these circumstances.
3   It seemed that Metternich was undermining the principle of national sovereignty!
    The view in Britain at the time was that 'we don't want any Cossacks in Hyde Park'.
       Can you explain this statement?
       Troppau was 'the parting of the ways'. The Great Powers could never agree on their role and function after this.

THE CONGRESS OF LAIBACH 1821

Here Castlereagh refused to approve Austria's intervention in a revolution in Naples. But in the middle of the Congress came news of the Greek Revolt against their Turkish masters. What would happen if the Tsar intervened (in his capacity as head of the Greek Orthodox Church)? The Russians would expand into South-East Europe and then into the Mediterranean. The Russians must be kept out. Castlereagh found a formula for doing this – but he committed suicide before the next Congress assembled. However, he had made notes and left instructions. The Duke of Wellington represented Britain at Verona.

THE CONGRESS OF VERONA 1822

Britain made her views crystal-clear:

1   She would not intervene to help anyone set up an independent state – it was up to the Greeks to achieve that for themselves.
2   But she would defend that state's right to exist once it had received international recognition.
    However, Austria, Russia and Prussia disagreed and authorised intervention in Spain (1823) – it had little effect.
       Foreign Secretary Canning made no effort to conceal the new British attitude. Of course, Britain could not act unilaterally and always had to try to persuade the other powers to act in a certain fashion. A good example is the Greek War of Independence.

THE GREEK WAR OF INDEPENDENCE 1821–7

Canning was anxious that Greeks should enjoy some measure of independence but remain within the Turkish (Ottoman) Empire. Eventually, Britain persuaded Russia and France to accept the idea. But the Greeks did not want this – they wanted full independence. This led to intervention against the Turks – the Battle of Navarino Bay (1827 – the year in which Canning died). Commanded by Vice-Admiral Codrington, a squadron of French, Russian and British warships sank about fifty Turkish ships. Many people in Britain thought this was a high price for Greek independence; without the Turkish navy to stop them, the Russians might move on Constantinople and sail into the Mediterranean.

The 1829 Treaty of Adrianople

This showed how strong the Russian influence was becoming. By this, the Turks were forced to leave Greece. Might not the Russians take advantage of the declining powers of Turkey who, later on, would be called 'the sick man of Europe'?

More immediately, the great powers were forced to concentrate their attention on the Belgian Revolt.

1 Map question

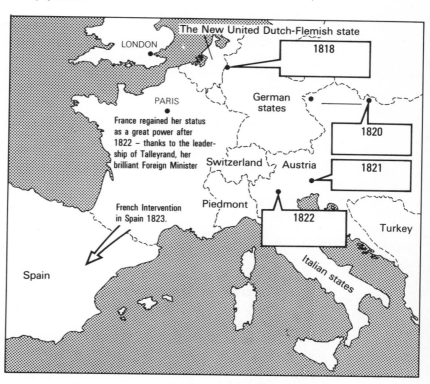

The Congress System

1   Mark the location of the four major Congresses in the boxes provided.
2   Shade in Austria.
3   Mark Karlsbad.

Multiple choice questions

1   The American President who published his famous doctrine that any European intervention in the Americas would be regarded as an 'unfriendly act' (1823) was:
   ☐   Monroe
   ☐   Madison
   ☐   Truman
   ☐   Eisenhower
2   The remark that 'it set out to divide among the victors the spoils taken away from the vanquished' was said about the Congress of:
   ☐   Vienna
   ☐   Aix-la-Chapelle
   ☐   Troppau
   ☐   Laibach
3   The remark that 'The ministry of Mr Canning marked an era in the history of England and Europe' was said by:
   ☐   Tsar Alexander I
   ☐   Talleyrand
   ☐   The Duke of Wellington
   ☐   Metternich
4   Tsar Alexander I proposed an alliance based on 'justice, charity and peace'. This was known as:
   ☐   The Triple Alliance
   ☐   The Quadruple Alliance
   ☐   The Holy Alliance
   ☐   The Dual Alliance
5   Before 1815 Belgium had been ruled by:
   ☐   Austria
   ☐   Spain
   ☐   Prussia
   ☐   Denmark

THE IMPORTANCE OF THE BELGIAN REVOLT

BACKGROUND TO THE REVOLT

Europe in 1815 was in an age of emergent nationalism. Yet the Congress of Vienna tried to unify the former Austrian Netherlands (Belgium) with the former United Provinces (Holland): 'a defiance of nationality'.

1   Castlereagh wanted the region ruled by a strong, reliable leader as it was vital to British interests: 'Whoever holds the Low Countries points a pistol at the heart of England.'
2   The new Dutch king, William I, was pro-Dutch:
   (a)   He favoured the Dutch language.

(b)   He used Dutch administrators to govern the south.
(c)   He ignored the religious split – Dutch Calvinists; Belgian Catholics.

3   Matters were not helped by an economic crisis during the 1820s. Textile prices fell and the Belgian workers suffered wage cuts; but as this coincided with a series of poor harvests, food prices went up. So the Belgians had plenty of grievances.

THE REVOLT 1830

These grievances came to a head when the Belgians heard that a French 'July Revolution' had toppled Charles X, replacing him with King Louis Philippe. On 25 August 1830 the Brussels audience joined in the opera they were watching – it was all about a revolution! The barricades went up in the city and in September the Belgian rebels had successfully resisted a Dutch army sent to restore law and order. The rebels produced their own Constituent Assembly with a new constitution demanding independence and a Belgian king.

The attitude of the Great Powers

Said the Duke of Wellington: 'It's a devilish bad business – the most serious affair that could have arisen for Europe.' However, France opposed intervention at this stage; Russia had to contend with the Polish Revolt; while neither Austria nor Prussia was prepared to act unilaterally. The Great Powers, who had originally favoured intervention to preserve peace, were now aware that intervention might cause a war. The situation required a very careful diplomatic solution and there appeared on the scene a new British Foreign Secretary, Lord Palmerston. His solution was based on the belief that France and all other Continental powers must be permanently excluded from the region – it should be permanently neutral.

The Five Power Conference, London 1830

1   The 1814 Union must be ended.
2   Belgium must become independent.

These were known as the 'January Protocols'. In this sense, the word 'Protocol' means the agreements made by the countries involved prior to the signing of a formal treaty.

However, the Belgians wanted to choose their own king and picked the Duc de Nemours – but he was the son of Louis-Philippe. Palmerston was appalled. The Belgians then agreed to have Leopold of Saxe-Coburg – but wanted Luxemburg included in Belgian territory. This led to another protocol – **the Eighteen Articles:**

1   Belgium to be neutral and independent.
2   There would be separate negotiations over the fate of Luxemburg.

WAR

William I refused to accept Leopold as King of the Belgians and invaded Belgium (1831). He defeated the Belgians at the Battle of Louvain. They appealed to France for help and a French army crossed the frontier and attacked the Dutch.

Said Palmerston: 'One thing is certain – the French must get out of Belgium or we shall have a general war, and war in a few days.'

PEACE

1 France withdrew her troops.
2 Palmerston negotiated the 'Twenty-Four Articles' guaranteeing Belgian independence.
3 Britain and France agreed to impose this solution on William I, with the full backing of Austria, Prussia and Russia:
   (*a*)   Anglo–French fleet blockaded Dutch coast.
   (*b*)   French troops moved in 1832–3.
   (*c*)   King William had to accept a definitive treaty – but wouldn't sign it!
   In 1838 he did agree to sign and on 19 April 1839 the Great Powers assembled in London to sign one of the most famous treaties in history – the **1839 Treaty of London.**

Its significance

1 It guaranteed the independence and permanent neutrality of Belgium.
2 It became known as the 'scrap of paper' when Germany ignored it in 1914 and invaded Belgium. Britain declared war on Germany.
   It was during this story of the Belgian Revolt that the British Foreign Secretary acquired his nickname – 'Protocol Palmerston'. His performance as a negotiator was always governed by British – not Belgian – interests. Yet he proved that it was possible to avoid a general war, that the Great Powers could (if they wished) gather together, change the map of Europe and preserve peace.

   The settlement of the Belgian Revolt therefore shows that the spirit of the Concert of Europe was still very much alive. Its death occurred because of the failure of the Great Powers to find a solution to the 'Eastern Question'.

THE EASTERN QUESTION AND THE CRIMEAN WAR

CONTENTS

WHAT WAS THE EASTERN QUESTION?

Three overlapping problems

1   The decline of the powers of the Ottoman Empire and attempts to maintain it (mainly by Britain) as a deterrent against possible Austrian and Russian expansion.

2   The attempts by the major powers to exploit Turkey's weaknesses for their own gain.

3   Attempts by peoples under Turkish rule to set up their own national sovereign states.

How did it become prominent?

The first major intervention of the Great Powers took the form of the Battle of Navarino Bay (1827) on behalf of the Greeks. Russia then forced the Turks to leave Greece (see p. 251). Mehemet Ali (1769–1849), ruler of Egypt since 1811, had lost a lot of ships during the Battle of Navarino Bay when he fought in support of his master, the Sultan of Turkey. Naturally, he now wished for some compensation. He fought the Sultan twice (1831–3; 1839–41). He conquered a great deal of Syria and his empire now stretched from Khartoum in the south well into the trade routes of the Mediterranean. Palmerston saw Mehemet Ali as a kind of eastern version of Napoleon who might easily upset the balance of power in the Middle East. He secured the agreement of Russia, Prussia and Austria to present an ultimatum to Mehemet Ali; and when Mehemet ignored this the Royal Navy bombarded Acre.

Result

The Great Powers agreed that Mehemet Ali should become the hereditary ruler of Egypt (i.e. Egypt had been effectively detached from the Ottoman Empire). But they also agreed that the Black Sea should be closed to the warships of all nations. This is the famous Straits Convention (1841) and was a setback to Russian plans. In a secret clause of the earlier Treaty of Unkiar-Skelessi (1833), the Russians had persuaded the Turks that, in the event of war, the Straits controlling the entrance into the Black Sea would be closed – but always open for the exit and return of Russian ships.

Implications

1   Britain had identified Russia as the main threat to Turkey and therefore as the most dangerous element in the Eastern Question.

2   When Tsar Nicholas I visited London in 1844 he proposed a partitic
of the Ottoman Empire (between Austria, Britain and France). But th
British refused and Russia did not seem to understand the growir
sense of partnership between Britain and France. Moreover, Britis
public opinion was becoming anti-Russian, especially after Lou
Philippe lost the French throne in 1848 to be replaced by Lou
Napoleon who became Emperor Napoleon III in 1852. Lou
Napoleon was popular in Britain and there was a form of *enten*
between the two countries during the 1850s.

THE HOLY PLACES

The ambitions of Napoleon III

Read the following account:

> Thirty years after Napoleon had died on St Helena, his
> nephew Louis Napoleon became Emperor of France. He
> desperately wanted the support of the Catholic vote and
> realised he could secure this if he could restore a sense of
> national pride – 'La Gloire!' But to regain her lost glory,
> France would have to destroy Russia's pre-eminence in
> international affairs. He needed to provoke a European war
> and that is why he intervened in a dispute involving the Hol
> Places of Jerusalem, then part of the declining Ottoman
> Empire.

1   When did Napoleon I die?
2   Why did Louis Napoleon need the Catholic vote?
3   Explain 'La Gloire'.
4   Where were the Holy Places?
5   Who ruled the Holy Places?

The attitude of the Turkish Sultan

He was aware that in the past the French had always claimed
protect the Holy Places but that for many years the Greek Orthode
Church had looked after Jerusalem's Holy Sepulchre and Bethlehem
Church of the Nativity. But there had been several quarrels betwee
the Catholic and Greek Orthodox monks who supervised the
(1851). So the Sultan:

1   Allowed the French to have rights within the Bethlehem Church.
2   Assured the Tsar of Russia that his rights within the Holy Places we
not infringed.
This was not in itself the cause of conflict. It was Russia's later actio
that drew Europe into war during 1854.

THE ORIGINS OF WAR 1853

The Tsar's next move was to send Prince Menshikov to Turkey wi an offer: Russia was prepared to protect all Greek Orthodox citizens residing within the Ottoman Empire. At the same time Nicholas I ordered the Russian Black Sea fleet to assemble at the brand-new naval base of Sevastopol.

1   The Tsar's actions were interpreted as warlike moves in the rest of Europe.

2   Turkey was sure she could depend on international support against the Russian threat and in fact British and French warships arrived in Besika Bay.

3   Louis Napoleon persuaded both Austria and Prussia not to intervene in the crisis – and by doing this he had effectively smashed the old Holy Alliance.

4   Tsar Nicholas now over-reacted by sending in troops to occupy the 'principalities' – these were the two provinces of Moldavia and Wallachia and are roughly equivalent to modern Romania. These two provinces straddled the mouth of the Danube and were seen by Austria as a threat to her trade once under Russian occupation.

The conflict begins

Ill-advisedly, the Sultan of Turkey now declared war on Russia. Read the following account of the Battle of Sinope:

> Admiral Nachimoff's Black Sea fleet immediately sailed south to attack the Turkish naval base at Sinope. Many of the Russian warships mounted French manufactured guns which fired high-velocity incendiary shells. These soon reduced the Turkish warships into a row of blazing hulks. News of this victory – emotively labelled the 'Massacre of Sinope' – aroused Russophobia in London and Paris. It was partly this, together with Russia's refusal to evacuate Moldavia and Wallachia, that persuaded Britain to join with France in a war designed to weaken Russian power in Europe. Yet this was easier said than done. Allied fleets tested the Russian coastline for its weak spots. They cruised off Kronstadt, attacked the fortress of Bomarsund, bombarded Sveaborg and raided the Finnish coast – later the British apologised to the Finns! They tried to attack the garrison at Petrapavlosk on the Pacific coastline of Russia and even sent help to Russian rebels in the Caucasus. Only in the Crimea did the Allies seem to have any chance of victory – through this was one of the most strongly defended parts of the Russian Empire.

1   Name the Russian admiral who commanded the Russian fleet at Sinope.

2   Who had manufactured the high-velocity Russian guns?

3   Explain the term 'Russophobia'.

4   Why did the Allies decide to attack Russia by sea rather than land?

5   Why do you think they eventually decided to attack in the Crimea?

Map question

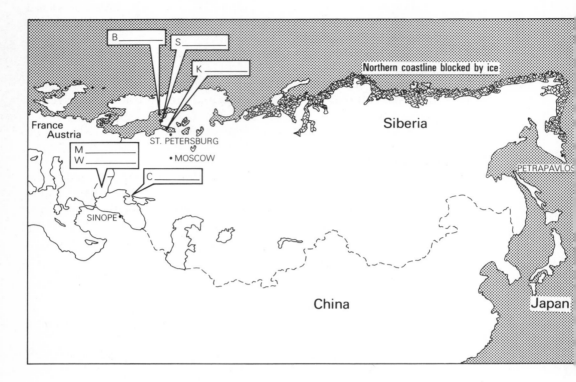

Russia on the eve of the Crimean War
N.B. Russia was rapidly expanding eastwards and imprisoning her political prisoners in
Siberia during this period.

1   Label Bomarsund, Sveaborg and Kronstadt.
2   By means of arrows, show the penetration of the Baltic and the Black
    Sea by Allied forces.
3   Mark Moldavia and Wallachia.
4   Mark the Crimea.
5   Shade in the extent of the Russian Empire.

THE WAR IN THE CRIMEA 1854–6

Failure of the first attack

On 14 September 1854 the Allies landed at Calamita Bay with the
intention of advancing south to capture the Russian base at Seva-
topol. They defeated General Menshikoff at the Battle of the River
Alma (September 1854) and then trudged southwards in an attempt
to outflank the huge base. As they did this the Allied fleets bore down
on the Russian fleet anchored in Sevastopol Roads. Perhaps the Allies
hoped they would repeat the tactics of the Nile victory (1798) – but
Menshikoff didn't give them the chance. He ordered his admiral

unship the guns from half the fleet and then scuttle these ships to block the harbour entrance. The rest of his ships then anchored close to the coastal batteries and, between them, poured down a rain of incendiary shells on the Anglo-French vessels. Before long, several British warships were ablaze and the Allies abandoned this part of the operation. Clearly, Sevastopol could only be taken by infantry assault.

Balaclava and Inkerman

The Russians tried to prevent this by launching a surprise attack at Balaclava. The British Heavy Brigade forced the Russians back into a defensive position, well-protected by artillery. Confusion among British officers then led to the heroic but futile Charge of the Light Brigade (25 October 1854). This twenty-minute epic saw the loss of 405 troopers out of the 600 who began the charge. A few days later the Russians attacked at Inkerman Heights. They were repulsed with heavy losses and fell back inside the main defences of Sevastopol.

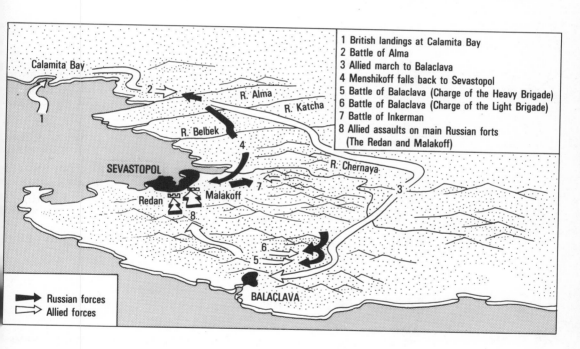

1 British landings at Calamita Bay
2 Battle of Alma
3 Allied march to Balaclava
4 Menshikoff falls back to Sevastopol
5 Battle of Balaclava (Charge of the Heavy Brigade)
6 Battle of Balaclava (Charge of the Light Brigade)
7 Battle of Inkerman
8 Allied assaults on main Russian forts
   (The Redan and Malakoff)

The war in the Crimea, 1854–5

The siege of Sevastopol

This took place during a bitter Russian winter. The Allies were ill-equipped and supply problems were a national disgrace – inadequate food and clothing led to misery and a great deal of disease. Florence Nightingale arrived at Scutari and there began the medical reforms that were to have such an impact upon nursing techniques. For the first time news of the administrative chaos that characterised the British campaign in the Crimea was readily available in Britain. William Russell, the first war correspondent, sent back his dispatches for *The Times*; Roger Fenton brought back photographs of the campaign, though his equipment was not able to record any 'action shots'. These were left to the artists, who glorified the war. There were significant changes in 1855: Tsar Nicholas I died, a victim of 'General February'. Palmerston became Prime Minister; General Pelissier arrived to take over command of the French contingent; Sardinia sent a small army to help the Allies.

In June there was a major assault on the two huge Russian forts – the Malakoff and the Redan. Both were repelled by General Todleber (1818–84) – probably the greatest military genius of the entire campaign. A Russian counter-attack (the Battle of the Chernaya River) failed. In September 1855 the French captured the Malakoff defences and the Russians decided to blow up the rest of their fortress defences. Most Russian soldiers then drifted north and the war in the Crimea ended.

THE PEACE OF PARIS, MARCH 1856

There were four very important points:

1   The Black Sea was now 'neutralised'. This meant that it was open to all merchant ships but banned as far as warships were concerned, while the Russians weren't allowed to rebuild their base at Sevastopol.
2   Russia had to give up any claim to be the 'protector' of Greek Orthodox subjects in the Ottoman Empire.
3   The Russian frontier along the Danube was now pushed northwards and the two provinces of Moldavia and Wallachia became Romania.
4   The Ottoman Empire was now considered to be part of Europe's international responsibilities and the great powers now agreed:

> 'to guarantee the independence and territorial integrity of the Ottoman Empire'.

EFFECTS OF THE CRIMEAN WAR

On Britain

There had been many critics of Britain's participation in the Crimea. Some made an anagram of CRIMEA = A CRIME. The war led to a reorganisation of the British Army, not least in the provision of good medical services. The ordinary British soldier was accorded rather more respect – previously he was always 'the scum of the earth'. Queen Victoria showed her respect by instituting the Victoria Cross – awarded to officers and other ranks alike. The middle classes showed theirs by adopting some of the 'fashions' of the Crimean campaign:

1   The beard and pipe became common in Victorian Britain.

2   The clothing trade named 'cardigans' and 'raglan coats' after British commanders; and the woollen 'balaclava' after the battle.

On Russia

The new Tsar was Alexander II – and his first task had been to make peace with the Allies, a shattering experience. He understood that Russia had suffered a major humiliation in European affairs and that her planned expansion westwards had been checked for many years to come:

1   It would take a generation to rebuild the Russian economy.
2   Russian expansion was now towards the east – the Russians founded their partially ice-free port of Vladivostock in 1861.
3   Their ambition was to link Vladivostock and St Petersburg with a railway – but it would be thirty years before they began the longest railway in the world, the Trans-Siberian.
4   Nevertheless, they began their policy of settling colonists in the east, to begin opening up the rich mineral wealth of Siberia.

On Italy

The Italians were later to say that the new nation of Italy was born out of the mud of the Crimea. Count Cavour (1810–61) had sent 15,000 soldiers to the Crimea not because he was fundamentally concerned with the Eastern Question but because he wanted to sit as an equal to France, Britain, Austria and Russia round the peace table – and in this way gain recognition for the movement to unify Italy.

On naval design

The Crimean War had highlighted the weaknesses of Allied warships. The Russian successes at Sinope and Sevastopol Roads were not forgotten. The French began building ocean-going frigates whose vulnerable wooden hulls were protected by iron plates – naturally, the first was called *La Gloire*! Britain then built the *Warrior* – bigger, faster and with an iron hull and forty guns. *Warrior* was a 'capital ironclad', the first true, modern battleship. After a chequered career, she was taken to Hartlepool in 1979 for restoration.

Politicians' assumptions after the Crimean War

1   The British stated that they went to war to defend Turkey against Russian aggression. But as the Duke of Cambridge was to say:

> The sick man is excessively sick, indeed, dying as fast as possible . . . and the sooner diplomacy disposes of him the better, for no earthly power can save him.

2   The British and French leaders always assumed that the main threat to Europe's peace was Russia. But critics of the day, such as Richard Cobden (1804–65), said that phrases such as 'the balance of power' and 'the integrity of the Ottoman Empire' were mere echoes of the past . . . 'admirably suited for the mouths of a senile Whiggery'.

3   The fact that Russia tried to undo the work of the 1856 Treaty of Paris
    – she actually denounced the Black Sea clauses during the Franco-
    Prussian War (see pp. 273–4) and thus revived the whole problem of
    the Eastern Question.

    But by then the political make-up of Europe had changed radically.
    New nations – notably Germany and Italy – had changed the old
    balance of power. Germany, not Russia, was to become the main
    threat to Europe's peace and, as the British were ruefully to admit,
    'we had backed the wrong horse'.

Multiple choice questions

1   The name of the eastern ruler whom Palmerston saw as a new
    Napoleon was:
    - ☐   Ibrahim
    - ☐   Abbas
    - ☐   Ali Pasha
    - ☐   Mehemet Ali

2   The Straits Convention was signed in:
    - ☐   1841
    - ☐   1842
    - ☐   1843
    - ☐   1844

3   Russia's new base in the Crimea was:
    - ☐   Kronstadt
    - ☐   Vladivostock
    - ☐   Petrapavlosk
    - ☐   Sevastopol

4   The first major Russian victory in the war (1853) was at the:
    - ☐   Battle of Alma
    - ☐   Battle of Balaclava
    - ☐   Battle of Sevastopol Roads
    - ☐   Battle of Sinope

5   The name of *The Times* correspondent in the Crimea was:
    - ☐   Roger Fenton
    - ☐   William Russell
    - ☐   Florence Nightingale
    - ☐   Richard Cobden

6   The peace treaty ending the war in the Crimea was signed in 1856 at:
    - ☐   Berlin
    - ☐   London
    - ☐   Paris
    - ☐   Vienna

7   Florence Nightingale's main hospital was at:
    - ☐   Sinope
    - ☐   Sevastopol
    - ☐   Scutari
    - ☐   Constantinople

8   The British Commander-in-Chief in the Crimea, a veteran of the
    Peninsular War, died from dysentery in 1855. He was:

- ☐ Lord Cardigan
- ☐ Lord Raglan
- ☐ The Duke of Wellington
- ☐ Lord Palmerston

9 The Church of Russia was known as the:

- ☐ Christian Church
- ☐ Catholic Church
- ☐ Greek Orthodox Church
- ☐ Reformed Church

10 The new nation that was said to be born out of the mud of the Crimea was:

- ☐ Germany
- ☐ Finland
- ☐ Italy
- ☐ Austria.

NEW NATIONS AND THE INTERNATIONAL ALLIANCES TO 1914

CONTENTS

In this chapter you will see how the German and Italian states unite to form the new nations of Germany and Italy; how Germany in particular intervenes to help settle another complicated stage in the Eastern Question; and how the German Chancellor Bismarck constructs a web of European alliances designed to preserve German security – alliances that ultimately operate to cause the First World War.

THE UNIFICATION OF ITALY

REVOLUTIONARY NATIONALISM

All over Europe men were determined to set up independent national states and 'revolutionary nationalism' exploded during 1846–9. 1848 is called the 'Year of Revolution':

1   Riots in Berlin and revolution in Frankfurt – crushed.
2   Revolution in Vienna and Galicia. Metternich forced to leave office. Rebellions crushed by Austria.
3   Revolution in Hungary – begun by Louis Kossuth (1802–94). The Russians drove him out in 1849 and he never saw Hungary again.
4   Revolutions in Tuscany, Venice and Sicily – crushed by Austria; revolution in Rome crushed by France.

Everywhere the cause of nationalism had failed. But in Italy the lone constitutional monarchy of Piedmont-Sardinia remained determined to unify the Italian people.

The leading personalities

King Victor Emmanuel II (1820–78) – 'the cavalier king'. He had become king of Piedmont-Sardinia in 1849 and was to rule as King of Italy from 1861.

Count Camillo Cavour (1810–61) was Prime Minister of Piedmont (1852–61) and was dedicated to the creation of a united, constitutional Italian monarchy. He had founded the newspaper *Il Risorgimento* (1847) and the word 'risorgimento' (meaning 'resurrection') signifies the process of the unification of Italy. He was a far-sighted statesman and a moderniser – railways, roads, canals, industrialisation flourished under his leadership. He tried to restrict the power of the Church in Northern Italy's society – he wanted 'a free church in a free state'.

Giuseppe Garibaldi (1807–82) was an outstanding soldier and patriot. T
Victorian England, he seemed to be the symbol of all that was desi
able in the expression of national rights and his exploits were we
reported in newspapers. Garibaldi is best known for his leadership
the 'Thousand Redshirts' who invaded Sicily and Naples (1860).

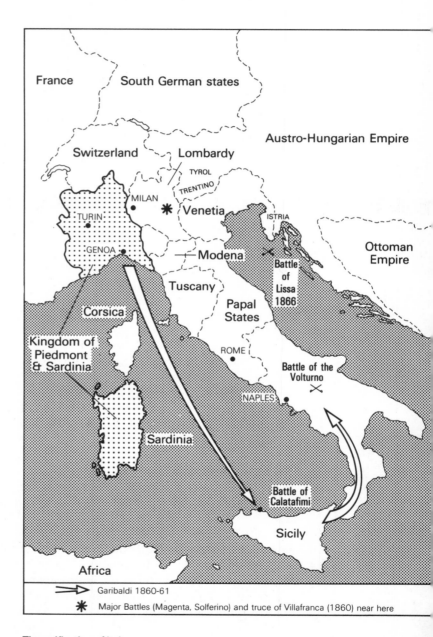

The unification of Italy

Main events in the Revolution

1858 Cavour negotiated the secret Pact of Plombières with Louis Napoleon of France who promised to support Cavour if he could have Nice and Savoy.

1859 Cavour and Louis Napoleon declared war on Austria and Franco-Sardinians won a string of victories – the Battles of Montebello, Palestro, Magenta and Solferino. These led to the Truce of Villafranca: France gained Nice and Savoy; Cavour gained Lombardy.

Britain was dismayed by these extensions of French power and anxious that the process of Italian unification should proceed without further foreign interventions. Palmerston was back in office this year and he was determined to preserve peace in Europe and maintain the existence of Austria; and positive that Louis Napoleon must not be allowed to engage in further military adventures.

1860–1 On 11 May Garibaldi and his Redshirts landed in Sicily to take advantage of a nationalist revolution that had broken out there. In the distance was a British fleet – implying protection for Garibaldi and a threat to anyone who tied to molest him. This was Britain's main contribution to the story of Italian unification and the British politician Lord John Russell told Parliament that he saw Garibaldi's landing in Sicily in the same light as he regarded that of William of Orange, who had landed in England in 1688 to begin the 'Glorious Revolution'. Garibaldi won the Battle of Calatafimi, crossed on to the peninsula of Italy and won the Battle of the Volturno. Garibaldi now handed over all his conquests to Victor Emmanuel II – who was now the ruler of Parma, Modena, the Kingdom of the Two Sicilies, part of the Papal States and Lombardy as well as his own kingdom.

1866–70 During these years the story of Italian unification was bound up with Bismarck's war with Austria (1866) and Bismarck's war with France (1870–1).

1   Cavour was dead (1861) and the thrust and drive that had characterised his war leadership was now lacking. Italian armies fought the Austrians in 1866 – but were defeated. Nevertheless, a grateful Prussia rewarded Italy with Venetia.

2   In 1867 Garibaldi tried to capture Rome. French and Papal troops, using the new chassepot rifle, defeated him (Battle of Mentana).

3   11 September 1870: Italian troops entered Rome while Louis Napoleon's attention was on the war against Prussia.

This effectively meant the end of the Risorgimento in the nineteenth century – Italy had emerged as a united country by the end of 1870. However, some Italians said that the Risorgimento did not end until 1919 when the treaties at the end of the First World War gave Italy the Trentino, Istria and the South Tyrol.

A note on the sea warfare (1866)

Between the Battle of Trafalgar (1805) and the Battle of Jutland (1916) there was only one sizeable battle between the fleets of two nations – and this was the **Battle of Lissa (1866)** between the Italian and Austrian fleets. The Austrians had six of the new ironclads; while nine of the Italian ships had the new rifled naval guns. The battle was a mixture of the old broadside tactics and the new ramming methods. The Italians lost their flagship and one other vessel.

The Italian *Palestro*, lost at the Battle of Lissa, 1866, eight months after she had been built. Note the broadside guns and the rather useless ram bows. These ships of the line still needed sails to supplement low-power steam engines

THE UNIFICATION OF GERMANY

There were many conflicting views in the nineteenth century about the nature of the Germany that could be formed by uniting German-speaking states:

1　Some supported *klein deutsch* (Little Germany), i.e. a union under Prussia without Austria.
2　Others favoured *gross deutsch* (Big Germany), i.e. a union including Austria.
3　Splinter groups of revolutionary nationalists favoured an overthrow of all the monarchies and the creation of a new 'German Republic'.
4　A few wanted a 'third Germany' made up of parts of the south and west.

But Bismarck, Chief Minister of Prussia in 1862, said that 'The great issues of the day are not decided by speeches and resolutions of majorities – that was the mistake of 1848 and 1849 – but by iron and blood.'

OTTO KARL VON BISMARCK (1815–98)

He visited Britain just before he became Chief Minister. There he remarked that he intended to make Prussia's army the strongest in Europe: 'I shall take the first opportunity of settling accounts with Austria and dissolving the German Confederation ... then I shall establish a united Germany under Prussia's leadership.' Few people in Britain paid any attention but Disraeli said, 'Take care of that man, for he means what he says.'

Bismarck's achievement

He fought four wars: against Denmark (1864), Austria (1866) and France (1870–1). He gained Holstein (1864), Schleswig (1866) and became Chancellor of a Prussian-dominated North German Confederation from which Austria was totally excluded. He defeated France in 1870; and in 1871 proclaimed the creation of the German Empire in the Palace of Versailles. From France he took the two rich provinces of Alsace and Lorraine. His Prussian king became Kaiser (Emperor) Wilhelm I, ruling from 1871 to 1888.

The War against Denmark 1864

Schleswig-Holstein were two ancient duchies with substantial German-speaking populations. Bismarck took advantage of a disputed succession during which the Danish king had suggested a union between them and Denmark. Bismarck, with Austria's help, then 'liberated' the two provinces. At the Convention of Gastein, Bismarck acquired Schleswig while Austria took Holstein (1865).

The War against Austria 1866

This is also known as the Seven Weeks War – though the main battles took less than a fortnight. Bismarck watched the decisive Battle of Sadowa (also called Königgratz) in 1866 in which the Prussians took 24,000 Austrians prisoner. His generals now wanted to march in triumph into Vienna, but Bismarck was unwilling to do this. He had demonstrated his superiority over Austria and now wanted her support in the future. Therefore he imposed a moderate peace. At the Treaty of Prague (1866) Prussia annexed Schleswig-Holstein and key regions such as Frankfurt and Hanover; Austria had to pay Prussia an indemnity of £3 million. Austria's greatest loss, of course, was to be excluded from the German Union now dominated by Prussia.

The Franco-Prussian War 1870–1

Bismarck worked hard to create a sense of unity in his new 'Germany', notably by introducing a customs union during 1866–9. But his strongest weapon was to encourage a fear of France, who was bound to object to the rise of a new and powerful nation on her eastern frontiers. Bismarck therefore deliberately created a 'crisis situation' by exploiting the sense of pride and honour so characteristic of the 'Second Empire' under Louis Napoleon.

The Ems Telegram 1870 This was the culmination of an argument over who was to succeed to the Spanish throne. One candidate was Leopold of Hohenzollern (the name of the Prussian royal family). France wanted Bismarck to withdraw Leopold as a candidate and Benedetti, the French ambassador, met Kaiser Wilhelm I who was 'taking the waters' at Ems, a famous spa near Coblenz. Benedetti was told to secure the withdrawal of Leopold – otherwise it is war'. The Kaiser refused and sent Bismarck a telegram, reporting the gist of the meeting. Bismarck deliberately edited the telegram and then published it. To the French, the telegram used insulting language. France declared war on Prussia 19 July 1870.

The campaigns It took less than a fortnight to mobilise the German armies – 450,000 men under the command of Wilhelm I. The main German thrusts came between Trier and Worth and on 2 September 1870 Louis Napoleon and an army of 83,000 men surrendered at Sedan. But the fighting went on under the command of a new Republican government in Paris. Soon the Germans were besieging Paris. Leon Gambetta (1838–82), who had set up the French Third Republic in 1870, now had to escape from Paris in a balloon. While German troops still surrounded Paris, Bismarck proclaimed the German Empire in the Hall of Mirrors in the Palace of Versailles.

The surrender of Paris The Germans had bombarded the French capital for a month and its citizens were suffering from starvation. The city surrendered on 28th January 1871.

The Treaty of Frankfurt 1871 France lost Alsace-Lorraine (including the two fortresses of Metz and Strasburg) – vital to her steel industry as well as to her defence. France also had to pay an indemnity of £200 million over the next three years.

So Bismarck had united Germany by means of war. The price he paid for this was the undying hatred of the French. Bismarck was well aware of this and thus he devoted a great deal of effort to the construction of an alliance system, beginning with an eastern version of the old Holy Alliance – the League of the Three Emperors or, as Bismarck called it, the Dreikaiserbund.

THE INTERNATIONAL ALLIANCE SYSTEM AFTER 1870

THE LEAGUE OF THE THREE EMPERORS 1873

Bismarck hoped to befriend both Austria and Russia in the hope that these two natural enemies would not come to blows over their rival interests in the Balkans. It was of little significance and collapsed during yet another crisis involving the Eastern Question – the Russo–Turkish War 1877–8.

Read the following account:

It was not long before trouble erupted in the Balkans. In 1875 Serbia's Slavs rebelled against their Turkish overlords and within two years Russia was fighting the Turks in Bulgaria and the Caucasus. Though Turkish defenders held the Russians throughout three fierce battles at Plevna (July–December 1877), the Russians broke through, won the battles of Plovdiv and Shipka, and entered Adrianople. To prevent the loss of Constantinople, the Turks accepted an armistice and in March 1878 signed the Peace of San Stefano. This treaty involved the creation of a new, large state of Bulgaria and it needed very little imagination to appreciate that the Bulgarian Slavs would look to Russia for future protection.

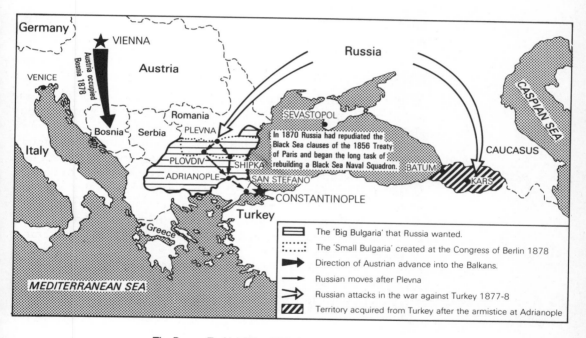

In 1870 Russia had repudiated the Black Sea clauses of the 1856 Treaty of Paris and began the long task of rebuilding a Black Sea Naval Squadron.

Legend:
- ▭ The 'Big Bulgaria' that Russia wanted.
- ⋯ The 'Small Bulgaria' created at the Congress of Berlin 1878
- ➤ Direction of Austrian advance into the Balkans.
- → Russian moves after Plevna
- ⇒ Russian attacks in the war against Turkey 1877-8
- ▨ Territory acquired from Turkey after the armistice at Adrianople

The Russo–Turkish War, 1877–8

1   This was as big an international crisis as the Crimean War had been. Bismarck now adopted the role of the 'honest broker' and invited all interested parties to attend the 1878 Congress of Berlin.

2   The powers agreed at Berlin to demand Russian sacrifice of the 'Big Bulgaria'.

(*a*)   Look at the map. What territory did Russia secure as compensation?

(*b*)   What evidence is there on the map that the great powers were highly suspicious of Russia's intentions?

(c)   What territorial gain did Austria make in 1878?

Read the extract again Who was the Russian military expert who finally captured Plevna? Where had he previously distinguished himself?

FROM DUAL ALLIANCE TO TRIPLE ALLIANCE

Tsar Alexander II was naturally indignant that he had had to make so many sacrifices at the Congress of Berlin and accused the German Chancellor of wrecking the Dreikaiserbund. Bismarck's reaction was to sign the Dual Alliance with Austria (1879) and then in 1882 to convert this into the Triple Alliance (Italy, Austria, Germany). At the same time, he persuaded the Tsar* to agree to the terms of the 1887 Reinsurance Treaty:

*Tsar Alexander III, who ruled from 1881–94.

1   Germany promised not to attack Russia.
2   Russia promised not to attack Austria.
    Then, quite unexpectedly, the young Kaiser Wilhelm II visited Turkey – Russia's eternal foe!

THE FRANCO–RUSSIAN ALLIANCE 1894

In 1890 Russian harvests were a failure and the threat of famine forced the Tsar to seek a foreign loan. France lent the money to buy grain. In the same year, when Kaiser Wilhelm II dismissed Bismarck as German Chancellor and failed to renew the 1887 Reinsurance Treaty, Russia turned to France for military security. The French fleet visited Kronstadt. The Russian fleet paid a courtesy visit to Toulon. Negotiations were in secret but at the beginning of 1894 the Tsar (now Nicholas II 1894–1917) and the French government confirmed that a defensive military alliance existed between the two countries.

1   If a Triple Alliance country mobilised its army then Russia and France would mobilise their armies.
2   Mobilisation was in effect a declaration of war.
    As a French general commented, the alliance had brought a completely new and potentially dangerous element into European affairs.

BRITISH REACTIONS TO CHANGES IN EUROPE

Britain had to accept Russia's repudiation of the Black Sea clauses (1870) – Gladstone was dedicated to 'Peace, Retrenchment and Reform' at almost any price. When Disraeli became Prime Minister in 1874 he was determined to give Britain a stake in the Middle East, especially with the revolution in transport that had accompanied the opening of the Suez Canal in 1869. Look at the sketch opposite of the first ships passing through the Suez Canal.

1   What do you notice especially about the way in which the ships are powered?
2   Why do you think the flag on the left is placed so prominently? A

Source: BBC Radio for Schools, Spring 1977

clue: the Canal was built by Ferdinand de Lesseps and was opened by the Empress Eugénie.

Egypt's ruler, the Khedive Ismail, owned nearly half of the shares in the Suez Canal. Short of funds, he decided to sell. Disraeli raised £4 million from his banking friends, the Rothschilds – one of the most remarkable financial investments ever made by Britain. The Mediterranean now became a key British interest, as did the defence of the Canal – the new link with India.

Thus, during the Russo–Turkish War 1875–7, Britain sent troops to Malta and the Royal Navy patrolled the Sea of Marmora. Disraeli returned from the Berlin Congress, bringing (he told the waiting crowds at Charing Cross station) 'Peace with honour' in the form of Cyprus as a new British naval base. But Britain made no formal alliances – she rejected Bismarck's offer (in 1889, just before he was dismissed) of an Anglo–German alliance.

Was Britain 'isolated'? Some British politicians thought so:

> Since the Crimean War nearly fifty years ago, the policy of this country has been a policy of strict isolation. We have no allies – I am afraid we have no friends.
>
> (Joseph Chamberlain)

But Goschen said in 1896:

> Our isolation is not an isolation of weakness, or of contempt for ourselves; it is deliberately chosen: the freedom to act as we choose in any circumstances that may arise.

Dangers for Britain

Britain became aware that Kaiser Wilhelm II was no friend of Britain.

1   During the abortive Jameson Raid into the Transvaal (1895–6), the Kaiser sent a telegram to President Kruger congratulating the Boers on their defeat of Cecil Rhodes' plans for the takeover of the Transvaal.

2   **The First German Navy Law (1898)** showed that Germany was ready to contest the mastery of the high seas with Britain. Said the Kaiser when the Boer War began in 1899:

> I am not in a position to go beyond the strictest neutrality and I must first get myself a fleet. In twenty years time, when the fleet is ready, I can use another language.

In 1899 came the Second German Navy Law – Britain was clearly facing a major challenge from a rapidly growing naval power.

REACTION – THE 1902 ANGLO–JAPANESE ALLIANCE

Because of Russian expansion in the Far East (a source of anxiety for both Japan and Britain) and the need to keep a large number of capital ships in home waters, Britain needed a friend in the Pacific, a friend capable of taking over naval security in the region. Clearly, this was Japan and in 1902 the Anglo–Japanese Alliance stated:

1   If either nation were attacked by a third power the other would remain neutral.

2   If either were at war with two powers, the other would give military assistance.

THE ENTENTE CORDIALE 1904 – A 'FRIENDLY UNDERSTANDING'

Though Britain may have felt that she had contained Russia in the Far East, France was now worried that she might find herself committed (as Russia's ally) to fighting Britain (Japan's ally) in a possible conflict between Russia and Japan. The French Foreign Minister Delcassé began talks with the British to try to develop good relations – not an easy task since the confrontation between the two countries over the Fashoda Incident (1898).* Delcassé succeeded and the Entente Cordiale was signed. It was not a military alliance.

1   It settled old grievances in Siam, West Africa and Newfoundland.

2   France recognised that Egypt and the Sudan were British spheres of influence.

In the midst of the Entente negotiations, the Russo–Japanese war broke out in and around Korea and Port Arthur. The Japanese fleet annihilated the Russian Baltic Fleet at the Battle of Tsushima and the Russians signed the Treaty of Portsmouth (USA) in 1905. Russian naval power in the Far East was no longer a threat to Britain.

*British troops under Kitchener, advancing up the Nile after the Battle of Omdurman, encountered a French unit commanded by Marchand who claimed the region as a French sphere of influence. The British were prepared to fight – and the French had to back down.

THE ANGLO–RUSSIAN ENTENTE 1907

During 1905 the Germans tested the strength of the Entente Cordiale in the First Moroccan Crisis. Aware that Britain had agreed to the future partition of Morocco by Spain and France, the Kaiser had arrived in Tangier to promote Moroccan independence. At the 1906 Algeciras Conference, Germany had to back down, having discovered that the Entente was very strong indeed. Britain and Russia, France's ally, now came to their own friendly understanding:

1   Persia divided into three zones with a neutral buffer zone separating Russian and British spheres of influence.
2   Tibet and Afghanistan to be left as neutral buffer states between the Russian and British Empires in Central Asia.

The Kaiser was infuriated. He now saw himself as encircled by the armed might of the Entente.

EVENTS LEADING TO THE FIRST WORLD WAR

A series of crises marked the period 1908–14:

1   Austria's annexation of Bosnia and Herzegovina 1908.
2   The Agadir Incident 1911 (the Second Moroccan Crisis).
3   The war between Italy and Turkey 1911–12.
4   The Balkan Wars 1912–13.
5   The Sarajevo assassinations 28 June 1914.
6   The German invasion of Belgium 4 August 1914.

They were not cumulative – there is no inevitability in history. Each one of the above crises, apart from the last two, was settled without resort to a major war. The most important area was the Balkans – Bismarck had once prophesied that if there were ever to be a major European war it would develop out of some unexpected event in the Balkans. Both Russia and Austria had dreams of expanding in the region and Austria actually annexed the two provinces of Bosnia and Herzegovina in 1908. Austria's motives were mixed – but the annexations did enable her to bring pressure on Serbia.

THE PROBLEM OF SERBIA

Many Austrians were Slavs and anxious to form their own, independent Slav states along the lines of Serbia. The Serbs fought the two Balkan Wars against her neighbours, including the Turks, during 1912–13. Austria saw the solution to several problems in the annexation of Serbia – but the Serbs had no intention of becoming part of the Austro–Hungarian Empire. They appealed to Russia who promised aid if the need ever arose.

Sarajevo 1914

Sarajevo is in Bosnia, annexed by the Austrians in 1908. On 28 June 1914 the Archduke Franz Ferdinand of Austria, together with his wife, visited the city. As they were driving in their car a student named Gavril Princip shot them both. Princip was linked to the Serbian terrorist organisation known as the Black Hand gang and the Austrians naturally believed that the Serbs had planned the assassinations. The Archduke had been next in line to the Austrian throne. So now the Austrians made some impossible demands of Serbia – had they been agreed to Serbia would have lost much of her independence. After more than three weeks, the Emperor of Austria, Franz-Josef, issued an ultimatum to Serbia – with Germany's blessing.

Mobilisation

The Sarajevo crisis led directly, though not immediately, to the First World War. It is important that you understand that there was little or no discussion between the political leaders of Europe during this crisis. The German and Austrian army general staffs play a great part in the timetable that led to the fighting – and their decisions had the approval of Kaiser Wilhelm II and Franz-Josef. The German General Staff had a plan (the Schlieffen Plan) designed to overcome the problem. Von Moltke, Schlieffen's successor, refined the plan.

1   A surprise attack through Belgium to force the French into surrender by taking Paris and then hitting the French fortress system in the rear – a matter of a few weeks.

2   The German army would then be moved by train to the Eastern Front where the Russians (who were likely to take weeks to call up their reserves let alone transport them to the battle zone) would be beaten in a series of short, sharp campaigns.

In this way, Germany 'solved' the problem of a war on two fronts and the German General Staff blithely applied the plan in July–August 1914.

28 July 1914	Austria declares war on Serbia.
29 July 1914	Russia orders mobilisation.
1 August 1914	Germany declares war on Russia.
3 August 1914	Germany declares war on France.
3 August 1914	German troops invade Belgium.
4 August 1914	Britain honours the 1839 Treaty of London

and declares war on Germany.

On the other side of the world Japan declared war on Germany and proceeded to occupy German colonies in the Far East.

Questions

1   Read the following newspaper announcement:

> Paris   January 14th 1858
>
> **Attempt to assassinate the Emperor**
> **and Empress of France**
>
> **Dramatic intervention on the route to the Opera**
>
> Tonight a bomb was thrown at the Emperor and
> Empress as they travelled to the Paris Opera. Their
> Royal Highnesses are safe. Innocent spectators were
> savaged in the attack and I saw at least two dead and
> many scores wounded. The perpetrator of this crime
> was a Felice Orsini, claiming to be a patriot in the
> cause of Italian freedom. I will send more intelligence
> tomorrow when we shall know more.

1   This is a description of the famous Orsini bomb plot. Name the
     Emperor of France involved.
2   What happened to Orsini?
3   What effect did the affair have on Anglo–French relations?

2   Throughout the nineteenth century the British were wary of France
     and twice feared a French invasion. Against which French emperors
     were the following precautions taken in Britain?
1   The building of Martello towers (small circular forts with massive
     walls designed to stop a seaborne landing).
2   The formation of large-scale volunteer rifle corps throughout the
     country. These were formed one year after the Orsini bomb plot:
     (*a*)   Date their formation.
     (*b*)   What name do we give to the their volunteer equivalents
     nowadays?
     (*c*)   Name the Liberal minister who set up the volunteers on a
     formal basis in 1907.

3   Look at the cartoon overleaf.
1   Why has the cartoonist drawn a Pyramid in the background?
2   What does the lion symbolise?
3   Why are the lion's paws resting on a key?
4   Who is the figure on the left?
5   What is he doing?

PUNCH, OR THE LONDON CHARIVARI—February 26, 1876.

THE LION'S SHARE.

"GARE À QUI LA TOUCHE!"

Source: BBC Radio for Schools, spring 1967, *The Victorian Age*

4 This drawing represents a very special ship launched by the British in 1906.

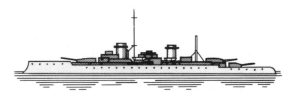

1 What was the name of this warship?
2 What was so special about her armament?
3 Name the British admiral who supported this design.
4 It has been said that the launching of this ship put all the navies on an equal footing. Can you explain what this means?
5 Did this particular ship have a distinguished career during the First World War?

THE FIRST WORLD WAR 1914-18

CONTENTS

THE GERMAN ADVANCE 1914

THE ATTACK ON BELGIUM

Within a few days of the outbreak of war it was obvious that every Belgian civilian, man, woman and child, as well as the soldiers, were in the firing line. As the Germans advanced in the glorious summer sunshine, any Belgian who showed resistance suffered death. The Germans were equally indifferent to the fate of their own men as they hurled them against the massive Belgian fortresses. Soon the Germans brought up their siege guns – the famous 'Big Berthas' made by Krupps and the 'Slim Emmas' made by the Austrian Skoda Works. These guns pulverised Liège and Namur, wiping their defence systems off the face of the earth. Artillery, with its high explosive shells, shrapnel and mortar bombs, would be the greatest killer of the First World War, far more deadly than gas and machine-guns.

Big Berthas in action, 1914

Eventually, the British and French armies managed to block the German advance but not before Moltke's men were well inside northern France. The British Expeditionary Force (BEF) first encountered the Germans at Mons. Its rapid rifle fire stopped the Germans in their tracks – then the BEF began its famous retreat from Mons, side by side with its Belgian and French allies. Moltke pressed his tired troops onwards until they were a mere fifteen miles (24 km) from Paris.

The Battle of the Marne 1914

General Joffre, commander of the French armies, co-ordinated an Anglo-French attack on the dangerously extended German lines (5–6 September 1914). Moltke correctly assessed that his troops were at risk.

1 They were weak from forced marches, many battles and poor food supplies.
2 Many units had been removed to East Prussia to stem an unexpected Russian invasion of Germany.

So Moltke decided to pull back from the Marne to prepared positions behind the River Aisne. For the French, this was the 'Miracle of the Marne'. Up to this battle, their resistance had cost them over 211,000 men – a casualty rate never to be equalled over the next four years. Now it seemed that the war was going in their favour. Had they chased after Moltke they might have turned his retreat into a rout. But they didn't. The battle line reached the Aisne and then both sides tried to turn each other's flanks in the famous 'race to the sea'.

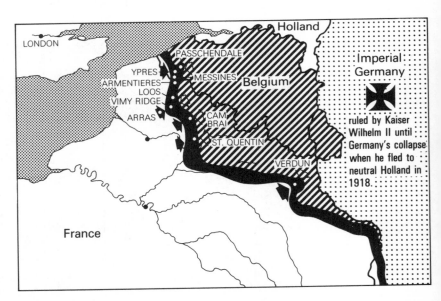

The Western Front, 1914–18, where the war was won, was a 'Sausage machine, because it was fed with live men, churned out corpses and remained firmly screwed in place...' (Robert Graves)

THE RACE TO THE SEA

Von Falkenhayn replaced Moltke and moved his troops forward to capture the Channel ports and thus stop reinforcements from reaching the BEF. But as each German unit moved the Allies outflanked it until the Belgians held the line from the Channel coast inland to Ypres, the BEF held the region between Ypres and Armentières and the French held the rest of this vast new front.

The beginning of trench warfare

By the end of autumn 1914 both sides were 'digging in'. From the Swiss frontier to the English Channel a line of trenches and fortifications developed into the static line of defence that men would call the Western Front. For the next three years the line would hardly waver as millions died in advances sometimes measured in miles but more often in yards.

BY THE END OF 1914

The war was truly global by December 1914. Cossack regiments had galloped into East Prussia as soon as war began – the vanguard of a well-equipped and well-trained Russian assault force. The finest units in the Russian Imperial Army, they defeated the Germans at Stalluponen and Gumbinnen. A rapturous British press hoped they would soon be in Königsberg and Berlin. It was not to be. German forces arrived from the west and stopped the Russian 'steamroller' at two battles: Tannenberg and the Masurian Lakes. Further south, the Austrians had swarmed into Russia only to meet five Russian armies plodding towards them. With their overwhelming numbers, the Tsar's troops pushed the Austrians out of Russia and won a major victory at Lemberg. So, in stark contrast with events on the Western Front, a huge war of movement swayed back and forth in the east. Elsewhere in the world, events took place at a bewildering speed. German warships seemed to be everywhere. *Goeben* and *Breslau* led a Turkish raid on Odessa; *Seydlitz* spearheaded the forays against British East Coast towns and eleven-inch shells smashed into Whitby.

In the Pacific, Admiral von Spee defeated the Royal Navy at the Battle of Coronel (December 1914) before he himself was defeated at the Battle of the Falkland Islands. *Emden* managed to escape the British for weeks and played havoc with the East Indies trade before being caught by the Australian cruiser *Sydney*. In East Africa, General von Lettow-Vorbeck held out against the Allies for the rest of the war – though British, West African and South African troops overran the other German colonies: Togo (1914), South-West Africa (1914–15) and Kamerun 1915–16. To the great disappointment of the British people there was no decisive sea battle. A few warships clashed at Heligoland Bight but the really decisive battles would be fought under the waves against the U-boats. Signs appeared that the air might be an important scene of warfare. Before the year ended, German aircraft had bombed Paris and Dover.

Document 1

CROQUIS DE GUERRE 1915
Forces anglaises se préparant pour l'action contre le Cameroun
473

This old postcard is captioned: 'An aspect of war 1915 – British forces preparing to attack the Kamerun.'

1   Where is the Kamerun?
2   What is its modern name?
3   What do you notice about the officers?
4   What do you notice about the soldiers and their NCOs?

Document 2

LA GUERRE DANS LE NORD
6 . Sur les grandes routes - La Chasse au Taube

This postcard is captioned: 'The War in the North – On the highways – the hunt for the Taube.'

1 In what part of Europe do you think the photograph was taken?
2 Do you think the soldiers are British?
3 What is the soldier on the left doing?
4 What is a Taube?
5 The picture might be called 'An early French AA gun'. In this context, what does 'AA' mean?

THE NATURE OF THE CONFLICT 1915–17

Both sides tried to break through on the Western Front and their early bull-headed attacks sacrificed thousands of men. Both sides learnt to envelop enemy positions in clouds of poison gas, eventually delivered with great precision. The British even tried a massive diversionary attack in an abortive assault on the Dardanelles (1915–16) in the hope of relieving pressure on the Western Front and of coming to the help of their long-suffering ally, Russia.

THE BATTLES OF 1915

By 1915 the Western Front was approximately 475 miles (765 km) long. It was not literally criss-crossed with defences throughout its length. There were large areas of marshland in the many river valleys that prevented men from digging even a slit trench. But regions that could be defended had the most elaborate earthworks and ferro-concrete 'pill-boxes' that soldiers could devise. One of the first 'all-British' offensives, the Battle of Neuve-Chapelle (March 1915) illustrates the problems encountered by the fighting men.

> A deafening barrage crashed down on German positions for 35 minutes, after which the infantry advanced on a front of 8000 yards (7.3 km). Within 3 hours they were pinned down by German fire and though the battle went on for the next 36 hours the British could not move beyond the outskirts of the little town of Neuve-Chapelle. The BEF suffered 12,900 casualties – roughly the same as the Germans. The British advanced 1200 yards – just over a kilometre.

The photograph on page 290 shows a German trench of this period. Note the high wall of sandbags and the duckboard along the trench floor. Why do think a bugler was so important in trench warfare?

When the Germans retaliated with their attack on Ypres (April 1915) they filled the Allied trenches with chlorine gas released from carefully concealed gas cylinders. The soldiers had no protection but the new weapon was dependent on wind direction and the Second Battle of Ypres soon fell into the pattern set at Neuve-Chapelle.

Verdun and the Somme 1916

General Falkenhayn decided to try to 'bleed the French white' by attacking Verdun – he knew that the French sense of national honour

would compel them to throw in every man they had. Thousands of *poilus* marched up the Voie Sacrée (the Sacred Way) to Verdun where the battle had begun on 21 February 1916. Generals Nivelle and Pétain, the defenders of Verdun, proclaimed, 'Ils ne passeront pas!' – 'They shall not pass!' Their casualties were so heavy that they appealed to the British to relieve the pressure.

Britain's Commander-in-Chief, Sir Douglas Haig, responded by attacking on the Somme – an area backed by open country through which advancing troops might move into 'green country' very swiftly and thus force a gap in the German lines.

After 5 days of bombardment, the first waves of British infantry (66,000) began crossing No Man's Land towards the German trenches. Within an hour half of these men were casualties, 'mown down like meadow grass', victims of the German machine-gunners. By noon 50,000 British troops had been killed or wounded; by the evening 21,000 British, Irish and Newfoundlanders had died, 35,000 were wounded and 600 were prisoners of war. Four officers and five 'other ranks' had won the VC. This was the first day of the Battle of the Somme – where the fighting went on until 14 November 1916. It had marginally helped the French, whose successful defence of the 'mincing machine' at Verdun went on until the middle of December. But neither side, at Verdun or on the Somme, had managed to break through the enemy defences – not even the British who had introduced the tank in

September in an effort to find a way of smashing the barbed wire, crossing the trenches and wiping out the deadly machine-gun posts.

1 Explain the term *'poilus'*.
2 Name the defenders of Verdun.
3 Who was the British Commander-in-Chief who planned the Battle of the Somme?
4 Did the Germans have any tanks at the Somme?
5 Look at this drawing of a British tank:

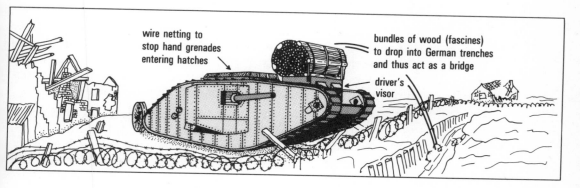

wire netting to stop hand grenades entering hatches

bundles of wood (fascines) to drop into German trenches and thus act as a bridge

driver's visor

A 1916 type Mark 1 tank. 32 feet long; 105 hp engine; 2 6-pounder guns; crew of 8 and a maximum speed of 0.5 mph over rough ground

(a) Why was their wire-netting on the top of the tank?
(b) What were fascines?
(c) How fast could it travel?
(d) Why was there a wheel behind the tank?

6 This is a British soldier's song of the First World War:

> Far, far from Wipers, I want to be
> Where German snipers can't get at me.
> Damp is my dug-out, cold are my feet,
> Waiting for whizz-bangs,
> To put me to sleep.

(a) Explain the meaning of 'Wipers'.
(b) Using the song as your source material and building on the knowledge of trench warfare you now have, write a typical soldier's letter home describing what it was like to serve on the Western Front between 1915 and 1916.

1917: ANOTHER YEAR OF ATTRITION

France had a new commander, General Nivelle. He decided to attack in 1917. But the Germans retreated to a brand-new set of defences (the Hindenburg Line) – and Nivelle attacked these new, untested defences. He suffered over 200,000 casualties and the *poilus* mutinied

Verdun and The Somme, 1916: The human cost

Verdun	740,000 casualties; the French lost 340,000 For the first time, the Germans used flame-throwers (February) and phosgene gas (June).
Somme	1,300,000 casualties; the British lost 400,000 The total advance achieved on the Somme was six miles (9.7 km). This took five months!

(elements of no less than fifty-four divisions were involved). Once more the British and their Commonwealth troops bore the brunt of the battle: the Canadians at Vimy Ridge, the British, Australians and New Zealanders at Messines – preceding the Third Battle of Ypres. The climax came in the attempt to capture Passchendaele Ridge.

> Marked by a flooded terrain and the use by the Germans of mustard gas, the fighting for Passchendaele Ridge began to lose all meaning and seemed to be helping no one. It didn't save the Italians from their defeat at Caporetto (October 1917) or prevent the Bolshevik Revolution in Russia (November 1917). The British suffered 244,000 casualties at 'Third Ypres' and when Canadian troops captured the little village of Passchendaele there was nothing to see there apart from 'a brick coloured stain on a watery landscape'.

HOW COULD SUCH A WAR BE ENDED?

Germany's new military leaders, Hindenburg and Ludendorff, put their faith in the U-boats. Although this wasn't their trump card, they hoped that unrestricted warfare against Britain might cut Britain off from her newest ally, the USA (who had declared war on Germany on 6 August 1917). With their vital sea lanes cut, the British might reach the verge of starvation – and be ready to surrender.

THE WAR AT SEA TO 1917   The U-boat war had begun in November 1914 when a German submarine sank a British merchant ship in the North Sea. The first 'unrestricted' U-boat campaign (February–August 1915) led to the sinking of 0.75 million tons of shipping, including the four-funneled *Lusitania* that sank in eighteen minutes within sight of the Irish coast (7 May 1915) – 1198 people died; 128 of these were Americans.

Elements of the German High Seas Fleet had raided East Coast towns in 1914; and when they tried again in 1915 Admiral Beatty's battle-cruisers intercepted them at the Battle of the Dogger Bank. In

1916 off Jutland Bank, the British and German fleets clashed in a battle unplanned by either side. The British came off worse in terms of loss of ships; but the German High Seas Fleet never again tried to lure the Royal Navy into a decisive naval action; though did make two uneventful sallies in August 1916 (when Scheer missed an encounter with British warships) and in April 1918 (when the Germans steamed close to the Shetlands).

The second unrestricted U-boat campaign (February 1917 onwards) brought America into the war and caused the British to take all sorts of precautions to defeat the U-boat:

1   The use of convoys – Prime Minister Lloyd George's great contribution.
2   The use of echo-sounders to find U-boats and better quality depth charges to sink them.
3   The use of Q-ships designed to lure a U-boat to the surface and then sink it with concealed guns.

The old postcard below shows two U-boats passing through the Straits of Gibraltar. Who were operating the searchlights?

An important sideshow: Lawrence of Arabia

A medieval historian and archaeologist, with a keen interest in the crusading Military Orders, T. E. Lawrence (1885–1935) was doing research in Syria in 1914. British Military Intelligence sent him to organise the Arab Revolt (it had broken out in 1916) so that it would, under his guidance, disrupt Turkish communications and tie down large numbers of Turkish troops. Lawrence worked with the Arab leaders, raided the Damascus–Medina Railway, and captured Akaba (1917). He fought on the right wing of Allenby's main 1918 offensive and captured Damascus in December. He represented the Arab point of view at the Paris Peace Conference (1919) and considered that the

1919 Treaty of Versailles – and especially the Palestine and Syrian mandates – betrayed everything for which the Arabs had fought. Later, he served in the RAF (he used the names Ross or Shaw) and the Tank Corps. He died when his Brough Superior motor cycle crashed near Bovington Camp, Dorset. His book, the *Seven Pillars of Wisdom*, is the classic account of the Arab Revolt.

ATTEMPTS TO BRING RUSSIA BACK INTO THE WAR

Lenin and Trotsky, the leaders of the successful 1917 Bolshevik Revolution had taken Russia out of the war via the Treaty of Brest-Litovsk (3 March 1918). Under British command, Allied troops reached Archangel in September 1918. They had three objectives:

1 To rescue the Czech Legion, stranded prisoners of war located on the Trans-Siberian Railway. These men wanted to resume fighting the Germans.
2 To re-establish a fighting front in Russia against the Germans.
3 to capture ammunition dumps before either the Germans or Bolsheviks reached them.

The entire operation was a massive failure and had absolutely no impact on the ultimate victory. Allied troops were fighting Russians long after the Armistice – even after the Treaty of Versailles had been signed!

THE FINAL CAMPAIGNS ON THE WESTERN FRONT

Meanwhile, the German General Ludendorff had planned one last attack on the Allies before the American reinforcements could arrive on the Western Front. His plan was called the Kaiserschlacht and its target was the destruction of the British 5th Army – Ludendorff intended to overrun it or force it to retreat so that he could capture the Channel ports. For three months the Germans battered the Allied lines and made substantial advances. However, their losses were appalling and by mid-July they began to pull back

Now the Allies struck back, their armies unified under a single commander, General (later Marshal) Foch. Americans arrived by the thousand to bolster the exhausted French armies in the south and centre; the élite of the British Army, spearheaded by tough Australian, Canadian and New Zealand divisions, bore the brunt of the fighting.

Yet it was hard to exploit this new war of movement, despite the large numbers of tanks now equipping the Allied armies. For example, on 'Black Day' (as far as the German army was concerned – 8 August 1918) 534 tanks led the British attack at Amiens. Four days later, only six of these were operational. No tank could break through St Quentin – the toughest part of the Hindenburg Line. But the infantry could, and on 29 September 1918 the British 46th Division crossed the canal at St Quentin in one of the most successful military operations of the First World War.

THE ARMISTICE

After weeks of fighting in a dismal, rain-sodden autumn, against determined German resistance and particularly vicious machine-gunners, the Allies forced the mighty German army to surrender. On 7 November a German armistice delegation drove their motor cars across the crumbling German front line and, under a white flag, reached the forward Allied positions. Simultaneously, the British First Army was force-marching towards Mons, determined to capture the town where the first British shots had been fired back in 1914. On 10–11 November the German and Canadian infantry clashed outside Mons. In the early morning Haig signed his last communiqué of the war: 'Canadian troops of the First Army have captured Mons.'

Haig's blunt words were echoed by Private James Tait of the East Yorkshire Regiment who had fought on the Western Front since 1916. He describes his experiences after one of the last German attacks in 1918:

> They were caught in a salient. That was the beginning of the end of the German army . . . thanks to a great French General, Marshal Foch . . . as our remnants marched on, footweary and worn out, we heard a fresh sound from a brand new American battalion, who yelled across at us, 'Where's this goddammed shootin' gallery?!' I finished up at Mons where it all began for the British and cried myself to sleep when the guns were silenced and the Armistice began in the town . . . and then I remembered that Jesus also wept.
> (From the Diary of Pte. James Tait, *Malet Lambert High School Local History Originals*, Vol. 8, 1982)
> Credit: P. N. Farrar

1 To whom did Pte. Tait give the credit for the Allied victories?
2 What evidence is there that the US battalion he met hadn't yet seen action?
3 Where was Tait at the end of the First World War?
4 Why was that spot especially significant to a British soldier.
5 Soldiers in combat are often deeply religious; do you think Tait was?

THE ARMISTICE TERMS (1918) AND THE 1919 TREATY OF VERSAILLES

THE ARMISTICE TERMS

A hastily created German government agreed to evacuate France, Belgium, Luxembourg and Alsace-Lorraine. It accepted that Allied troops would occupy Germany west of the Rhine, together with Cologne, Coblenz and Mainz. The German army would surrender 2,500 heavy guns, 30,000 machine-guns and 2000 aeroplanes. The German Navy would allow 6 battle-cruisers, 10 battleships, 8 light cruisers and 50 destroyers to be interned; and it would hand over all its U-boats. Additionally, 5000 railway locomotives, 150,000 wagons and 5000 lorries would be transferred to the Allies.

The Germans now had to shift 183 divisions out of the battle zone, across the German frontier and then east of the Rhine. This involved 2 million soldiers and reflected great skill on the German officer class who were clearly willing to work with the new government of Socialist Germany.

1 What had happened to the Kaiser?
2 When did he die?
3 Who was the British Prime Minister who now went to Paris 'to make Germany pay'?
4 The German fleet went into internment at Scapa Flow. What then happened to it?
5 Who was the first President of the new Germany?

THE TREATY OF VERSAILLES 1919

Both Lloyd George of Britain and Clemenceau of France wanted compensation for the damage suffered during the war. Woodrow Wilson, the US President, wanted everyone to agree to no more wars – and to join the League of Nations that he hoped would spring up after the Germans signed the treaty:

1 Germany lost West Prussia, Eupen, Malmedy, Posen, part of upper Silesia, Northern Schleswig, Alsace-Lorraine, the Saar coalfield and all her colonies.
2 The Allies confiscated her High Seas Fleet and Merchant Marine.
3 There would be no conscription and the army had to be reduced to 100,000 men.
4 The German Air Service was abolished – no more Zeppelins or fighting aircraft to be built.
5 All lands west of the Rhine to be occupied; and there would be no military fortifications to a depth of 50 km east of the Rhine (the 'demilitarised zone').
6 Any union (*Anschluss*) between Germany and Austria was forbidden.
7 Germany must accept full responsibility for causing the war and for all the suffering that followed.
8 Germany would have to pay compensation – this was called 'war reparations' and the sum was fixed in 1921 at £6,600 million.

BRITISH POLICIES TOWARDS EUROPE 1919–39

CONTENTS

AN OVERVIEW

Britain:

(*a*)   exploited post-war conditions in Europe to benefit her own industries wherever possible;

(*b*)   tried to create the illusion of a system of 'collective European security' with the minimum of effort;

(*c*)   with France, used the League of Nations as an arbiter of disputes between relatively small or economically weak countries.

Britain's Prime Ministers

Lloyd George (1863–1945) won the 1918 General Election and continued the wartime coalition government. Had to resign over the collapse of his foreign and Irish policies (1922).

Bonar Law (1854–1923) was first Conservative Prime Minister after the war (1922–3).

Ramsay MacDonald (1866–1937) led two minority Labour Governments: 1924 and 1929–31; led two National Governments: 1931; 1931–5.

Stanley Baldwin (1867–1947) Prime Minister on three occasions: 1923–4; 1924–9; 1935–7. (National Government)

Neville Chamberlain (1869–1940): Continued the National Government into the Second World War 1937–40.

The main events

1 The reconstruction of the German state and the Locarno Treaties (1925).
2 The Spanish Civil War (1936–9)
3 The collapse of the European Security System.
4 Appeasement.
5 Outbreak of the Second World War 1939.

THE RECONSTRUCTION OF GERMANY

Still filled with a hatred of Germany, both Britain and France took every chance they could to extort the maximum gain from this defeated country.

British coal exports flourish

Both Polish and German coal exports declined during the period 1921–4 and Britain immediately seized the European coal market.

1 War between Poland and Russia 1920–1 led to end of Polish exports.
2 Franco-Belgian invasion of the Ruhr (1923) led to the closedown of many German coal-mines.

The Franco-Belgian invasion had been caused by the failure of post-war Germany (the Weimar Republic) to meet its reparation payments. Publicly condemned by Britain; but, in fact, Britain had made no effort to prevent the invasion. The French stayed in the Ruhr for over two years and withdrew when it was obvious that Germany was going to sign the Locarno Treaties.

THE COLLAPSE OF THE GERMAN MONETARY SYSTEM

The occupation of the Ruhr and the German reaction (passive resistance) had led to:

1 political disorder (Hitler's unsuccessful 'putsch' – Munich, 1923);
2 financial chaos (inflation reached unprecedented levels).

Aid to Weimer

The American General Dawes and a team of experts drew up plans to place Germany's finances on a brand new footing. In 1924 they devised a new currency and lent Germany's industrialists $200 million. This gave Germany the chance of modernising her industries. Germany now paid her reparations until 1929 when another team of US experts led by Owen D. Young came to the rescue and arranged a plan so that Germany could repay her reparations over the next fifty-nine years! This reflected the hopes that Europe would remain at peace, hopes enshrined in the treaty signing that had been going on since 1925.

The Locarno Treaties 1925

Several treaties were signed at Locarno in December 1925.

1 The most important guaranteed:
   (a)   the frontiers between Belgium and Germany;
   (b)   the frontiers between France and Germany;
   (c)   the permanent demilitarisation of the Rhineland.

British and Italy (now led by the Fascist dictator Benito Mussolini) guaranteed these treaties.

2 France also signed treaties guaranteeing the defence of Poland and Czechoslovakia, new states that had been set up after the First World War.

   In 1926 Germany joined the League of Nations and in 1928 was one of sixty-two nations who signed the famous Kellogg-Briand Pact. This was a general renunciation of war 'as an instrument of national policies' negotiated by US Secretary of State Kellogg and the French Premier, Aristide Briand.

THE DEPRESSION

Within a few weeks of the Young Plan the Wall Street Crash (1929) heralded the depression that would shatter the world's trading system and demolish the delicate structure of war debts and reparations. Everyone now said they couldn't possibly meet their payments to America. Consequently, the USA had to write off most of its reparation and war debt investments and recall its overseas investments in industry. The American people became very bitter about the unreliability of Europe and most of them agreed with their President, Calvin Coolidge (1923–9), who – when criticised for calling in American overseas investment – retorted: 'Well, they hired the money, didn't they?'

THE SPANISH CIVIL WAR 1936–9

The most dramatic effect of the years of depression 1929–33 was the rise to power of Adolf Hitler, Chancellor of Germany in 1933 and Führer or Leader in 1934. Yet far more attention was given by Britain to events in Spain and the progress of the Civil War that began in 1936.

CAUSES OF THE WAR

The deep-rooted cause of the war was the discontent and distress among agricultural workers, the landless *braceros* who – when they had the chance – worked on the vast estates known as *latifundia*. Powerful landowners made up about 5 per cent of the population and owned about 70 per cent of the land. Supported by the Catholic Church and the army, they kept the vast majority of the Spanish people in a state of permanent subjugation. There was nothing new about this. As one Spaniard noted in 1930, there was 'little in the Spanish countryside which was not already known and denounced more than a century ago'. A dozen different governments tried to tackle Spain's fundamental problems 1918–23. Then Primo de Rivera (1870–1930), a distinguished soldier, took over – a dictator who tried to modernise Spain (King Alfonso XIII used to call him 'my Mussolini'). Rivera's dictatorial rule led to widespread opposition and he resigned in 1930. Within a year Alfonso XIII had followed him into exile and the Spanish Republic was born. Before long Spain, so long divided between the landowners and the landless, had its own political labels to highlight the differences:

The Left Republican, Socialist, Communist and Anarchist Parties united in 1936 to form a 'Popular Front' against the Right.
The Right Catholics, landowners and Fascists (followers of José Antonio Rivera, the ex-dictator's son who had founded the Falange Espanola).

On 16 February 1936 the Popular Front won the general election. Did this mean that Spain would now go communist? The Spanish army feared that it would – and rebelled against the Republican Government on 17–18 July 1936. The revolt of the army began the Spanish Civil War.

The early campaigns

The army revolt began in North Africa but rebels in Spain quickly gained about a third of the countryside. The problem was: how to transport the army from North Africa to Spain? Hitler and Mussolini soon came to the Spanish army's rescue.

1   German Ju-52 transport aircraft ferried the first of the troops across the Straits of Gibraltar.
2   Italian ships transported the bulk of the 'Nationalist Army' (as it was now called) and provided air cover using aircraft of the Regia Aeronautica.

Unexpectedly, General Francisco Franco (1892–1975) became the nationalist leader when his superior, General Sanjurjo, died in an air crash. On 1 October 1936 the army proclaimed Franco as Generalissimo and 'Head of State', with supreme power. This meant that Franco was the Nationalist dictator in those parts of Spain controlled by the army.

Aid to the Republic

The Spanish Republic received direct military assistance from the Soviet Union and the International Brigades.

Russia's aid was mainly material – it sent only a small number of propaganda experts, military advisers and political commissars. Altogether 1409 Soviet aircraft were sent to help the Republic (General Smushkevich commanded 'Stalin's Falcons'); while several troops of Russian T-26 tanks were tried out in Spain – usually they were outgunned by Nationalist tanks and very easily caught fire.

The International Brigades came from all over Europe and the United States. They were recruited by the Communist Party and they were all volunteers. Walter Ulbricht and Klement Gottwald would one day head Soviet satellite governments in East Germany and Czechoslovakia; non-Communist recruits were usually funnelled through the Paris office run by Josip Broz (later Marshal Tito). Altogether, twelve International Brigades served in Spain and, as the Republican leaders used them as shock troops, they took heavy losses. They defended Madrid against Franco and forced the dictator to lay siege to the city – for the next twenty-eight months!

Support from the arts Picasso's *Guernica* became one of the twentieth century's most famous paintings – an art form that captured the horror of the German bombing raid on the little Basque town of Guernica in 1937. Ernest Hemingway produced one of his best novels, *For Whom the Bell Tolls*, as a result of his experiences in Spain. George Orwell, who had fought in a Trotskyite militia unit, wrote his *Homage to Catalonia* and *Animal Farm*. Benny Goodman gave concerts to raise money. British fund-raising activities, noted one cynic, paled in comparison with the amount of money spent every week by the British working class on their football pools.

More aid to the Nationalists

Franco didn't hold the industrial regions – so he couldn't manufacture the weapons needed to fight the war. Hitler and Mussolini again came to his aid.

1 Both Hitler and Mussolini recognised Franco as the legal ruler of Spain.
2 Mussolini defined the war as a 'crusade against Bolshevism' and sent four divisions (they fought and lost the Battle of Guadalajara in 1937) who were later integrated into the Nationalist Army and fought with distinction. So did Italy's new Fiat CR-42 fighters and Savoia–Marchetti three-engined bombers.
3 Much better known was the German Condor Legion. It kept a force of

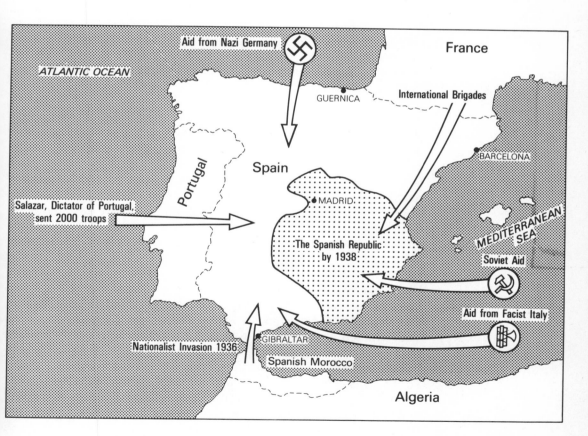

The Spanish Civil War, 1936–9

one hundred aeroplanes in Spain and tested out the new Heinkel 111 bomber and the Ju-87 'Stuka' dive-bomber.

THE NATIONALIST VICTORY 1939

Both Nationalists and Republicans conducted a wholesale slaughter of their political opponents during the Spanish Civil War. Prisoners of war rarely survived and most of these horrors took place behind the frontline – a line that moved ever closer to the Republican heartland in 1937–8.

During 1938 most of the International Brigades left Spain. In Barcelona, the famous Communist broadcaster Dolores Ibarruri (known to everyone as La Pasionaria) paid tribute to the many foreigners who had helped the Spanish Republic:

> Today they are leaving us. But many of them, thousands of them, remain with us with the Spanish earth for their shroud. All Spaniards remember them with the deepest of feelings.

Their absence gave Franco the edge and he forced the Republican 'Army of the Ebro' into exile during 1939. The first German Panzers rumbled into Barcelona (25 January 1939) and soon Catalonia was in Nationalist hands. Four columns advanced on Madrid (General Mola had boasted many months before that he had a 'Fifth Column' of secret supporters inside the city – Mola was killed in an air crash). Madrid fell on 27 March 1939 and Franco announced the end of the Civil War on 1 April 1939.

THE SIGNIFICANCE OF THE SPANISH CIVIL WAR

1 It was of immense importance in the history of Europe and the world as it involved:
(*a*)   a struggle between a legitimate Spanish government and a rebellious right-wing Nationalist organisation;
(*b*)   the armed forces of the Soviet Union, Fascist Italy and Nazi Germany;
(*c*)   immense public sympathy for the suffering of the Spanish people;
(*d*)   the International Brigades.
Yet Britain and France wanted no part of the affair.
1 Both feared for the safety of their colonies – the British base at Gibraltar and the French possessions of Algeria and Tunisia.
2 They wanted to contain the war and preserve – no matter who was the victor – the unity of the Spanish state.
Britain and France therefore supported a 'Non-Intervention Policy', i.e. an arms embargo on both sides for the duration of the hostilities. They set up the Non-Intervention Committee in London. Germany and Italy were members of the committee! It kept talking but did nothing.
2 It totally discredited the League of Nations. The Non-Intervention

Committee was not an instrument of the League but the League was quite happy to endorse its recommendations.

(a) No steps were taken to stop the flow of arms.

(b) Prime Minister Chamberlain wanted to do nothing that might provoke the dictators – so his point of view made a great impact on the League. The Royal Navy and the French Navy did, however, patrol the Spanish coast after an Italian submarine tried to torpedo a British destroyer. However, there was no protection given to Spanish ships or shore installations – fair game for the German pocket battle-ship *Deutschland* and various Italian warships operating in the Mediterranean. So the League made no impact, in the same way as it had made no impact over the Manchurian crisis (1931–2) and the War in Abyssinia (1935–6). This was not because its fundamental principles were unsound but because its senior member nations – Britain and France – refused to adopt a resolute policy that would have denied the foreign weapons on which the Republicans and Nationalists depended.*

*For details of these events see Pan Study Aid History 1

3 Quite exceptionally, the Spanish Civil War enabled three dictators to test and develop their latest weapons under modern battle conditions. The war – especially through the newsreels – reinforced the idea that the future would be won by those nations who had the biggest number of bombers. Perhaps what was not noticed was the remarkable resilience of civilian populations under persistent terror attacks from the air. Madrid, for example, endured intense bombing for well over two years.

THE COLLAPSE OF THE EUROPEAN SECURITY SYSTEM

THE THREAT FROM ADOLF HITLER

Far too little attention had been given to the menace of Adolf Hitler, dictator of Germany since 1933.

In his book, *Mein Kampf,* he had specifically blamed Jewish politicians and Jewish war profiteers for the collapse of the German army on the Western Front in 1918:

> If at the beginning of the war, and while it was going on, 12,000 or 15,000 of these Jewish corrupters of the people could have been exposed to poison gas, just as hundreds of thousands of our best German manpower from all walks of life had to suffer poison gas on the battlefield, then the millions who died in the war would not have died in vain.
> (*Mein Kampf* (1938 edition), p. 772).

He also wrote:

> We must put a stop to this ceaseless German march towards the South and the West and turn our eyes instead to the lands of the East . . . So when we speak of new territory in Europe

nowadays we must think mainly of Russia and the border states under her control . . . This colossal Empire in the East is ripe for dissolution and the end of Jewish rule there will also mean the end of Russia as a state.

(*Mein Kampf*, pp. 742–3)

DISMANTLING THE VERSAILLES TREATY

Slowly and methodically, Hitler dismantled the Versailles Treaty. In 1935 the people of the Saar voted to return to German rule; and in the same year Hitler announced conscription for a new German army to be called the Wehrmacht. Hitler had thus renounced the disarmament clauses of the Versailles Treaty, and Britain, France and Italy formed a defensive 'Stresa Front'. This was the result of the Stresa Conference 1935 – all it did was to issue a protest against Hitler's act. Within a matter of months the Stresa Front had collapsed because of Italy's involvement in Abyssinia.

Then, on 7 March 1936, three German battalions marched across the Rhineland bridges and headed for Aachen, Trier and Saarbrucken.

Read the following account:

It has often been said that this was the moment when Hitler could have been stopped. Thirteen French divisions were standing by along the Franco-German frontier; while Britain, despite her rundown army and airforce, could have sent some troops and aircraft against such a tiny force. In fact, Cabinet papers released in 1968 showed that no one in the British Foreign Office intended to block Hitler's reoccupation of the Rhineland. People were anxious to please Hitler and to preserve peace in Europe. Foreign Secretary Anthony Eden was even prepared to hand over the Cameroons to the Führer. Eden's opposite number, Pierre Flandin, came to London after the reoccupation had begun in search of advice. Eden said that although Hitler had dealt a heavy blow at 'the sanctity of treaties', we 'have no reason to suppose that Germany's present action threatens hostilities.'

1   What evidence is there that Britain did not intend to oppose Hitler over the Rhineland in 1935?
2   What was Britain's main interest?
3   Why would Eden suggest handing over the Cameroons to Hitler?
4   Explain the term 'sanctity of treaties'.
5   Do you think that Eden was also an 'appeaser'?
    In 1938, Hitler repeated his success – by demanding territories that, although they contained substantial numbers of Germans, were not legally his. In 1938 he summoned the Austrian Chancellor, Kurt von Schuschnigg, to Berchtesgaden (12 February) and demanded an *Anschluss* (union) between Germany and Austria.

Document 1

I will blow up the frontier system of Austria and spill German blood in the process. Don't think for one moment that anyone on earth is going to thwart my decision. Italy? I see eye to eye with Mussolini. England? England will not move one finger for Austria. France? She could have stopped us in the Rhineland and then we would have had to retreat. But now it is too late for France.

(Hitler, berating Schuschnigg)

Document 2

Austrian men and women! I cannot countenance the spilling of German blood. We have ordered our troops in the event of a German attack to withdraw without resistance.

(Schuschnigg's broadcast to the Austrian people).

1. What was significant about Berchtesgaden as a choice of meeting Schuschnigg?
2. What is the significance of the use of the expression 'German blood' in these two extracts?
3. Why was Hitler confident about Italy?
4. Did Hitler have any respect for Britain?
5. Why was it 'too late for France'?
6. How did Schuschnigg react to Hitler's threats?
7. A plebiscite was held to see if the Austrian people approved of the union; 99% of the Austrians voted one way. Which way?
8. List the ways in which Hitler had now broken the Versailles Treaty.

APPEASEMENT OVER CZECHOSLOVAKIA

ANGLO–FRENCH REACTION TO GERMAN MILITARISM

In many ways, Britain had condoned the rise of German military power by:

1. The 1935 Anglo-German Naval Agreement that:
   (a)   set up the '35 per cent formula' allowing Germany to build up to 35 per cent of the tonnage of the Royal Navy;
   (b)   but allowed the Germans to build 45 per cent or more of submarine tonnage.
2. Her willingness to accept German territorial expansion (Rhineland and Austria) in complete defiance of the Versailles Treaty.

Britain's answer was to continue her policy of appeasing Hitler but at the same time building up her armed forces. Though there was still a National Government in Britain, the Labour leader, Clement Attlee, stated that his party's policy was 'not one of seeking security through rearmament but through disarmament'.

France's policy had been far more consistent. She had maintained very strong defence forces, pouring money into the Maginot Line's complex defence system. Her army was fairly small but very professional; her air force had very few modern aeroplanes but a lot of old fashioned designs; her tanks (especially the Somua S-35) were among the best in the world; the navy had sleek battleships such as the *Richelieu* and *Dunkerque* and remarkable submarines such as the monster *Surcouf*.

Chamberlain's brand of appeasement

In its political sense, the word 'appeasement' was first used in the 1920s to describe the general process by which international problems might be worked out around the conference table. After Hitler came to power in 1933, appeasement was the term used to describe the concessions France and Britain made to the German dictator in the belief that the Führer was only reoccupying 'his own back garden'. Chamberlain had a certain amount of sympathy with Hitler.

1 He agreed that some of the Versailles decisions about frontiers had been basically unsound.
2 He also recognised that the rise of dictators such as Hitler and Mussolini represented new forces in Europe that the Versailles treaty makers had never anticipated.

Hitler was one of the first political leaders to realise the value of travelling by aircraft. He often flew around Germany, speaking at meetings so that as many people as possible could see him. The man in the background (right) was in charge of Hitler's propaganda machine. What was his name?

3 Chamberlain also mistakenly believed that both Mussolini and Hitler

were fundamentally reasonable men who could be satisfied once their various frontier problems had been settled. His views were true for most western politicians and probably for most of the British and French people.

4   So Chamberlain failed to understand that he was dealing with men whose values were entirely different from his, who had no respect for the principles of democratic government and who had no belief in human rights and popular self-determination whatsoever.

CZECHOSLOVAKIA SACRIFICED TO HITLER

Hitler made up his mind to smash Czechoslovakia 'in the near future'. He gave his service chiefs a deadline: **1 October 1938.** On 19 May the international press carried reports of German troop movements close to the heavily defended Czech frontier. Two days later the Czechs ordered partial mobilisation of their army. However, the British Foreign Minister, Lord Halifax, hinted to the German ambassador that Britain might not stand by if a 'general war' broke out over the Sudetenland where 3.25 million Germans lived.

1   There was every chance that the determined Czechs, located in very strong defensive positions and with thirty-five divisions equipped with the latest weapons, would fight Hitler.

2   Chamberlain saw his mission in life as preventing such a war. He therefore asked if he could see Hitler in Berchtesgaden.

The idea caught public imagination Britain's elderly Prime Minister, who had never been in an aeroplane, was making his first flight to preserve the peace of Europe.

1   At Berchtesgaden Hitler promised on 16 September 1938 not to attack Czechoslovakia until Chamberlain had worked out some sort of deal with the Czech leader, Dr Beneš.

2   Chamberlain flew back to Germany and met Hitler at Godesberg (22 September). He could have most of the Sudetenland!

3   Quite unexpectedly, Hitler refused the deal – he wanted it all, or he would take it by force.

Gloomily, Chamberlain flew back to Britain. The Labour Party urged the support of Czechoslovakia; the Trades Union Congress urged Chamberlain to join with France and the Soviet Union against Hitler. War seemed inevitable and on 27 September 1938 Chamberlain made the following broadcast to the British people:

> How horrible, fantastic, incredible it is that we should be digging trenches and trying on gas-masks here because of a quarrel in a faraway country between people of whom we know nothing . . . I would not hesitate to pay a third visit to Germany if I thought it would do any good.

On 28 September – two days before the deadline – Chamberlain was addressing the House of Commons. A note was passed to him. He glanced at it and then told the House: 'I have been informed by Herr

Hitler that he has invited me to meet him in Munich tomorrow morning.'

In Munich (29–30 September, twenty-four hours before the deadline – Chamberlain and Daladier (the French Prime Minister) agreed that Hitler could have all the Sudetenland. A joyful Chamberlain now flew back to Britain.

Chamberlain returns from Munich, 1938
Source: BBC Hulton Picture Library Catalogue, p.6

As he drove back to Downing Street, the crowds shouted, 'Good old Neville!' He spoke to them from his window:

> My good friends! This is the second time in our history that there has come back from Germany to Downing Street peace with honour. I believe it is peace for our time.

Questions

1 To what event was Chamberlain referring when he spoke of 'peace with honour'?
2 Who was the Prime Minister then?
3 Look at the map opposite:
   (*a*)   Name the three places where Chamberlain met Hitler in 1938.
   (*b*)   Name two other countries that received parts of Czechoslovakia in 1938.
   (*c*)   Note the location of the Maginot Line. Which country in particular (bearing in mind the history of the First World War) did it fail to protect?

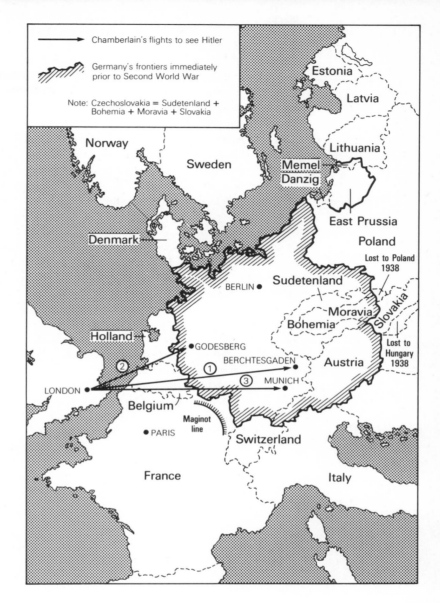

Appeasement, 1937–9

WAR OVER POLAND

By March 1939 there were fresh fears of a war developing in Central
Europe.

HITLER'S NEW GAINS

Hitler annexed Bohemia and Moravia, occupied the Czech capital of Prague, and took over the Skoda armaments factory. He allowed 'Slovakia' to exist as a separate state under German protection and let Hungary gobble up the rest of Ruthenia. On 21 March 1939 he scored another triumph – Lithuania gave Germany back the port of Memel. Simultaneously, he offered Poland a twenty-five-year non-aggression pact if the Poles would return Danzig to Germany and let the Nazis control the railway that crossed the Polish province of Pomorze between Germany and East Prussia (everyone except the Poles called this the 'Polish Corridor'). When the Poles refused this led to a revolution in British foreign policy.

British reactions

Britain and France now guaranteed Polish independence – and from now on this became the crucial issue for Europe and, ultimately, for the world. Danzig became the scene of many Nazi demonstrations and tension ran high.

In August the Germans and Russians signed their totally unexpected Non-Aggression Pact (23rd); on the 25th Gauleiter Forster became Danzig's 'Head of State'; and on the same day Britain and Poland signed an Agreement of Mutual Assistance – Britain would come at once to Poland's aid if she were attacked. Hitler was shaken and postponed the invasion of Poland, scheduled for the 26th. Then he reconsidered – the British wouldn't dare to intervene. But if they did, how could they help Poland? So he took the risk and sent his armed forces into Poland on 1 September 1939.

On 3 September 1939 Britain and France declared war on Germany. The Second World War had begun.

THE SECOND WORLD WAR 1939–45

CONTENTS

THE DEFEAT OF POLAND 1939

Battered by Stukas and the fast-moving German Panzer divisions, the Poles staked everything on a desperate counter-attack against the Nazi invaders along the River Bzura. It lasted a week and the Germans themselves called it a great battle of annihilation. After days of fighting the Polish survivors regrouped, hoping there would be some sort of intervention from Britain and France. But the Western Allies did nothing: there was virtually no activity in the zone between the Maginot Line and its German equivalent, the Siegfried Line. When Soviet armies invaded Poland on 17 September, Polish resistance began to collapse. Warsaw held out for three days under attack from 1000 German bombers and then surrendered. Many Polish soldiers managed to escape into Hungary and Romania but on 6 October 1939 all fighting against German and Russian troops ended.

Significance

Undoubtedly, the speed of victory gave Hitler too much faith in the effectiveness of *blitzkrieg* (lightning war) tactics but for the time being his skill as a military leader won almost total and thoroughly enthusiastic support among the German people. His success was a stern warning to Britain and France, neither of whom had lifted a finger to help the Poles. The importance of combating the Stuka (no match for any Allied frontline fighter) and the vulnerability of the Panzers to armour-piercing and incendiary shells should have imprinted an indelible lesson on the minds of the West's military planners. The RAF did begin to increase the strength of Fighter Command and to improve the reliability of the radar and Observer Corps early warning systems. But apart from this the western allies did very little over the next seven months, months that have gone down in history as the 'phoney war'.

German stamp: Stuka dive-bombers

German stamp: Panzer

THE 'PHONEY WAR' 1939–40

IN FRANCE

Though there were some incidents, some serious, the hostilities that existed between the Allies and Germany bore no resemblance to those that had gone on in France and Belgium during 1914–15. The BEF (British Expeditionary Force) of 152,000 and 9,500 RAF ground crew sailed in convoy across the Channel and seventy-two French divisions and four British divisions glared at their opposite numbers in the Wehrmacht – but from a safe distance.

ON THE SEA

The Royal Navy was not so lucky. On 14 October the U-47 penetrated the British naval base at Scapa Flow, fired three torpedoes and sank the 31,000 ton battleship *Royal Oak*. This disaster came hard on the heels of the loss of the aircraft carrier *Courageous*, sunk in the Bristol Channel by U-29 the previous month. The Navy's great success was the Battle of the River Plate when three British cruisers, the *Exeter*, *Ajax* and *Achilles*, forced the German surface raider *Graf Spee* to put into Montevideo harbour for repairs. On 17 December the *Graf Spee* steamed out of Montevideo harbour into the River Plate and then, in a moment of high drama, scuttled herself on the direct orders of Adolf Hitler.

IN THE AIR

RAF bombers also made war on the German navy. On 4 September 9 Squadron's Wellingtons took part in the famous raid on the German battleships at Brunsbuttel; while RAF Spitfires defended the Royal Navy base at the Firth of Forth against reprisal raids by German bombers (26 September and 16 October). Most effort went into the RAF's leaflet raids. Yorkshire-based Whitleys flying as far afield as Warsaw (16 March 1940) performed incredible feats of navigation and endurance in the early days of night operations.

1   Look at the first stamp on page 315. Write a paragraph explaining the tactics adopted by the much-feared Stukas.

2   Look at the second stamp on page 315. What main differences were there between Hitler's Panzers and the sort of tanks used by the British in the First World War (refer back to p. 291)? One important clue is suggested by the German artist.

3   How did the Stukas and Panzers work together to create the *blitzkrieg*?

4   Why do you think there were no attacks by Britain and France along the Western Front in 1939?

5   Why do you think there was no effort to give direct aid to Poland? Is there any evidence in the description of British air activity (above) to suggest that the RAF might have helped the Poles?

THE GERMAN BLITZKRIEG IN THE WEST 1940

DENMARK AND NORWAY

Late in March 1940 Britain and France came to the conclusion that the most important part of Western Europe, from the strategic point of view, was Scandinavia. Norway's coast with its main fiords, so useful as potential U-boat and surface raider bases, was vital for British defences; while the port of Narvik held a special significance: most of Sweden's high-grade iron-ore, on which Germany depended, was shipped through here. Nevertheless, it sounded very odd to British ears to hear their first Lord of the Admiralty, Winston Churchill, announce that the Navy was mining neutral Norway's coastal waters; and even stranger to learn that an Allied task force was heading for the Norwegian coast. But compared with Hitler's own plans, the Allied efforts were puny.

Read the following account:

> 'Operation Weser' required the German armed forces to carry out a combined invasion of Denmark and Norway. Early on 9 April 1940 the people of Copenhagen were going to work. German ships nosed into the harbour; Junkers 52 transports roared overhead. Spilling out of the ships were squads of German bicycle troops who mingled with Danish cyclists in the morning rush hour. By the afternoon a German officer had politely informed the Danish king that his country had been occupied. Simultaneously, ten German destroyers were heading for Narvik while heavy units of the German Navy off-loaded their assault troops on Trondheim, Bergen, Stavanger, Kristiansund and Oslo. British and French troops tried and failed to match German versatility and skill. As Churchill later said, they were 'baffled by the vigour, enterprise and training of Hitler's young men'.

THE LOW COUNTRIES AND FRANCE

While the fighting was still going on around Narvik, Hitler put into operation the second and third stages of his *blitzkrieg* in the west: the attack on the Low Countries and the invasion of France.

1 Junkers 52 transports towed German glider troops to key targets in the Low Countries.
2 Stukas bombed Dutch airfields.
3 Paratroopers swamped the bewildered Dutch and Belgian defenders. In Britain, on the same day – 10 March 1940 – Chamberlain resigned, to be replaced by Winston Churchill. He could do nothing to save the Dutch and Belgians from the devastating air raids that would lead to their surrender:
1 **14 May** 57 Heinkel He-111 bombers dropped their high-explosive loads on Rotterdam. The city surrendered two hours later.

2   **17 May**   Brussels endured similar attacks and surrendered.
Already, France was in desperate trouble. Tanks led by the brilliant German Panzer leader, General Guderian, reached the Meuse and, under the cover of a thousand ground-attack aircraft, crossed the river and began to fan out towards the south and the Channel ports. The Panzers took Gravelines, Boulogne and Calais and pushed on to Dunkirk – where they were halted by Hitler.

Dunkirk – Operation Dynamo

The British had decided the pull out of France. Admiral Ramsay was in charge of the entire operations from his headquarters in Dover. With great foresight, he had sent 80,000 gallons of drinking water, stored in cans, to the sand dunes of Dunkirk's beaches so that the exhausted BEF – who would have to wait some time before being taken off to waiting destroyers – would not suffer from thirst.

The rescue mission began on 26 May. Cut off inside an ever-tightening perimeter, nearly 350,000 troops had to suffer constant air and mortar attack. The Luftwaffe systematically levelled the port installations and then began bombing the town itself. Long lines of soldiers gathered on the sand dunes.

Read this soldier's account of Dunkirk:

> We fell back after three days on the perimeter. We brought our Brens and the last two anti-tank guns with us, hauling them through the burning Bedfords on the edge of Dunkirk sands. We had some food and the French had given us lots of money. I saw one chap throw away pocketfuls of coins when he went into the water. We dug some shell-scrapes and they were all right against the bombs which went deep into the sand before going off. What we didn't like was the way Jerry shovelled hand grenades at us. I took pot shots at one bomber that did this with my Colt. I was in the water at least eight hours. I think I was sunk five times. I came home in the *Icarus*.

1   Who was in charge of Operation Dynamo?
2   How had he acted with 'great foresight'?
3   How many troops were inside the Dunkirk perimeter?
4   Why were there so many 'burning Bedfords' on the edge of the sands?
5   Why did soldiers have to stand in the water for so long?
6   How did they manage to reach destroyers such as the *Icarus*?

THE FALL OF FRANCE 1940

Hitler's *blitzkrieg* had thrown the British Army out of the France and thus spared the BEF the horror of a repeat performance of the First World War style of trench fighting. But to the French, Britain's evacuation seemed more like desertion in the face of a superior enemy.

1　General Weygand took command of the depleted French forces (the Germans had taken 200,000 prisoners during the crossing of the Meuse; the entire First Army surrendered at Lille; 100,000 *poilus* escaped with the British from Dunkirk).

2　General de Gaulle, who had already fought Guderian, urged Weygand to assemble all the 1200 French tanks and attack Guderian's flank – but Weygand had no time to do this.

3　Mussolini declared war on Britain and France (10 June) and invaded France.

4　Prime Minister Reynaud fell from power and Marshal Pétain formed a new government. His first act was to ask the French people to stop fighting.

5　Hitler agreed to an armistice and France was divided into an occupied and an unoccupied France (a 'free zone' with its capital at Vichy). Pétain became Head of State; he was now convinced that Hitler would win the war and Britain would have her neck wrung 'like a chicken'.

THE BATTLE OF BRITAIN 1940

HITLER'S AIM

He intended to invade Britain but knew that he would have first to gain control of the air over the English Channel. This meant that he would have to destroy the RAF's fighters.

Hitler's methods

First he sent in bombers to crater RAF fighter bases and destroy the radar network – in the main, these attacks were far more successful than was admitted at the time. Then the Luftwaffe began its direct assault on the Hurricanes and Spitfires of Fighter Command – often outgunned by the powerful Me-109s that had long-range cannons fitted for 'strafing' and air combat. During the period 24 August–7 September Fighter Command lost 103 pilots killed and 128 seriously wounded; 466 Spitfires and Hurricanes were destroyed or seriously damaged. Out of the thousand RAF pilots about 25 per cent had been lost; the Operational Training Units couldn't keep pace with the losses – 260 were available, but not all had completed their training.

What did this mean?

During August and early September the Luftwaffe had gained air superiority over 11 Group – the Group defending the south-east 'invasion area'. But in no way did this superiority mean that Hitler could actually invade Britain. Sea conditions were too rough for his invasion barges, the British had mined the Channel, the Royal Navy could obliterate an invasion force if it ever appeared, and in the last resort, the RAF still had a lot of fighters in the north of Britain. So

Hitler, at this crucial moment in the Battle of Britain, changed his tactics.

The bombing of London

Hermann Goering, head of the Luftwaffe, now ordered his fighters to stop their deadly low-level attacks and escort the bomber force to London. On 17 September 300 bombers with nearly 600 fighter escorts appeared and the British were sure that this was the beginning of the invasion. Britain's newly formed Home Guard moved to action stations. But the invasion did not come.

1 For a week the Luftwaffe concentrated on London, its docks, East End and Croydon.
2 Many night attacks took place.
3 On 15 September Goering launched his biggest attacks and RAF controllers committed every squadron in 11 Group to the fray, since commemorated as 'Battle of Britain Day'.
4 Scores of German bombers limped back to their bases with dead crewmen, smoking engines and hydraulic failures. Behind them sixty Luftwaffe aircraft had crashed in the sea, on English fields or in the middle of London. That day the RAF lost twenty-six fighters and thirteen pilots; but it had broken up the mass German attack and forced Goering to reconsider his tactics once again. He would now attack by night – the blitz began.

Look at the illustration opposite.
1 Label the first two aeroplanes – the RAF's Spitfire and Hurricane.
2 Label the second two – an Me-109 and a Heinkel He-111.
3 The fifth aeroplane is a Focke-Wulf 190. Was this used during the Battle of Britain?

THE NIGHT BLITZ

Coventry was one of the first cities to suffer the ordeal of the blitz – Londoners, of course, were veterans by November 1940.

Coventry 14–15 November 1940

The air raid alert lasted eleven hours. Throughout the night 500 tons of high explosives and 30,000 incendiaries destroyed or damaged 70,000 houses, most of the local factories and virtually the entire transportation system. Over 1400 civilians were dead or injured in a city that could no longer look after itself. The army moved in troops to keep law and order, to provide emergency repairs and to run mobile kitchens. The Women's Volunteer Service later set up communal feeding centres and the Ministry of Food shipped in special rations. Some of the scenes were so full of suffering and despair that the government censored newspapers. Photographs of the Coventry blitz showing the horrors were banned – many were not shown to the British public until a year later.

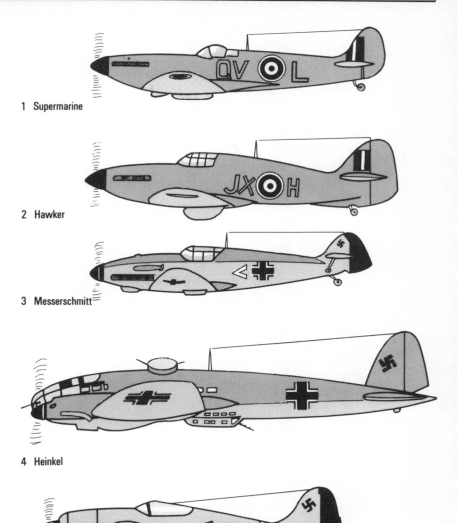

1 Supermarine

2 Hawker

3 Messerschmitt

4 Heinkel

5 Focke-Wulf FW 190

Battle of Britain aircraft

The technology of the night war

British searchlights, anti-aircraft guns and barrage balloons did not deter the German bombers and soon the RAF converted some of its day fighters into makeshift night fighters. But they were ill-equipped to search out and destroy enemy aircraft on dull, cloudy winter nights. And in 1940 Britain did not have the technical skill to 'bend' the beams pioneered by Kampfgruppe 100. Fortunately, the new

Beaufighter was capable of locating and shooting down all the main types of German bombers. Night fighter crews became skilful in the use of GCI (Ground Controlled Interception) radar and one pilot, John Cunningham, emerged as a night-fighter 'ace'.

The attack on London 19–20 April 1941

The Luftwaffe sent 712 bombers to attack London. Night fighters shot down twenty-four of them. Scientists were now able to 'bend' the beams and so lead the enemy bombers away from their planned targets.

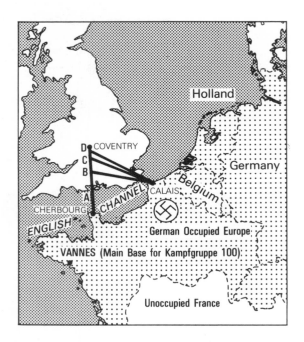

The X-beam system used for the bombing of Coventry, 14–15 November 1940
1. The pilot of a specially equipped HE–111 of Kampfgruppe 100 flew along the director beam **A** Towards Coventry
2. He listened to the beam – a continuous buzz – to stay on track. 'Dots' and 'dashes' meant he was straying left or right.
3. His bomb aimer listened for the 'cross' signals – **B** alerted him; **C** told him to start his computer so that when the bomber crossed at **D** (5 km away from target) it could drop the bomb load automatically on the target

Slowly, the air raids began to diminish – but not simply because the RAF and the scientists were beginning to get the measure of the bombing force. Hitler had already made up his mind to invade Russia and gradually the German bomber groups began to slip away from their bases in France and the Low Countries to prepare for 'Operation Barbarossa'.* By 10 May 1941 only four groups were left in the west

*For an account of Barbarossa and the war on the Russian front, see *Pan Study Aid History 1*, Chapter 6

out of the original forty-four that had conducted the night-time blitz against the British people.

FIGHTING MUSSOLINI

IN AFRICA

As soon as Mussolini declared war on Britain and France in June 1940 the island of Malta found itself in the frontline of the Mediterranean war. It remained in a state of siege until September 1943. Mussolini also attacked British Somaliland, Egypt and Greece.

1 British, Australian and New Zealand troops captured most of Libya.
2 Troops from the Gold Coast, Nigeria and South Africa over-ran Italian Somaliland.
3 British convoys began to reinforce Malta, despite constant air attack and daring missions by Italian frogmen.

ON THE SEA

The Fleet Air Arm knocked out part of the Italian fleet when Swordfish torpedo aircraft attacked the naval base at Taranto (11 November 1940). This incensed Hitler – he ordered Mussolini to challenge the Royal Navy. At the Battle of Cape Matapan (28 March 1941) Italy lost three of her cruisers – *Zara*, *Pola*, *Fiume* – and two destroyers.

HELP FROM HITLER

German Stukas began to assemble in Sicily and Sardinia and in February 1941 a remarkable German general named Erwin Rommel arrived in Libya to begin the formation of the Afrika Korps. Other German units invaded Greece and forced the British to evacuate the 'Imperial Army' to Crete. Hitler then sent in German paratroopers and glider forces and forced the British to evacuate Crete – one of the most humiliating and deadly operations of the war:

1 Britain lost three cruisers and six destroyers.
2 There was no air cover against the Stukas.
3 5000 troops had to be left behind.
4 Most Royal Navy ships suffered damage.
5 One in four of the German paratroopers who dropped on Crete died in action. This was their last airborne battle – the survivors were whittled away in infantry assaults in the later Russian and Italian campaigns.

El Alamein to Cape Bon 1942–3

Rommel twice tried to smash his way into the oilfields of the Middle East. At the Battle of El Alamein (1942) General Montgomery pushed

*After Japan attacked the USA at Pearl Harbor (7 December 1941) Hitler had declared war on America. See *Pan Study Aid History 1*, Chapter 6.

him back through Libya. At the same time an Anglo–American force* landed in North Africa. Rommel defeated it at the Battle of Kasserine Pass (February 1943) but failed to stop the Allied advance. He flew back to see Hitler who ordered the Afrika Korps to fight to the last man. The German and Italian armies surrendered at Cape Bon in Tunisia, May 1943.

THE INVASION OF ITALY 1943

Over 2500 ships and landing craft put an Allied invasion army ashore in Sicily (July 1943). Mussolini fell from power and Marshal Badoglio formed a new government. As the Allies crossed the Straits of Messina, Hitler sent his troops into Northern Italy. Italy surrendered on 8 September but by then the Germans were in the south, contesting every foot of the way.

PROSPECTS FOR A SECOND FRONT

THE CALL FOR A SECOND FRONT

Stalin was loud in his demands that the Anglo-Americans should invade Europe in 1943. In fact, British and Canadian troops had already waded ashore at Dieppe in 1942. This was Operation Jubilee, designed to test the German defences. It turned into a disaster. The invaders were pinned down; 3379 Canadians died; all the new Churchill tanks were lost; above the beaches, in one of the biggest air battles of the war, the RAF lost eighty-eight Spitfires.

Lessons from Dieppe

The Germans defending Dieppe were never seriously worried. They didn't even need to summon a nearby Panzer division to come to their help! The raid taught the Allies two lessons:

1. An invasion must be preceded by total command of the air.
2. The Allies must have the ability to land large forces on the beaches.

Could the Allies have invaded in 1943?

Jubilee had taken place in 1942. Up until the Battle of Kursk in Russia (July 1943) the Germans were at the peak of their power. General Guderian, now Inspector General of all Panzer forces had built up a strategic reserve of:

    5 Panzer divisions;
    3 SS Panzer divisions;
    the Gross Deutschland Division – the best-equipped of all.

Had these been available in another Dieppe-style landing in 1943 then the disaster would have been repeated but on a much greater scale.

THE U-BOATS

The Battle of the Atlantic began on 3 September 1939 when a U-boat torpedoed the SS *Athenia* off the Irish coast; it ended on VE-Day, 8 May 1945, when Admiral Doenitz (Hitler's successor) surrendered at Rheims. All ships coming to Britain had to pass through the perilous Western Approaches – running the risk of attack from 'wolf-packs' of U-boats.

THE CONDORS

Focke-Wulf Condors were long-range reconnaissance bombers flying from France. They located convoys for the U-boats and sometimes attacked the fast merchantmen that sailed by themselves. Merchant ships sometimes carried Hurricane fighters launched by catapult to shoot down these attackers. The British pilots had to land by parachute and hope to be rescued.

Sinking the *Bismarck*

The German battleship *Bismarck* was the greatest threat to the Atlantic convoys. It broke out into the Atlantic (May 1941) in company with the *Prinz Eugen*. Britain's most glamorous battlecruiser, *Hood*, intercepted them and blew up after *Bismarck*'s fifth salvo. Aided by Swordfish torpedo-planes the Navy caught *Bismarck*, reduced her to a wreck and then finished her off with torpedoes from HMS *Dorsetshire*.

Beating the U-boats

New weapons, aircraft and superior technology began to beat the U-boats during 1943 when the U-boats were mangling the Atlantic convoys. Using new radar and the Squid and Hedgehog depth charges, the escort ships began to sink U-boats. Doenitz lost forty of his crews in May 1943. Many of them died in an attempt to sink Convoy ONS-5, regarded as the turning point in the Battle of the Atlantic.

THE NATURE OF THE RESISTANCE

Resistance was a response made by peoples of Occupied Europe to the imposition of Nazi rule, control, ideas and atrocities. Its aim was to win freedom from this horror and to create secret armies that would one day overthrow the occupation power.

Control

A great deal of resistance activity came under the control and direc-

tion of partisan headquarters in Moscow and the SOE (Special Operations Executive) in London. Some resistance groups, such as the
Maquis in Central France, the fighters in Poland, Greece and Yugo-
slavia, fought specifically to set up Communist governments – and
fought consistently throughout the war. But this was not the case for
most members of the resistance. There was nothing very romantic
about their work; they were ordinary people. They carried messages,
they hid Allied airmen, they provided bicycles or vans.

Arms and advice

Britain was active in supplying arms and equipment to resistance
groups; and in parachuting agents to help them e.g. Harry Rée was
an expert in sabotage and parachuted as an SOE agent into France
during 1943. They tried to help people to undermine German rule:

1   The Poles, who waged a bitter war in the marshes and forests; but
who in the towns would change a Nazi poster
from: Deutschland *siegt* an allen Fronten (Germany is winning on all
Fronts)
to: Deutschland *liegt* an allen Fronten (Germany is losing on all
Fronts)

2   The Czechs who were allowed to wear the badge of one Germany
approved organisation – National Solidarity (NS). But they wore the
badge upside down – SN = Smrt Nemcun (Death to the Germans).
Sometimes the British intervened directly, as in the SOE raid by glider
on the German heavy water installation at the Vemork factory in
Norway (a total failure in 1942); then the SOE asked the Norwegian
resistance to knock it out, which they did with great efficiency in
1943. When the Germans tried to ship out their stocks of heavy water
in 1944 via a local ferry the resistance sank it.

Thousands of Allied servicemen owed their lives to the network of
safe houses and escape routes all over occupied Europe. Local people
had to avoid attracting the attention of the local Gestapo, the Wehrmacht and, all too often, the pro-Nazi local police forces.

Perhaps the greatest form of resistance was the passive resistance
of the Jewish people. One of Tito's own resistance leaders, Vladimir
Dedijer, acclaimed their dignity as they walked into the gas chambers
of Auschwitz, Dachau and Sobibor, victims of the horrific Nazi 'Final
Solution'.*

*See *Pan Study Aid History
1*, Chapter 2.

BRITAIN STRIKES BACK

THE AIR WAR

RAF Bomber Command attacked Germany by night; the US 8th Army
Air Force based in East Anglia attacked by day. Covering the entire
war theatre were the elaborate German Himmelbett radar chains,
capable of locating Allied bombers when they took off from their
British airfields. Thus the German defenders had plenty of advance
warning of Allied attacks – though they still lost heavily when they

attacked the Allied formations. Memorable RAF attacks included the 'dambuster' raid 1943, the sinking of the German battleship *Tirpitz* and the destruction of the Dortmund-Ems Canal – both in 1944. The important effects of the air war over Germany were:

1 It secured air superiority for the Allies through the destruction of the German fighter force.
2 It enabled the Allies to invade Europe in 1944 without Luftwaffe interference.
3 It forced Hitler to rely more and more on missiles – the V-1 doodlebug and V-2 supersonic rocket. Though they caused great damage in Holland and Britain, they could not be aimed properly and therefore did not cause any serious dislocation to troop movements or industrial production.

D-DAY: THE NORMANDY LANDINGS 6 JUNE 1944

The project, code-named 'Operation Overlord' was under the command of General Eisenhower, later President of the United States. It didn't go entirely to plan. The weather and the shortage of landing craft meant that Eisenhower had to put back the date for the invasion: 'June 1944 saw the highest winds and the roughest seas experienced in the English Channel for twenty years.' On the strength of a good weather forecast, he sent in the troops on 6 June 1944.

1 The British attacked at Gold, Sword and Juno beaches.
2 The Americans landed at Utah and Omaha beaches.

The US 82nd and 101st Airborne suffered heavy casualties as did the Americans on Omaha, where the seas were exceptionally rough. Tough Canadian infantry soon took Juno while the British moved out of Gold. Partisans sabotaged the French railways and when the Panzers, deprived of their low-loaders on the railways, tried to move across country they were often destroyed by the RAF's deadly Typhoon tank-busters. When the Allies managed to move out of the bridgehead they killed thousands of Germans at the Battle of the Falaise Gap and then moved on towards Paris, Antwerp and the Siegfried Line. They hoped for a rapid victory – if they could secure the bridges across the Rhine. This was object of the Arnhem landings in September 1944.

ARNHEM

Montgomery's plan was to move into northern Germany across the key bridges of Nymegen and Arnhem. The Americans captured their objectives but the British 1st Airborne, supported by Polish paratroopers, failed to hold the bridge at Arnhem. The Red Devils fought for over a week – the planners had not realised that a crack German division (the IX Hohenstaufen) was refitting in the area of the British drop zone. Of the 10,000 men dropped at Arnhem, about 2400 managed to escape.

THE YALTA CONFERENCE

This was the last of the great conferences concerning Europe, held before the final Nazi surrender. It was held in the Crimea early in 1945. It decided:

1　The partition of Germany into three zones (later into four, to include France).

2　That Poland would be shifted westwards – Russia would take over most of East Prussia and the Polish state for which Britain and France went to war back in September 1939.

This was the last time the three leaders, Churchill, Stalin and Roosevelt, met. Roosevelt died on 12 April 1945 and Harry S. Truman became President of the United States.

The defeat of Germany 1945

The Soviet Red Army had borne the bulk of the fighting against the land forces of Nazi Germany. Now Russia was in the heartland of Europe. Soviet troops captured Berlin and met the Anglo-American forces on the River Elbe at Torgau. On 30 April 1945 Hitler committed suicide and the German surrender followed a week later.

*For detail, see *Pan Study Aid History 1*, Chapter 6

The defeat of Japan*

Apart from the valiant British effort to hold the Japanese in the Arakan (Burma), where Japan's land advance was halted by British Gurkha, West African and American troops, the victory in the Pacific theatre was largely an American achievement.

Questions

1　The Lancaster was the most famous RAF bomber during the Second World War, but this aeroplane had an equally distinguished career. What was it called?

2　This graph shows the battle of the sea-lanes 1941–3:

The Battle of the Sea Lanes 1941–3

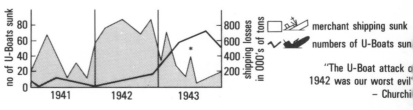

merchant shipping sunk

numbers of U-Boats sunk

"The U-Boat attack of 1942 was our worst evil"
– Churchill

*the turning point – mid 1943

(a)   In what year did the Allies suffer the greatest loss in merchant shipping?
(b)   When was the worst month for shipping losses?
(c)   In what year did the Allies sink hardly any U-boats?
(d)   In what year were the most U-boats sunk?
(e)   The turning point was in 1943: describe the convoy action that was probably the most critical of the war.

3   On this map of the D-Day invasion:
(a)   Mark the five landing beaches.
(b)   Explain the two parachute symbols.
(c)   Name the three primary targets marked with a star.
(d)   Name the two Channel ports B and C where the Germans were expecting the invasion.

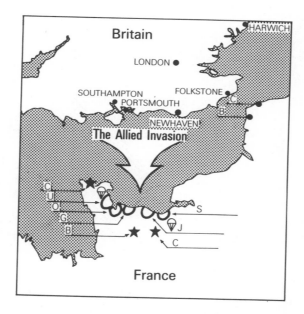

D-Day, 1944

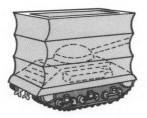

DD = Duplex Drive which operated propellers at rear of tank. The men in the turret were protected by the air-filled envelope which kept the tank afloat

4   This is a sketch of a 'DD' tank used on 6 June 1944.

(a)   What was its main function?

(b)   What type of tank was used?

(c)   Was it an American tank?

(d)   The British had AVREs (Armoured Vehicles, Royal Engineers. These were called '*funnies*'. Explain what the following were:

1 Crocodiles;

2 Flails.

(e)   Once the fighting went inland, the tanks encountered the Normandy *bocage* – high hedgerows. A device called the 'Rhino' was used to cut a way through these. How did it work?

5 This is a map showing the defeat of Germany.

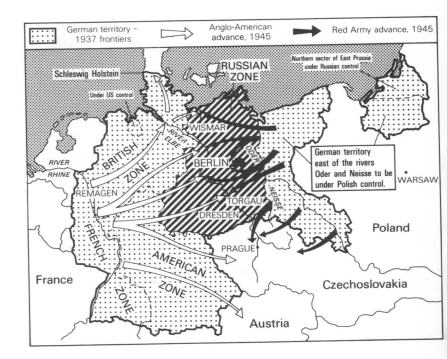

The destruction of the Third Reich, 1945

The map shows the extent to which the Anglo-American armies penetrated the Russian zone of Germany. These armies withdrew into their own zones when hostilities were over.

American views of the Russians in 1945 are interesting:

General Eisenhower: 'In his generous instincts, in his love of laughter, in his devotion to a comrade, and in his healthy, direct outlook on the affairs of workaday life, the ordinary Russian seems to me to bear a marked similarity to what we call an "average American".'

Harry Hopkins: 'We find the Russians as individuals easy to deal with – they like the United States. They trust the United States more than they trust any other power in the world . . .'

(*a*)   Name two countries, besides Germany, penetrated by US troops.

(*b*)   'Poland was shifted westwards': western Poland now extended to two important rivers. Name them.

(*c*)   Montgomery ordered the capture of Wismar because, he said, 'So far as I was concerned, the oncoming Russians were more dangerous than the stricken Germans.' What was the strategic importance of Wismar?

(*d*)   One German city, very badly bombed in February 1945, is named on the map. What was it?

(*e*)   Note the views expressed by Eisenhower and Harry Hopkins. Do you think their estimates of Russia and its people were correct?

6   This is a photograph of Winston Churchill making one of his famous radio broadcasts. He is dressed in what was called a 'siren suit'.

Source: Imperial War Museum

(*a*)   When did he become Prime Minister?

(*b*)   To whom was he speaking when he made one of his first, famous speeches?

> I have nothing to offer but blood, toil, tears and sweat. You ask what is our policy? I will say: It is to wage war by sea, land and air, with all our might and with all the strength that God can give us; to wage war against a monstrous tyranny, never surpassed in the dark, lamentable catalogue of human crime. That is our policy.

(*c*)   To whom was he referring when he said:

> Never in the field of human conflict was so much owed by so many to so few.

(*d*)   At the end of the war, Churchill visited Berlin to attend the Potsdam Conference. Afterwards, he was to state: 'My hate died with their surrender'. About whom was he talking?

(*e*)   Churchill lost the 1945 General Election. What was his political function 1945–51?

7   This photograph shows three Nazi leaders.

     (*a*)   What were their names?

     (*b*)   What was their fate in 1945–6?

EUROPEAN CO-OPERATION SINCE 1945

CONTENTS

In this chapter you will see that the enmity towards Germany that persisted after 1918 quickly evaporated after 1945; and that a new spirit of European co-operation grew up in matters political, economic and social. Very soon, Western Europe had its own defence organisation (NATO) and its own common market (the EEC).

A NEW MOOD

CHRISTIAN DEMOCRACY

On 4 May 1944 Italian Fascists had executed several young resistance fighters. One of them, eighteen year-old Giordano Cavestro, said these words just before he died: 'The great beacon of freedom will arise upon our graves.'

One year later, after VE-Day (8 May 1945), these words began to come true. As Churchill put it, people 'came . . . back from the jaws of death, out of the mouths of hell'. Survivors of the 27 million displaced people taken from their homes by the Nazis began looking for shelter, relatives and jobs. Prisoners of war trekked homewards. Thousands of concentration camp inmates, saved by the advancing Allied armies, emerged in their striped prison suits in search of the humanity and civilisation that had vanished from Europe during six years of war. Despite the prominence of Communists in the resistance movements, Europe did not go communist. The new Christian Democracy made a much greater appeal. It offered:

1 Recognition of man's natural freedom and intellectual abilities.
2 The chance of making up for the past (especially in Germany) and a return to the old Christian values and Christian culture.

A SHORT REVENGE

Retribution for the Nazis and pro-Nazis came swiftly.
1 Prominent politicians who had worked with the Nazis (e.g. Pierre Laval of France and Vidkun Quisling of Norway) were executed.
2 The French condemned Pétain to death but General de Gaulle commuted the sentence to life imprisonment.
3 Girls who had gone out with Germans had their heads shaved.
4 Collaborators were often shot.

The Nuremberg Trials 1945–6

Twenty-one Nazi leaders were put on trial at Nuremberg on four major counts:

1 Conspiring to engage in an aggressive war.
2 Destruction of the peace.
3 War crimes.
4 Crimes against humanity.

Three Nazis – Schacht, von Papen and Fritzsche – found not guilty; seven were jailed (Deputy Führer Hess died in Spandau Prison in 1987); the rest received death sentences – including Martin Bormann, Hitler's powerful secretary, who couldn't be found. Goering evaded the hangman – he took poison. The rest were hanged and their bodies cremated in Dachau.

THE ECONOMIC MIRACLES

WEST GERMANY

There were two remarkable post-war leaders: Konrad Adenauer and Ludwig Erhard.

Konrad Adenauer (1876–1967) He formed the German Christian Democratic Party and became the first Chancellor of the Federal Republic of Germany (1949). Up to 1948 Germany was flooded with worthless currency and the black market flourished. On 20 June 1948 the new Deutsche Mark became the only form of legal tender – and from this moment one can date the *wirtschaftswunder* (economic miracle).

Ludwig Erhard (1897–1977) He became a prominent Christian Democrat and Director of the British and US Zones (in economic matters) after 1947. He freed German industry from all military rules and regulations and the pace of industrial change was swift:

1 By 1950 Germany had passed the 1936 gross national product.
2 Volkswagen's huge plant at Wolfsburg sold its 'beetles' all over the world.
3 German industrialists had to pay high taxes but Erhard gave them big rebates if they ploughed the money back into research and development.
4 He used Marshall Aid far more intelligently than did the British – he rebuilt old 'smokestack' industries in modern forms and with modern equipment.
5 He offered the trade unions (they combined into the Confederation of Trade Unions in 1949) high wages, low inflation and stable prices. There were few strikes and before long Germans had a very high standard of living – when Britain was emerging from the 'Age of Austerity'.

FRANCE

Louis Armand was France's equivalent of Erhard. A resistance fighter who had specialised in railway demolition, he rebuilt the French railways into the finest in Europe. Other industrialists imitated his modernising techniques:

1 Coal mines were highly efficient.
2 The newly nationalised Renault factory began challenging Volkswagen.
3 The new aviation industry centred on Toulouse became a world leader.

The Fourth Republic collapsed politically in 1958 and General de Gaulle came forward to establish the Fifth Republic. The change did not hamper French productivity.

General de Gaulle (1890–1970) enjoyed almost unlimited powers 1958–68:

1 He ensured that the Economic Community protected French agriculture.
2 He kept Britain out of the EEC.*
3 He transformed France into a nuclear power.
4 He came close to defeat in 1968 (student and workers' rebellions) and called a referendum, urging the French to support him. They turned him down.

*See pages 337–41.

ITALY

Italy became a Republic in 1948. The man who personified Italy's 'economic miracle' was Enrico Mattei (1906–62). He concentrated on finding new sources of energy.

1 In 1946 Azienda Generale Italiana Petroli (AGIP) found natural gas near Milan.
2 In 1949 AGIP found oil in the Po valley.

Cheap fuel helped Italy develop shipbuilding, state radio and TV, the autostrade, steel manufacturing, the huge FIAT car industry and the Alitalia airline. However, not all Italians shared in the prosperity. Italy was still a 'divided land' – the north-south split that blighted the Italian people. The overcrowded, agricultural South couldn't cope with the galloping inflation of the 1950s and 1960s. Consequently, the overall economy was not as healthy as the French and German economies and the Italian lira remained a weak currency.

THE EUROPEAN ECONOMIC COMMUNITY

A NEW SENSE OF UNITY

In 1947 Britain and France signed the Treaty of Dunkirk, promising to help one another in the event of another German war of aggression – though there seemed very little risk of that happening. In 1948 this

treaty grew into the Western Union (Belgium, Netherlands, Luxem
burg, France and Britain), guaranteeing one another against any
source of attack. It was natural for this to grow into a European
Defence Community. John Foster Dulles, the US Secretary of State
urged the western nations to unite for defence – and the North
Atlantic Treaty Organisation (NATO) was formed in 1949 at the
height of the 'Cold War'.

In 1954 Britain, France, Italy, Belgium, Netherlands, Luxemburg
and West Germany signed the 1954 WEU (Western European Union
Treaty – the treaty that permits the stationing of British troops on the
European mainland. In 1955 West Germany entered NATO.

The Treaty of Rome 1957

This was preceded by Benelux – a new economic union formed by
Belgium, Netherlands and Luxemburg (1948). Men of vision, such as
Robert Schuman (1886–1963), saw Europe's future as an even bigger
economic union and the 'Schuman Plan' united West Germany
France, Italy and the Benelux countries into the European Coal and
Steel Community (ECSC) in 1951. The success of the centralised
planning policies encouraged member states to meet at Messina
(1955) to discuss a free trade area in Western Europe. 'The Six' signed
the Treaty of Rome that set up the European Economic Community
(EEC) or Common Market.

The EEC at work

The EEC was a free trade area, dedicated to the protection of its own
industrial and agrarian products. This meant that the EEC imposed
high taxes on goods coming in from outside the frontiers of its six
member states. These taxes subsidised the controversial Common
Agricultural Policy (CAP) that guaranteed EEC farmers:

1   huge subsidies;
2   minimum prices for their products.

All of the Six sent representatives to the Council of Ministers; Council
decisions about EEC policies were then implemented by the EEC
Commission. The EEC also had a European Parliamentary Assembly
and in 1979 direct elections were set up to send Euro-MPs to the
parliament. There was also an EEC Court of Justice, set up to deal
with infringements of EEC law by individuals, firms and even
governments.

EFTA 1959

In December 1959 Britain, Norway, Denmark, Sweden, Austria
Portugal and Switzerland set up the European Free Trade Association
(EFTA). EFTA had strong links with the British Commonwealth and
because of this the EEC was unwilling to link up with EFTA.

Expansion of the EEC 1973–86

Charles de Gaulle resigned in 1969. The pro-British Georges Pom
pidou became President of France (1969–74). Simultaneously, the

equally pro-British Willy Brandt became Chancellor of West Germany (1969–74).

On 1 January 1973 Britain, Ireland and Denmark became full members of the EEC.

In 1981 Greece joined – bringing the number of EEC states to ten.

In 1986 Spain and Portugal joined the EEC.

Farming – gains and losses

There are over five million farmers in Europe – most of them very small farmers making small profits. The EEC guaranteed these farmers high prices for their arable and dairy products. During the 1970s farmers' incomes mounted and more and more food had to be stored in EEC warehouses: about 1.5 million tons in the 'butter mountain' and a million tons in the 'skimmed milk mountain'. In 1984 the EEC decided to cut back on milk production – and fined any farmer who exceeded his quota.

Expansion of the EEC 1957–86

1　The original Six are shaded. Colour in the additional six that joined the EEC after the Treaty of Rome.

2　Mark Strasbourg, the location of the European Parliament.

3　Draw an arrow to show which country receives surplus, heavily subsidised food from the EEC.

4   Why did Britain suffer far more than France from the 1984 decision to cut back milk production?

5   Why have farmers been able to re-equip their farms with very expensive machinery and forms of personal transport?

Unemployment in the EEC

The 1973 OPEC decision, to reduce oil production and at the same time quadruple its price, was the main cause of the worldwide industrial recession for the next decade. It:

1   encouraged inflation;

2   led to the rapid shedding of work-forces;

3   resulted in the rapid installation of robots, computers and word processors to make EEC industry competitive with Japan, Taiwan, South Korea, Singapore and the Philippines (where labour was cheap and plentiful). This made unemployment worse in the EEC.

	Unemployment
1973	nearly 3 million
1984	nearly 12 million
1986	over 13 million

Outside the EEC (in Norway, Austria, Sweden and Switzerland) unemployment and inflation figures were significantly lower, leading some people to question the validity of belonging to the EEC. However, British markets in the EEC were now so important that the issue became a matter of political dispute.

1   Prime Minister Margaret Thatcher urged reform of the budgetary system (British contributions were very high), the ending of cheap food sales to the Soviet Union and the abolition of 'butter mountains' and 'wine lakes'.

2   The Labour opposition wanted to make *membership* of the EEC the main issue.

The effects on foreign workers

France, West Germany and Britain had developed a tradition of dependence on immigrant workers long before 1957. Read the following account:

> Between 1945 and 1955 most of the foreign workers were either refugees or immigrants from the former colonial empires. After the Treaty of Rome well over 15 million foreign workers came to take jobs in Western Europe. Most were from the Mediterranean countries – especially Turkey, Greece, Spain, Italy, Algeria, Portugal and Tunisia. West Germany was the biggest employer of foreign workers (the Germans called them *Gastarbeiter* or 'guest workers') and even hired nurses from as far afield as South Korea and the

Philippines. To house them the Germans built 'workers' camps' attached to big industrial firms such as Bosch, Siemens and Mercedes-Benz.

1   Who were the original foreign workers during 1945–55?
2   Where did most come from?
3   Where did Britain find most of her immigrant workers?
4   What did the Germans call their foreign workers?
5   Where did the Germans hire their nurses?

After 1980 there was hostility to foreign workers in Western Europe:

1   Chancellor Schmidt (West Germany) offered financial inducements to Turks and Yugoslavs to return home.
2   President Giscard d'Estaing stopped immigration into France (1974) and offered bounties to Africans who would go home.
    (a)   Was this discriminatory?
    (b)   How would a Turkish family, who had taken out West German citizenship, feel?
    (c)   Was it reasonable to assume that foreign workers hired to do specific jobs were denying British, French or West German workers their jobs – just because they had different ethnic origins?

UNITY ON DEFENCE

For over forty years the West European powers have enjoyed peace within their national frontiers – unlike the East European nations who have on several occasions had to suffer invasions from the Soviet Union and its Warsaw Pact (1955) allies e.g.:

1956   Hungarian Revolt
1968   Invasion of Czechoslovakia

However, West European powers have been involved in military action on several occasions (excluding colonial wars).

KOREA 1950–3

After the North Korean invasion of South Korea (1950) thirty-two members of the UN sent troops to help South Korea. The first sixteen to respond were:

> USA; Belgium; Netherlands; Luxemburg; France; Britain; Greece; Turkey; Philippines; Thailand; Australia; Canada; New Zealand; South Africa; Colombia; Ethiopia.

Others – notably India, Italy and Norway – sent medical aid.

1   Why do you think West Germany couldn't send any aid?
2   Which nation sent the most aid to South Korea?
3   Look at the photo overleaf. You will probably have seen the programme on TV called *MASH*, featuring characters such as Hawkeye and Radar. MASH really did exist in Korea. Which country do you think set up this particular MASH?
4   What do the letters MASH mean?

SUEZ 1956

When President Nasser of Egypt nationalised the Suez Canal in 1956
Britain, France and Israel decided to try to overthrow him by force
Israel attacked Egypt on 29 October 1956 (the Second Arab–Israel
War); then Anglo-French forces attacked Port Said and blasted the
way into the canal zone. The world was horrified by these events an
the UN hurriedly formed its own Emergency Force (it pointedly di
not use Europeans but chose Indians, Yugoslavs and Canadians to a
as an occupation force) to take over from the Anglo-French troop
The Suez affair was a failure for Anglo-French policies. Never aga
did they act jointly in an attempt to impose their will on othe
countries.

THE FALKLANDS CAMPAIGN 1982

In 1982 Argentine troops invaded the Falkland Islands. Every effor
short of using UN forces, was made to settle a long-standing dispu
between Argentina and Britain over the ownership of the Falklan
(called the Malvinas by Argentina). Britain tried to persuade Arge
tina to withdraw – the *moral sanction* – but nothing the US Secretary
State (Alexander Haig) and the Secretary-General of the UN (Perez
Cuéllar) could say would budge the Argentine soldiers. Then No
way, New Zealand, all the EEC countries and the USA applied t
economic sanction and refused to undertake new trade agreemen
with Argentina until the crisis was resolved. Finally, Britain had
choose the *military sanction*. A task force sailed to the Falklands a
landed at Port San Carlos. There followed a short but bitter war

which the British armed services defeated the Argentine forces. The results included:

1 The collapse of the junta that governed Argentina.
2 A failure for the UN – it had failed to implement its policies successfully, i.e. the invader was not persuaded to surrender his spoils peacefully.
3 Britain was left with an expensive military commitment to maintain the defence of the Falklands at a very high level – the 'Fortress Falkland' policy.

CRUISE AND PERSHING

At the request of European NATO countries, NATO decided in 1979 to site 464 Tomahawk Cruise and 108 Pershing II missiles in Western Europe during 1983. There was nothing new about stationing nuclear missiles in Europe; but Pershing and Cruise were direct responses to the 200 Soviet SS–20s (each equipped with three nuclear warheads) that the Russians had deployed against Western Europe by 1979. Many West Europeans believed that they might be the victims of a superpower decision to fight a limited nuclear war in Europe and began to clamour for nuclear disarmament in both Western and Eastern Europe. During 1986 President Reagan and the Soviet leader, Mikhail Gorbachev, met for a 'mini summit' in Reykjavik to discuss disaramament. By then most of the Cruise and Pershing weapons were in position – though some NATO/EEC countries were reluctant to go ahead with installation.

Multiple choice questions

1 The new political movement common to many Western European nations after 1945 was:
  ☐   Revolutionary Socialism
  ☐   European Conservatism
  ☐   Christian Socialism
  ☐   Christian Democracy
2 The pro-Nazi leader of Norway during the Second World War was:
  ☐   Vidkun Quisling
  ☐   Marshal Pétain
  ☐   Pierre Laval
  ☐   Admiral Horthy
3 The first Chancellor of the Federal German Republic was:
  ☐   Ludwig Erhard
  ☐   Konrad Adenauer
  ☐   Willy Brandt
  ☐   Chancellor Schmidt
4 In 1958 General de Gaulle founded the:
  ☐   Second Republic
  ☐   Third Republic
  ☐   Fourth Republic
  ☐   Fifth Republic

5   Italy became a Republic in:
☐   1945
☐   1946
☐   1947
☐   1948

6   In 1947 Britain and France signed a treaty to protect themselves against a future war with Germany. It was called the Treaty of:
☐   Calais
☐   Boulogne
☐   Dunkirk
☐   Cherbourg

7   In 1947 the west set up the OEEC to administer the Marshall Aid funds. In 1960 it changed its title to the Organisation for Economic Co-operation and Development, abbreviated to:
☐   OECD
☐   OECOD
☐   ORGECD
☐   OECOP

8   Sweden was a member of:
☐   the EEC
☐   Benelux
☐   the ECSC
☐   EFTA

9   Britain joined the EEC in:
☐   1970
☐   1971
☐   1972
☐   1973

10   The European Parliament is held in:
☐   Bonn
☐   Berlin
☐   Paris
☐   Strasbourg

11   The Headquarters of NATO are in:
☐   Brussels
☐   Paris
☐   Bonn
☐   Strasbourg

12   The British 'jump-jet' that distinguished itself in the Falklands campaign was the:
☐   Harrier
☐   Pucara
☐   Sea-king
☐   Lynx

ANSWERS TO MULTIPLE CHOICE QUESTIONS

PAGE 18

1 Coal
2 The North-East
3 Improvements in infant mortality
4 Woollen manufacture

PAGES 72–3

1 The Six Acts
2 Arthur Thistlewood
3 The Copyholder
4 Lord Grey
5 .25 million
6 Jeremy Bentham
7 £20,000
8 Hull
9 1 January 1808
10 New South Wales and Tasmania
11 Strike action
12 1839, 1842, 1848

PAGE 79

1 Twenty shillings (20/–)
2 ounce
3 £14 million
4 change their notes into gold
5 it failed totally

PAGES 93–4

1 Swansea
2 Gilchrist Thomas
3 Michael Faraday

  4　the USA
  5　Alexander Graham Bell
  6　a decrease in the cost of food and manufactured goods
  7　limited times for the opening of factories
  8　picketing
  9　the match girls
 10　The Taff Vale Judgement 1901

PAGES 119–20

  1　Crewe, Swindon and Rugby
  2　William Huskisson
  3　1910
  4　'Pullman cars were not introduced in the 19th century' – they were!
  5　'had a wooden hull' – in fact, the *Great Eastern* had an iron hull.
  6　*Titanic* and *Mauretania*
  7　Five times as much – and probably more when war began in Augu
     1914.
  8　City and South London Line
  9　1909
 10　1896
 11　used exhaust gases to operate two pistons
 12　1903–4

PAGE 148

  1　30
  2　Baldwin
  3　British Gazette
  4　Invergordon
  5　George V

PAGES 181–2

  1　Graf Spee
  2　1941
  3　Operation Dynamo
  4　1940
  5　Coventry
  6　6 June 1944
  7　Cologne
  8　the PX
  9　Social Security
 10　Attlee
 11　'Food wasted is another ship *lost*' – not *gained*!
 12　Bread

PAGES 206–07

1. 1948
2. Ellen Wilkinson
3. Sir Stafford Cripps
4. The Korean War
5. 1955
6. Macmillan
7. Prior and Tebbit
8. Michael Foot
9. Scotland
10. 1973

PAGE 252

1. Monroe
2. Vienna
3. Metternich
4. Holy Alliance
5. Austria

PAGES 264–5

1. Mehemet Ali
2. 1841
3. Sevastopol
4. Sinope
5. William Russell
6. Paris
7. Scutari
8. Lord Raglan
9. Greek Orthodox Church
10. Italy

PAGES 343–4

1. Christian Democracy
2. Vidkun Quisling
3. Konrad Adenauer
4. Fifth Republic
5. 1948
6. Dunkirk
7. OECD
8. EFTA
9. 1973

10   Strasbourg
11   Brussels
12   Harrier

NDEXES

PART II BRITAIN AND EUROPE SINCE 1789